MUD HOUSES AND BRICK WALLS

REBUILDING LIVES IN QUETTA AND NILOKHERI

MUD HOUSES AND BRICK WALLS

REBUILDING LIVES IN QUETTA AND NILOKHERI

BISHAMBAR DAS NANDA (1903-1982)
WITH SANJIV NANDA

With Forewords by

Lt General Bhopinder Singh (Retd)
PVSM, AVSM

Prof Deepti Gupta *nee* Dhamija
Panjab University

ZORBA BOOKS

ZORBA BOOKS

Published by Zorba Books, December 2023
Website: www.zorbabooks.com
Email: info@zorbabooks.com

Title: **Mud Houses and Brick Walls**
Authors Name: Bishambar Das Nanda (1903-1982) with Sanjiv Nanda
Copyright © Bishambar Das Nanda (1903-1982) with Sanjiv Nanda
Printbook ISBN :- 978-93-5896-632-9
Ebook ISBN :- 978-93-5896-397-7

All rights reserved. No part of this book may be reproduced or transmitted in any form or by any means, electronic or mechanical, except by a reviewer. The reviewer may quote brief passages, with attribution, in a review to be printed in a magazine, newspaper, or on the Web—without permission in writing from the copyright owner.

The publisher under the guidance and direction of the author has published the contents in this book, and the publisher takes no responsibility for the contents, its accuracy, completeness, any inconsistencies, or the statements made. The contents of the book do not reflect the opinion of the publisher or the editor. The publisher and editor shall not be liable for any errors, omissions, or the reliability of the contents of the book.

Any perceived slight against any person/s, place or organization is purely unintentional.

Zorba Books Pvt. Ltd. (opc)
Sushant Arcade,
Next to Courtyard Marriot,
Sushant Lok 1, Gurgaon – 122009, India

MUD HOUSES AND BRICK WALLS

REBUILDING LIVES IN QUETTA AND NILOKHERI

VISHAV BHAVAN

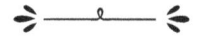

≥——⸱——≤

LESSONS IN GANDHIAN SOCIALISM

SWARAJ, SARVODAYA, SEVA, SADACHAR
DIGNITY OF LABOUR, UPLIFT OF ALL, SELFLESS SERVICE, MORAL RECTITUDE

Nilokheri

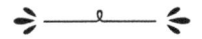

It had been built by the muscles of refugees who had been uprooted from their homes as a result of the Partition and put in a camp commanded by the great visionary, SK Dey. He decided to construct Nilokheri as an agro-industrial township as well as a focal point for rural development by linking the adjoining villages with it. It could claim to be the first planned township of North India. The township had been divided into Kisan Basti and poultry, hospital and school area. Its Gole Market was based on the model of the Connaught Place of New Delhi.

...

Nehru had once declared Nilokheri as his daughter! He had also desired that at least 10,000 Nilokheris be built up in various parts of India. But the tragedy is that today nobody bothers about this orphan of Nehru. Dey has also been completely forgotten. No institution could be named after him, despite the strenuous efforts of his daughter, Purbi Pandey, in 2006 — the centenary year of that great visionary.

Excerpt from
Dey is forgotten, Nehru's 'daughter' too
by Ranbir Singh
Musings, *The Tribune* (Chandigarh), Oct 12, 2019
https://web.archive.org/web/20231015125337/https://www.tribuneindia.com/news/archive/musings/dey-is-forgotten-nehru-s-daughter-too-845884

Life is a struggle, Death a complete calm
The City is bustling, the Tomb silent
(Our hearts are not empty of
memories of bygone days)

— *Bishambar Das Nanda*
Couplet in Urdu, translated by Mohd. Bilal Sidiqqui
and Sanjiv Nanda

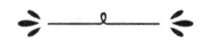

※ ——— ※

To
The entire youth of the world

~

This book is dedicated in the hope that their
generation may capture the spirit of secularism

— *B. D. Nanda*
July 1967 - July 1982

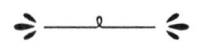

※ ——— ※

For our shared love of the world of books,
and our commitment to volunteerism and
social justice, dear Urmi

— *Sanjiv Nanda*

دل کی بات — یہ کتاب دنیا بھر کے نوجوانوں کے نام
(دعا ہے کہ ان کی نسل روحِ سیکولرازم سے بہرہ ور ہو سکے)

To

The entire youth of the world

This book is dedicated in the hope
that their generation may capture
the spirit of secularism.

Kishwar

July ~~November~~ 1982

We are faced with periods if not ages of conflict and confusion, in which the victory of constructive forces is by no means assured. It is the purest fantasy to imagine that we can leap with one bound from all complexities of the contemporary system to an equalitarian Utopia, even if anything of the sort is socially or biologically desirable. — H. G. Wells

The movement of humanity all these centuries has been towards human brotherhood. The various forward thrusts that have become manifest in different parts of the world, the ideals of justice, equality & freedom from exploitation of which men have become increasingly conscious, the demands of the common man against perversions & compulsions that were perpetually developing to restrain him & hold him back. The progress of the consciousness of freedom is the essence of human history. — KISHWAR KALHANI

~ x ~

We are faced with periods, if not ages of conflict and confusion, in which the victory of constructive forces is by no means assured. It is the purest fantasy to imagine that we can leap with one bound from all complexities of the contemporary system to an egalitarian utopia, even if anything of the sort is socially or biologically desirable.

— *H. G. Wells*

The movement of humanity, all these centuries has been towards human brotherhood. The various forward thrusts that have become manifest in different parts of the world, the ideals of justice, equality and freedom from exploitation of which men have become increasingly conscious, the demands of the common man against perversions and compulsions that were perpetually developing to restrain him and hold him back.... The progress of the consciousness of freedom is the essence of human history.

— *Sarvapalli Radhakrishnan*

Contents

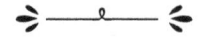

Foreword by Lt Gen Bhopinder Singh	xvii
Foreword by Prof Deepti Gupta nee Dhamija	xx
Preface	**1**
Pitaji	3
The Spirit of '77	11
Letters to Sanjiv on his departure for IIT Kanpur	14
Letter I: Human Kaleidoscope,	15
Letter II: The Indian Scene	18
Letter III: Thirty First Year of Our Republic	21
Vishav Bhavan	23
Editorial Note	31
Introduction	**33**
Part I: Kakrali	**39**
My Heritage	41
The Setting	46
Childhood Education	51
Servants	57
My True Guide	61
Traditions	68
Individual Existence	76
Part II: School Days	**81**
Education at Daulatnagar	83
At the District Headquarters	92
A Digression	98

The Reign of Terror and After	100
The Arya Samaj	106
Some Random Childhood Reminiscences	112
Maternal Uncles	118
Gandhiji	121

Part III: My Youth — 127

Two Indias (Urban and Rural)	129
My Grandfather's Death	137
My Uncle Shiv Nath	142
Boyhood Anecdotes	145
The Influences of Political Upsurge	151

Part IV: College Days — 159

Lahore and University Life	161
Influences of an Ascetic	170
The Survival of the Fittest (Random Thoughts)	175
Recuperation of Health	179
Simultaneous Hectic Activity	184
Journey Westward	195

Part V: England — 205

Experiences in England	207
Tramping in Europe	219
Farewell to England	225
Back to India	228
Random Thoughts	236
From Free Country to Enslaved Land	241
London As I Saw It	250

Part VI: Civil Engineer and Businessman — 253

The Maharaja's Service	255

Feelings and Incidents	263
The New Setup	272
1946 - 48	287
Part VII: Partition and Resettlement	**293**
Nilokheri	295
The Community Projects	305
Multifarious Experiences of Interest	309
The 'Underground Movement' in the War	319
I Build My New Home	327
Retirement from Business	331
Part VIII: Social Service	**335**
Bharat Sewak Samaj	337
Since Sixty-first Birthday	349
Being Metaphysical	353
Heart Attack	356
My Life's Inspirations	360
Pandit Nehru's Passing Away	367
My Aunt Lakshmi Devi	369
Vishav Bhavan - A Family Album	372
Thirty Five Years of Independence	378
Fight Corruption Through Moral Regeneration	385
Our Country	391
Now and Then in Retrospect	395
A Final Word	401
Epilogue: Seventy Years of Vishav Bhavan	**403**
Glossary	**405**
Author Biographies	**409**

Foreword by Lt Gen Bhopinder Singh

Leo Tolstoy once said, "There is no greatness where there is no simplicity, goodness and truth." No three adjectives can succinctly capture the essence of the life of Shri Bishambar Das Nanda, more eloquently than celebrating his thoughts and life as one of simplicity, goodness and truth.

A hidden treasure penned and forgotten in the humdrum of daily tribulations, finally emerged from the dark corridors of time as a priceless labour of love and affection by a doting grandson, Sanjiv Nanda. We are enriched and bettered for reading the same.

The lovely book ensures that the wistful words of a bygone era find a restorative place in our lives and imagination, almost half a century after they were beautifully handwritten. A story that starts in the quaint village of Kakrali in modern day Pakistan, is in many ways the story of the multiple wounds, dreams and seeding of the glorious 'Idea of India', by a generation that was uniquely giving, sacrificing and noble, like none since. The dreamy innocence and sheer dint of hard work that exemplified that generation's effort to fructify the proverbial 'tryst with destiny' comes through so vividly, so mellifluously, and ever so gently – in a manner and expression that is certainly lost to the vicissitudes of the times, that be.

In a world and a time, when even a Gandhi or a Nehru are getting increasingly and recklessly questioned for their relevance, it is truly healing and reassuring to see the impact of those great founding fathers through the eyes and words of Bishambarji, who exemplified the very best of those values, instincts, and aspirations, to which we owe the greatness of India, that exists today. He was after all a visionary who carried that goodness so lightly on his sleeve, as only the truly humble can.

The best tribute to the great man Bishambarji and his fine legacy is in the living reality of his extended family that continues to thrive across cities, countries, and continents. A thoroughly distinguished, genteel and dignified spirit that was nurtured so lovingly by Bishambarji has now been passed down generations, with the same sense of restrained decency and culturality, that we have known about the Nanda family, our neighbours in Chandigarh.

It is only befitting that the noble souls' final years were spent in the 'City Beautiful' or Chandigarh, a city that encapsulates the refinement of aesthetics, orderliness and aspirations that ought to be the entirety of India, but sadly isn't, as yet. Bishambarji's house was amongst the first and foremost to stand tall in the new city and it wouldn't be out of place to acknowledge the same as a veritable 'museum' or an 'institution' in its own right, given its antiquity, significance and design sensibilities that is quintessentially one of Le Corbusier's minimalism with clean lines.

Every reader would find a personal echo of their own 'India' seen through the eyes, heart, and soul of their own ancestors – a moving sepia-tinted memorabilia that must be treasured as a must-read for all those, who despite so many lingering issues, inequities and excesses have not given up on the majesty of the 'Idea of India'. My heartfelt *shradhanjali* to a great man, great writer, and amongst the greatest inspiration that one can read about today – simply put, a life full of simplicity, goodness, and truth. It is, as Mahatma Gandhi himself said, "Live simply that others might simply live."

Kudos to Sanjiv Nanda to share this priceless treasure with the world at large. My heartfelt and best wishes for this necessary endeavour, and deep reverence to the noble soul.

Lt Gen Bhopinder Singh (Retd), PVSM, AVSM
Former Lt Governor of Andaman &
Nicobar Islands & Puducherry

Foreword by Prof Deepti Gupta nee Dhamija

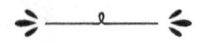

Visualise a child who enters a home that feels like a palace. Every nook and cranny carries the magical imprint of some great moment from the history of India. There are *objets d'art* scattered across every inch. The residents of the *haveli* are vibrant beings, ready with magical tales for any young, impressionable mind. Flights of fancy take off regularly. Colourful guests keep walking in and out. Meal times embody the horn of plenty, a virtual cornucopia of delicacies. Lo and behold, the feast doesn't end here. Every member of this gifted family is capable of guiding a school child in all the fields of study; with a smile and a pat of encouragement.

There is Lalaji, the great grandfather who can talk about the great land of undivided India. Pitaji, the grandfather who has lived every bit of the history of the created nation. Mataji, the grandmother who rules the household and the neighbourhood with love and discipline. Vinod uncle, the father from whom we learnt so much that the debt can not be added up by the best device. Shashi auntie, the mother, ever charming, gracious hostess and perfectionist, presiding deity at every kiddy celebration.

The boys, Sanjiv and Vipul, companions of so many childhood adventures and the go-to friends of our adulthoods. Let me not forget the constant stream of accomplished visitors and relatives from all walks of life, adding a bit of colour and design to the glorious canvas that is Vishav Bhavan.

Fitting every feeling, thought and moment associated with this house that is an institution unto itself is a formidable task even for a wordy professional! Yet, as the bard puts it in words: "We know what we are, but know not what we may be."

Kudos, Vishav Bhavan for guiding so many souls towards what they may be!

Prof. Deepti Gupta *nee* Dhamija
Department of English, Panjab University, Chandigarh

VISHAV BHAVAN

Preface

– Sanjiv Nanda

Pitaji

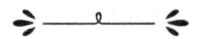

⇢――◦――⇠

Pitaji, my grandfather, Bishambar Das Nanda penned the words in this book over fifteen years between the mid-1960s and 1982. He breathed his last on August 15, 1982, just short of his seventy-ninth birthday.

Born on December 10, 1903, in Kakrali, a small village about one hundred and eighty kilometres north of Lahore, he tells the story of his early rural childhood of privilege, as a young boy, the grandson of the local landlord, spoiled by both family members and village people. He describes being sent away from home for middle school and high school in the district headquarters, then college in Lahore, in a period during which revolution was in the air. He describes his small acts of insubordination in school, as the British instituted laws designed to punish the locals in response to the cross-currents of revolution – both non-violent civil disobedience and violent insurrection, that were sweeping Punjab and beyond.

The year 1925 was hectic and pivotal. His uncle decided that he must go for further studies to England. He went on to study Civil Engineering at King's College, London. As well, to ensure that the young man did not stray, a month before he was to depart by ship from Bombay in October 1925, he was married on September 29, 1925. The bride was from village Chopala, 44 km away. The wedding party travelled by foot, to and fro, between the two villages. As the bridegroom, young Bishambar got to make the trip on a tall white steed. Pitaji paints a wonderful portrait of a wedding in rural Punjab in the early twentieth century.

The narrative moves on to his journey west by ship via the Suez Canal, disembarking in Marseille. Three years hence, Marseille would also be his port of embarkation for the return journey, returning as a man having gained rich worldly experience and a sense of confidence about his future. He narrates his observations of the class system in London, his opportunity to 'tramp' through the countryside and learn about British society. On his return journey, with little money, he took some time to 'tramp' through western Europe on the return trip. He relates his observations about travelling with a rucksack and nothing else through France, Belgium and Germany, countries that seemed alien. When he got to Italy, and with a few days remaining before he would depart for India, he felt that he was getting:

> ...nearer and nearer to my country. I loved simple village life more than the hustle and bustle of big cities. Here I found a small room in a very cheap little boarding house. The village had narrow streets with lines of washed clothes and lines upon lines of macaroni and spaghetti stretched from the windows of houses on either side of the alleys. Here the donkeys trotted along with their panniers on each side whilst the men and women carried their loads on their backs.

As a newly qualified civil engineer with a degree from the prestigious King's College, London, he hoped to join

Government service in public works, building roads and bridges. But it was not to be, there were few open positions and he failed the entrance examination.

After an extended stint of unemployment, he got his first job as an assistant engineer in the Government of the Maharaja of Kashmir, in charge of buildings and roads, as well as the Maharaja's palaces. With a good job and a steady income, he started to make a life for himself, and soon a growing family. Daughter Sarla arrived first in 1930, followed by son Vinod in 1932, and son Kailash in 1934. The household included his parents (my great grandparents), and a widowed aunt, the elder sister of his mother. Soon after the birth of Kailash, *Mataji*, my grandmother, fell seriously ill with tuberculosis. Meanwhile, to appease the locals, the Maharaja of Kashmir decided that jobs in government were to be reserved for those who were born in the state. In 1937, he found himself newly unemployed, with a large family of eight to support.

Confident about his abilities, he moved to Karachi aiming to become an independent architect and contractor in the construction business. He negotiated employment with Messrs. Herman and Mohata, and soon started winning and delivering large contracts for the firm, not just in Karachi, but in Lahore as well. He was supervising the construction of a large army contract for a slaughterhouse in Lahore to supply meat for the armed forces throughout the country, when protests broke out and the project had to be shelved. This is when he first noticed that he was doing all the work, bringing in all the money for the firm, while Herman and Mohata were getting rich on the fruits of his labour.

Quetta, in Baluchistan, was being reconstructed following the 1935 earthquake that had destroyed much of the town. Pitaji obtained construction contracts and moved the family to Quetta. With all this experience under his belt, he left his employers and finally established his own business as an architect and contractor. With more funds at his disposal, he branched into new businesses, first as a local supplier of electrical goods for the German company Siemens, and then when the Second World War brought about bans on German goods, switched his business to selling products from General Electric. He expanded his retail business to additional towns in Punjab and Sindh. His eminence in Quetta grew along with his bank balance, and the number of cars in his garage (four). He writes:

> The *Khaksars* gave me a march past and made me the local president. *Bazem-i-Iqbal*, Quetta, an organisation comprising the Urdu poets of Baluchistan made me to head the society, regardless of the fact whether I could compose any poetry myself. The *Arya Samaj* made me a member of the Managing Committee of the local D.A.V. School. The lovers of Hindi held a Hindi Sammelan and I presided over the meeting.

But clouds were on the horizon. The country would be divided into two, and as the date of Independence drew near, the prospects of a peaceful Partition, in which there would be two countries with Hindus and Muslims peacefully coexisting in both as they had for hundreds of years, started to diminish and then vanished. A few months prior to August 1947, Pitaji moved his family first to Dehradun and from there to Mussoorie in U.P. He enrolled his sons, Vinod and Kailash to boarding school in Nainital – Birla Vidya Mandir. Sarla had already appeared for and completed her matriculation exam in Lahore.

The family emerged safe from the bloodshed of Partition, but the eminent businessman from Quetta would have to start life over in newly independent India. Independence unleashed a spirit of service and a dedication to hard work among the millions of displaced families, the refugees. Pitaji drew inspiration from the freedom fighters and dived into public service. S.K. Dey became a mentor, and Pitaji his protégé, and together they pursued a vision of community development with the village or the block as the locus of development for an India that was largely rural. Prime Minister Nehru, and other leaders and planners had other ideas. Their vision was to pursue large projects, heavy industry in the public sector, hydroelectric dams, and the like. Rural development was subordinate to this larger vision, and eventually neglected and forgotten.

In his experience with rural development living and working with menial labour, Pitaji drew lessons about the dignity of labour, about self-sufficiency as a motivating force, the virtue of putting in an honest day's work, and in return, a remuneration sufficient to ensure that the 'Five Needs of Life' were met: Nutrition, Shelter, Clothing, Health and Education. While continuing to work for the Planning Commision in crafting Five Year Plans of Nehru's top-down socialism for the Central Government, he took over the reins of Bharat Sevak Samaj, an organisation outside government, dedicated to a bottom-up social upliftment.[1] He believed that the latter approach offered dignity and self-worth, and was more effective for social uplift than government programmes that invited inefficiency and corruption.

There was no rest for this public servant. The country was young, fifteen years had elapsed since independence, he was full of ideas and in a position of influence. Without regard to his own health and well-being, he was immersed in the work of making life better for his countrymen. But the body has a will of its own.

---

1 *Sevak* translates to servant, or in this case a social worker.

On February 10, 1964, the body delivered a message for him to slow down. He suffered from a coronary thrombosis. It was time to step back.

But the public servant could not give up. Over the preceding year, Bharat Sevak Samaj had gained prominence and vast government funds. With this visibility came scrutiny, audits and questions were raised about governance. The heady days of the newly-earned independence were being replaced with cynicism. Unhealthy practices and corruption were creeping into public life. He held those that lived austere lives in high esteem, and remained optimistic about our future.

> There was a difference between material progress which was desirable and materialistic outlook on life which was undesirable. Both are not synonymous and the whole of our own past history has shown that material progress is absolutely compatible with a non-materialistic view of life. The Indian mind, history proves, has always been inspired by men and women of integrity and renunciation, not by persons holding high positions living a life of luxury and personal bodyguards to protect them. I felt certain that there was still a large number of sincere men and women in the country, who can be centres of inspiration and produce a cadre of missionaries.

With his mentor, Union Home Minister Gulzari Lal Nanda, Pitaji launched the Sanyukta Sadachar Samiti.[2] An opinion piece that he wrote in 1965, *Fight Corruption through Moral Regeneration* is reproduced later in this book. There he wrote:

---

2   *Sadachar* translates to good conduct or good behaviour, in this case, in the public sphere.

Sadachar in society is valuable not because it adds to the good of the community but because it is eternally good. Corruption, as opposed to *sadachar*, spells great harm to the community. In fact, it is a form of theft which, on this account, should not be tolerated anywhere. It is contrary to the laws of organised societies.

To wage a relentless all-out war against corruption in all its various aspects, the people must mobilise their reserves of honesty and integrity, and their emotional resources as well. Corruption must die so that honesty can flourish.

In his sixties and seventies, Pitaji saw that moral decline of the Nation was at hand. He started penning his memoir, less an autobiography, more a series of vignettes that painted a picture of life, observations and lessons of his seventy years on earth. In the midst of this period, in 1975, fearing loss of power and exposure of corruption, Prime Minister Mrs. Indira Gandhi declared a state of Emergency, suspended fundamental rights, imposed censorship of the press, threw opposition politicians in jail and encouraged the portrayal of herself as the Saviour of the Nation. By surrounding themselves with sycophants, authoritarian leaders come to believe that they are synonymous with the Nation itself, the Nation's progress can only come with their leadership. Narcissism is a heady drug.

Those of us reading this book, who are now in our sixties and seventies, realise that our years have brought us some wisdom, but the confidence is gone that we can be effective agents of change based on the lessons we have learned. Our energy has diminished, and we start looking towards the youth who will have to make the essential changes needed for humankind to prosper. Today, I am inspired by our youth, activists against climate change, that have clarity of vision. As well as the fight for democracy around the world that we thought we had won, but needs to be won again.

In 1967, Pitaji started writing this memoir, and continued to write over the next fifteen years. The last words were written just a few months prior to his death in 1982. He desired to share his wisdom with the youth of the world in whom he was pinning his hopes. He dedicated the book to:

> The entire youth of the world. This book is dedicated in the hope that their generation may capture the spirit of secularism.

In 2023, the ideal of secularism has become cynically reviled by neo-Nationalists. Thus the dedication of his memoir is newly relevant today.

I completed Class X (ICSE) in December 1976, and would be starting pre-university in July 1977. Mrs. Gandhi was feeling confident about the popularity of the programs that she had rolled out during the Emergency. Moreover, the opposition was in jail, and censorship was in place, she felt that she would easily win reelection and firm up her authoritarian rule. She declared fresh elections and I jumped in as a local worker for the Janata Party, a coalition of opposition parties. Jay Prakash Narain, the Sarvodaya leader, came to speak at the Sector 17 parade ground, and I got to see him up close.

The Spirit of '77

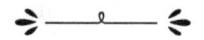

1977 was a watershed year in the history of our Nation. The Nation had rebelled against the autocratic regime that Prime Minister Indira Gandhi had attempted to install by suspending constitutional rights and throwing opposition politicians in jail without trial. Newly graduated from 10th class, I spent the months of January through June of 1977 volunteering for the Janata Party, went to rallies at which Jay Prakash Narayan ("JP") spoke, printed and distributed leaflets door-to-door, speaking to people about the chance to save the nation from dictatorship. The Spirit of '77 succeeded, and for the first time in the history of independent India, thirty years after Independence, a new 'opposition' coalition Government was installed at the Centre.

In July of 1978, I left home to go to college in Kanpur. I was seventeen, good at school, good at sports. The events of 1977 had resulted in establishing idealism as my guiding faith, more naive than pragmatic. The one quality that was deeply ingrained in me was honesty to a fault. To such an extent that I could not grasp the concept of a white lie sometimes told to protect someone emotionally. This is something I still struggle with at age 62. Idealism survives, naivete remains.

Weeks before I left for college, my grandfather Bishambar

Das Nanda, correctly surmised that his opportunities to impart his ideas and ideology to me were dwindling. He would turn out to be right, as part way through my stay at Kanpur, in August of 1982 I received the news of his passing away. We would never get to spend more time together than we did in the summer of 1978.

Writing in those days demanded focus and clarity of thought. Pitaji wrote longhand using his fountain pen. Every sentence that I write today, including this one, is started and deleted, restarted, spellchecked, and backspaced over and over. Pitaji's manuscript written in longhand shows few words on any page that are crossed out or overwritten, now and then a word inserted for clarification. In the years after his heart attack, he spent time writing down his story, his observations, and his ideas, that are the content of this volume.

Here's a paragraph from Pitaji's writings that captures the life lesson that I received. My father learned this from his father (Pitaji) and growing up in the presence of both, this lesson has been both my strength – what I have achieved in life – as well as responsible for what I have failed to achieve. He wrote,

> Both my wife and I were watchful of our children in their childhood to see that they do not go unchecked on heedless trails. I did not encourage them to be 'clever' nor would I accept falsehoods or small acts of dishonesty which could form firm habits over the years. After the death of my mother and my father's indifference towards family affairs I had taken upon myself the position of the head of the family. I concerned myself mainly with the inherent integrity of all members . Even little twistings of truths, 'minor' thefts of small things, and intended wrong impressions irritated me. I had it plainly known

to everyone that by freedom from corrosive sham and blurred values which accompany deceit, honesty will find firm roots in the whole family. It did work.

Indeed I can confirm that it did work. Growing up in Vishav Bhavan with Pitaji and my papa Vinod Chander Nanda, both disciplinarians, each with his own style, honesty did root, and firmly.

In 1978, Pitaji felt a sense of urgency and in May of that year he wrote three 'letters' to me that would help me on my journey in the world even when he was no more. I am so grateful that he wrote his thoughts on paper, as that has the gift of longevity compared to the conversations that we had. There is also a sense of urgency in his words and his writing in these letters, while the rest of his life story was written over a longer period, with more time and planning. [Another difference is that he used a ballpoint pen in 1978, instead of his fountain pen.]

I reproduce these letters here. They are prescriptive, directed to a young man lacking maturity and heading out into the world. They carry a message to inspire subsequent generations towards morality in public life and a life of service. Although these words were written in 1977, and they are written somewhat hastily, they are an introduction to his world view and who he was. The rest of his life story can then be read as how he and we came to be.

His message to me also tells you who he wanted me to be, and who I have tried to be.

Letters to Sanjiv on his departure for IIT Kanpur

26/8/76

Human Kleidoscope

Man is almost triumphant over Nature. He has established his mastery over earth, water & space. There is hardly any limit to his wisdom & courage & now he is well on the path to conquer even the starry kingdom. There have been such wonderful developments in the field of science that if they are beneficially harnessed in the service of mankind, they can easily drive out hunger, disease, and poverty root and branch. The world is no doubt full of natural resources, which if usefully mobilised & employed, there will be no want. Technologically it is not very difficult to provide the basic needs of life to all but it is a strange dilemma that the technologists do not enjoy control over production. Instead Statesmen and Politicians have usurped this right and control in our world and do not allow humanity to reap the advantage of scientific progress for raising the standard of living of the masses. Caught in the whirlpool of politics, these Statesmen continue to spend their valuable time extravagantly in raising new controversies & issues.

Inspite of the fact that a large number of universities and Research centres exist and are manned by a corps of thoughtful & ethical-minded elite who are constantly influencing human society with their piercing wisdom and yet the man is overshadowed by the constant fear of total extinction. Humanity is at the cross-roads, being goaded by an unexpected future and haunted by regrettable past.

In the international arena the political leaders of developed country are mainly devoted to either growing strongholds in underdeveloped countries or aim at justifying their territorial claims. In this way the nations

Letter 1: Human Kaleidoscope,

Dated: 26/5/78

Man is almost triumphant over Nature. He has established his mastery over earth, water and space. There is hardly any limit to his wisdom and courage and now he is well on the path to conquer even the starry kingdom. There have been such wonderful developments in the field of science that if they are beneficially harnessed in the service of mankind, they can easily drive out hunger, disease and poverty, root and branch. The world is, no doubt, full of natural resources, which if usefully mobilised and employed, there will be no want. Technologically, it is not difficult to provide the basic needs of life to all, but it is a strange dilemma that the technologists do not enjoy control over production. Instead statesmen and politicians have usurped this right and control in our world and do not allow humanity to reap the advantage of scientific progress for raising the standard of living of the masses. Caught in the whirlpool of politics, these statesmen continue to spend their valuable time extravagantly in raising new controversies and issues.

In spite of the fact that a large number of universities and research centres exist and are manned by a corps of thoughtful and ethical-minded elite who are constantly influencing human society with their piercing wisdom, and yet man is constantly overshadowed by the constant fear of total extinction. Humanity is at a crossroads, being goaded by an unexpected future and haunted by a regrettable past.

In the international arena, the political leaders of developed countries are mainly devoted to either gaining strongholds in underdeveloped countries or aim at justifying their territorial claims. In this way, these nations are mostly caught in the race of establishing superiority over underdeveloped countries. Their statesmen often talk like angels, but their hearts are full of sin. If they, on the other hand, seriously try to solve the problems facing humanity with a view to accelerate its progress based on humanitarian grounds, the world will become truly human. It should then break all artificial barriers between one country and another.

Within the borders of each country, each nation comprises the powerful 'haves' and the poor 'have nots', and the root cause of conflict among them is the amassing of wealth through all means at their disposal by the rich. Then it is also a fact that the 'have nots' are made tools by the rich to maintain fissiparous tendencies under one garb or another – communalism, provincialism, linguism and casteism. The atrocities committed on the poor and the innocent in the name of these 'isms' should bring tears even in the eyes of God.

It is a misleading notion that by making the poor more poor, the rich can enjoy better. In fact, if the rich do not offer proper opportunities of rise and advancement to the poor, they too, have no peace and tranquillity. Most of the political leaders are drawn from the well-to-do, and are mainly engaged in the process of grabbing political power for financial gains. Wealth and excessive enjoyment are regarded as the greatest power and man in the pursuit of these objectives has become very selfish and uncontrollable. This ever-increasing lust for power and self-gain generates corruption. While it may also be correct that sometimes poverty and starvation compels people to commit crimes, but lust and avarice are responsible for more heinous crimes.

The destruction of the morals of the people, particularly of the rich, is well noticeable – they have amassed wealth largely through illegal means, have become benefactors of religious preachers who act as hirelings in chanting hymns in praise of their masters. These wealthy masters of each religion utilise their ill-gotten wealth in the construction of religious places like temples, mosques, etc. Even when the fundamental principles of each religion are similar, fissiparous tendencies over trifles are excited by the vested interests for their personal motives. The individual is by and large surrounded by a particular society or religion and is thus disbarred from having a broader view of the vast humanity. There is, therefore, a view that the individual should be tutored to emerge out of the darkness of ignorance so that foundations of a strong world society may be laid.

Letter II: The Indian Scene

Dated: 27/5/78

The length and breadth of India is about two thousand miles either way with a coast line of four thousand miles. This is about the size of Europe without Russia. If one is struck by the variety of climate, the diversity of languages and customs while travelling through Europe, he would be equally struck by similar contrasts in India.

The land boundaries are West Pakistan, USSR, China, Burma, Bangladesh, from west to north and thence to east. The Himalayas in the north are a part of a great mountain region where range follows range. The farthest range is nearly a hundred miles from the plains of Punjab, Uttar Pradesh and Bihar and in this mountainous region there are minor regions intersected by streams and valleys. Behind the high mountain region is a deep depression in which the Brahmaputra and the Indus rivers are fed by glacial streams which flow into India and terminate into Bangladesh and Pakistan. To the north of these depressions is the table land of Tibet (Chinese territory) which is 15000-18000 feet above sea level and is 300 to 400 miles wide.

The regions of heaviest rainfall: i) western slopes of the western ghats, ii) the southern slopes of the Himalayas. The rainfall varies from nothing to 900 inches in a year, this is as much as 40 inches in a day!

Geographically, India has been described as the country that is enclosed by the Himalayas in the north and the sea in the south. Those who dwell within these areas, whatever may be their creed or colour and whatever their religion, all belong to this country, but very few are willing to accept the total heritage of India. On the other hand a large majority are content to take pride in only certain sections or aspects of Indian history and culture. Diversity is inescapable in a country so large in area with large differences in landscape and climate. Further, different people came to this area at different times and this has added to the complexity. And further, lack of communications encouraged local variations. Besides, various kingdoms within the country developed sub-nationalities.

After the achievement of our Independence, the first few years passed in framing a constitution for India and in giving stability to the State after the shock of Pakistan, when we went through inhuman massacres. The Partition has not solved even the Hindu-Muslim problem and in fact caste has suddenly assumed a sort of respectability and communalism lurks in the dark recesses of most people's mind with occasional public eruptions. Further, regionalism too has been born which has given birth to the brood of linguism and localism. Adult franchise and political power arising therefrom have revived caste in an unexpected way. Increase in population without a corresponding increase in national wealth has made local conflicts sharper. Many discords arise from differences of language, religion, caste or community. Social and economic backwardness is responsible for many of the fissiparous tendencies that come to the fore from time to time.

The process of secularism and unity of the Nation seems to be in transition. A consciousness of belonging to one another and the entire Indian community being a united whole has yet to grow. Unless every individual cultivates the habit regarding himself as an Indian first and everything else afterwards, it would be difficult to avoid disintegration and to safeguard the future against forces of disruption.

It would not be correct to say that we have not made any progress in material achievements but we have had a setback in our moral and social standards. Those who instinctively believe in a selfish outlook on life, have helm on the increase since Independence. Thus the people with utilitarian values as their motive power are apt to discard the moral values from their life and have no hesitation in becoming corrupt and they make an unhealthy impact on the rest of society. Prior to Independence when we were engaged in driving the British out, our leaders had practised self imposed poverty, simplicity in outlook, higher code of conduct and devotion to ideals. Need has, therefore, arisen for discouraging prestige attached to wealth and restoring dignity to ideals, honesty and labour.

Letter III: Thirty First Year of Our Republic

Over thirty years have already gone by since India became a Parliamentary Democratic Republic. During this period considerable progress has been made in developing the country through various measures by making the people more literate, expansion of scientific education and research, by increased industrialisation and a consequent urbanisation, by introducing intensive and extensive cultivation, by construction of large dams and irrigation works, by extensive power supply for industries and tube well irrigation, by reforming agrarian land and partial demotion of the privileged class in society and security of labour. In spite of these achievements the general standard of living of the masses has hardly improved and has been inadequate in proportion to the growth of population and abnormal rise in prices particularly of consumer goods. As such our masses do not still have the requisite wherewithals by which they can maintain themselves and one notices among them a sense of frustration with the struggle for existence becoming acute, the moral guideposts seem to have crumbled, resulting in corruption, adulteration, hypocrisy, lust, etc. Can we or should we contemplate such a situation with equanimity?

It is hazardous to predict the future even one year, and it is not within the competence of any individual, even of an astrologer of eminence to make a correct prophecy. Personally

I have no faith in astrologers. Statesmen do, however, make forecasts about immediate popular national interests or about likely international happenings on the basis of some data, but there are innumerable examples of false prophecies having been conspicuously made by statesmen of even the highest rank. The distant future of a country is so unimportant by the side of its immediate needs that even if 'the men in possession' would be reasonably certain that a particular evil ought to be guarded against by an immediate sacrifice they would not have the moral force required for the effort. For instance, those who hold the view that the present tendency of an expanding public sector is harmful to individual liberty and the development of initiative, have no power to give effect to their views in present day India. Statesmen will, therefore, make such forecasts as would be in keeping with popular sentiments for their own survival and to avoid powerful opposition.

The drafting committees of the Constituent Assembly deliberated on various aspects of the Constitution from Oct 1947 to Feb 1948, borrowed freely from the American and British Constitutions and from the Government of India Act 1935, but did not mention the word *Panchayat*. Not until Nov 1948 and almost as a second thought, was a clause added on *Panchayats* and it became Article 40 of the Constitution, while Gandhiji used to say that the essence of non-violence, was decentralisation and that the aim should be development of self sufficient, self governing village communities. Above the village *Panchayat* was to come a hierarchy of *Panchayats*, indirectly elected, at the *Taluka*, District, Provincial and finally the All India *Panchayat*, the Parliament. Gandhiji often said, "The State that governs best, governs least." Nehru and Patel believed that a strong Central Government and a highly industrialised economy were essential to safeguard national independence and to rid the country of poverty and backwardness.

Vishav Bhavan

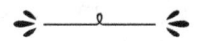

On the introductory page of this memoir, Pitaji writes:

> I am not even conceited to suppose that the details of my life or those of my near relations, who are mentioned in it, could be of any interest to the reader. It just occurred to me that the evolutionary progress in North India for the period (1903-82) as observed by me recorded in the form of an autobiography might be acceptable.

While the binder itself was embossed with the words 'Vishav Bhavan', he chose not to talk about life at Vishav Bhavan. On the other hand, it is my view that life at Vishav Bhavan during the period when he penned this book is of relevance, so I will take a couple of pages to talk about it.

From age three to seventeen, I grew up in Chandigarh. The doors to Vishav Bhavan,[3] the name Pitaji gave to our house, which I have loosely translated as *'A Shelter To The World'*,

---

3   *Vishav* translates to the (whole) world and *Bhavan*, a building or a house, or *A Shelter To The World*, or a *sarai* that offered a roof and a hearth to all who came. Vishav is also the first part of Pitaji's name as written in Hindi - Vishvambar, which in colloquial Punjabi transliterates to Bishambar.

were never locked. Someone was always home. Over the last seventy years, Vishav Bhavan has hosted thousands as overnight guests. At times there were weeks, when there were no visitors or overnight guests, we lived as a family with four generations under one roof. Lalaji (my great grandfather) had a bedroom downstairs and Bebeji (the sister-in-law of my great grandfather, the elder sister of Pitaji's mother) occupied a room under the staircase which was no bigger than a little alcove. Upstairs, Pitaji and Mataji occupied one bedroom and my parents occupied another. The common kitchen was downstairs, and there were both an indoor kitchen and an outdoor kitchen where food was cooked on an open flame.

Not only close family members, uncles and cousins from near and far, would come to visit for extended periods, but Pitaji's professional colleagues and acquaintances would visit and stay overnight as well. When holy men, wandering or directed to visit us by out-of-town family members, showed up at Vishav Bhavan, Mataji would never turn them away. Food and a bed were provided at any time of day. As I think back, Vishav Bhavan should have been called a *sarai*, an inn.

Growing up, I was unaware of how special it was that I was living with my great grandfather, a great grandmother, my grandfather and grandmother, and my parents. Unknowingly, I was absorbing so much lived experiences, and lived wisdom. Bebeji would tell me long stories every night, with funny and scary characters from villages of old. The lessons were obscure to me at that age. Lalaji would sleep for just a few hours every night and go off wandering for hours. I later learned that he would take his blankets and leave them with the families that were sleeping in the streets. When guavas or mangoes or figs or loquats would ripen in the trees, Lalaji would sit in the verandah for hours on end, shooing away the scavengers – the crows or the parrots, while singing tuneless melodies. Mataji, my grandmother spoiled me immensely. When I would refuse to eat, which was every day, she would lovingly feed me *churi*, smashed *roti*, loaded with *ghee* and sugar.

My parents were both professors, my father at Panjab University, Department of Mathematics, and my mother taught Hindi at Mehr Chand Mahajan D.A.V. College for Women.

My father was a number theorist, dedicated teacher, a storyteller par excellence, a mime with a ready wit and a supply of Urdu *shayari*. He inculcated in me the love of mathematics through puzzles and tricks, and he did the same for any child that happened to be in his presence.

As a true superwoman, my mother had hardly any rest. In addition to preparation and grading for her teaching job including writing for the college magazine and preparing students for inter-collegiate debates, at home she was responsible for getting me ready for school, and helping me with my homework. She was also the innkeeper for the *sarai* that was Vishav Bhavan. Growing up in Vishav Bhavan was also a life-long lesson in frugal living. Every night, my mother would update her notebook with daily expenditures. My weekly pocket money was one rupee, which I would save all week and enjoy an orange ice on the way home from school, on Fridays. Movie tickets for the cheap front rows (the lower stalls) were Rs. 1.50, a week and a half of pocket money, a lesson in savings.

When schools were on summer vacation in Delhi, Sarla *phuphi*, Balbir *phuphaji*, and their children, Sumant *bhaiya*, Sarita *didi*, and Geeta *didi* would come and stay for weeks. I remember those days with delight. While these cousins were older, Sarita and Geeta would spoil me immensely and I became very close to them. They were elder sisters to me, not cousins. Along with *phuphi*, Sarita and Geeta would spend weeks planning and organising a party for my birthday in July. When I went and stayed with them in Delhi, at Pusa Road and in Ramakrishnapuram, Sarita and Geeta would take me sightseeing around the capital city, and continue to spoil me. In 1975, Geeta and I travelled by tempo with the newlyweds Sarita *didi* and Satinder Puri, to help get them settled in their home in Ganaur, Haryana, a distance of 75 kilometres, all four of us singing (screaming and laughing) an obscure film song at the top of our voices.

I must have loved being the focus of attention of so many. My younger brother Vipul arrived in March 1968, and became the new focus of our collective attention. Lalaji would sit in the verandah for hours, just watching Vipul sleep while gently swaying a *pakkhi*, a hand fan, so that flies did not wake him up. Summer vacations were also an opportunity to develop strong family bonds as my mother and her sisters gathered their brood in Ferozepur. Some of these cousins would later come to study in Chandigarh and get to experience Vishav Bhavan.

With Panjab University, the PGI (the Post Graduate Institute of Medical Sciences and Research), and a half a dozen colleges, Chandigarh was a centre of higher education. Children of family members and acquaintances from around the country came to study and board in these colleges. Vishav Bhavan was where they could be assured of a home-cooked meal on any weeknight or weekend, accompanied by a ready supply of papa's jokes, elderly wisdom and intelligent conversation to supplement their education. This tradition started as early as the sixties with Indu *massi*, my mother's younger sister, and Ashok *mamaji*, mummy's cousin, and then continued for five decades. As teachers and educators, my father and mother played a role in the education of these college students, in their formative years. Even today I run into graduates who availed themselves of this Vishav Bhavan diploma, while collecting their formal education at college.

In 1978, I left for IIT Kanpur, a first step that took me away from Vishav Bhavan for good. Pitaji passed away in 1982. After 1978, I never stayed in Vishav Bhavan for more than a few weeks at a time. But, the tradition of Vishav Bhavan as a *sarai*, continued for many more decades.

The opening paragraphs of Pitaji's book are about his own grandfather Ram Shah, a somewhat autocratic head of the joint family that provided both social security for the members and enforced social norms. A story Pitaji does not include in this memoir is worth recounting here. *"Pandrah tiye, ik so panj, te painti, ik sau sath, das tennu chhade..., aithe angutha laa de."* "Fifteen times three is a hundred and five, plus thirty-five, a hundred and sixty, I'll forgive you ten..., place your thumb print here." The illiterate and innumerate residents of the village walked away grateful for the ten rupees that the benevolent Shah ji had forgiven, and remained forever in Ram Shah's debt. This turned his son, my great grandfather, Lalaji (Mathra Das), into the lifelong ascetic who never owned anything other than the clothes on his back.

Based on Pitaji's lived experiences – first the joint family in the little village of Kakrali where he grew up, later the joint family that helped him raise his children in Srinagar, Karachi, Lahore and Quetta, the joint family that helped him pursue his career when the children were young, and when Mataji was unwell. After Partition, having reestablished his career, he was in a position of being an elder statesman to a much larger family of his cousins scattered around the country, in Ahmedabad, Meerut, Faridabad and Delhi, all of whom were in the process of standing up on their own two feet after being displaced during Partition, and whose own families were growing.

Pitaji thus came to see the joint family as a model for social security and development in the wider community setting.

He writes:

… the joint family, in which the members of the family grew up under one shelter, provides social security to them whether members earned or not. They would not lack food as long as the joint family had the capacity to provide and they shared the plight of hunger if the joint stock dwindled to nothing. Unemployment, sickness and the like were not quite frightening when the common pool of the family was adequate…

…

Enlarging upon this simile, the Nation, which ought to function as a joint family in a democratic set up, would normally impose certain duties to be observed by its members strictly for them to pull together – the living expenses of well off members should be reduced with regard to the economic conditions of the whole family so as to provide food, clothes and shelter as also education and medical aid.

…

The community development programme, in which I had a hand, is a movement on a large scale similar to the joint family system with which I was quite familiar.

He concludes:

In the absence of any system which would provide the individual an insurance against old age, handicap, widowhood, loss of parent, etc, the joint family, however imperfectly, gave shelter and security.

My career as an electrical engineer took me to the forefront of the wireless and cellular revolution starting in the nineteen nineties, working first at the prestigious Bell Labs, and later at Qualcomm. I became a believer in technological advancement as the path to societal uplift. My father, Vinod Chandar Nanda, had become steadily more politically active, and after he retired from his position as professor of mathematics at Punjab University in 1992, he took on progressive causes. Over the next twenty-five years, as an activist, he led a call with high schools to boycott carbonated soft drinks and genetically modified foods, he wrote a booklet to oppose the Indo-US nuclear deal, and took up many more causes with the Gandhian socialism inspired organisation, *Azadi Bachao Aandolan*, to oppose the takeover of the world's economies by global corporations.

Interesting conversations and debates on globalisation and the mal-influence of global corporatisation would repeat during my twice-yearly visits to Vishav Bhavan, some partially paid for by my corporate employer (as I would combine my visits to Chandigarh with official visits to our offices in Bangalore). I wanted papa to see that you couldn't turn back the clock on technological progress. I felt that my father was unwilling to see both sides of the coin, but he held firm to his Gandhian ideals, to the end.

Today, it is more clear than ever to me that the economic model of capitalism, that has led to a century of technological breakthroughs, is based on the growth of consumerism, more and more production of goods, and more and more exploitation of the earth's resources. The key to a sustainable future lies in consuming less, a *mantra* from Gandhian socialism which is antithetical to the way we measure progress through the gross national product and stock market gains. Nature's fury is in evidence in the headlines today, making Gandhian philosophy ever more relevant to our future. While the technological genie cannot be shoved back in the bottle, how new technologies should be put in the service of 'less' – less consumption, less production, less exploitation of natural resources, is an exercise for the reader, and for the next generation of visionary leadership.

Gandhian socialism includes the tenets of *Swaraj*, the self-sufficiency of each human being to live a life with dignity of labour and a concomitant birthright to nutrition, shelter, clothing, health and education; *Seva*, where those with greater means serve those who have less; *Sadachar*, morality in public life and a society free of corruption; and *Sarvodaya*, uplift of society as a whole, starting from the grassroots, from the villages.

I suppose you have to be of a certain age to understand the truths that my father and my grandfather were trying to impart to me. The publication of this volume is my dedication to what I learned from them. *Der aaye, durust aaye,* better late…

Editorial Note

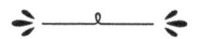

While typing up and editing my grandfather's neatly handwritten manuscript, I have scrupulously tried to keep his words, his language constructs, and his voice, unfiltered by newer 21st century sensibilities. Amazingly, in the entire manuscript there were just a dozen or so words that I found to be illegible. I have italicised most words or phrases that may be unfamiliar to non-English speakers, especially those not from India. In cases that a meaning of a word or phrase is not provided nearby, or words that appear frequently or need a lengthier explanation, I have placed them in a glossary that appears at the end.

To not interrupt his flow of words, I have limited editorial insertions within the text, except very rarely. When I have, it's through footnotes. I sincerely hope that I have succeeded in keeping a very light touch.

It's been a labour of love for me. I knew my Pitaji as a presence in my life as I was growing up, to be held in awe, not to be disturbed even if he was playing solitaire. He always dressed in white *khaddar* (handloom cotton) *churidar-kurta,* a *Nehru topi* on his head, a *shervani* when it was cool or if a formal occasion demanded it. He commanded respect from all.

In this book I discovered that he was a somewhat sickly lad, the spoiled grandson of the village landlord. I discovered his vagabond travels in England and Europe. It was through writing up this manuscript that I discovered how he gained, and then during Partition, lost a fortune in Quetta. I have found letters that he wrote to the Governments of India and Pakistan over a quarter century following Partition, demanding recompense for his property and business in Quetta. There is no mention of this pursuit of refugee reparations, in this manuscript.

His life experiences and the overarching influence of Gandhi led him to a life of service (*Seva*), a guiding philosophy of grassroots rural community development (*Sarvodaya*), the dignity of labour, and the significance of full employment as a national goal (*Swaraj*). Late in life, he lamented the loss of moral rectitude (*Sadachar*) in the public sphere.

I hope I have succeeded in my endeavour to bring a good story and an enjoyable read to you, dear reader.

– Sanjiv Nanda

VISHAV BHAVAN

Introduction

The following narrative is not exactly an autobiography but a record of some recollections and reflections of my experiences in life. I am not even conceited to suppose that the details of my life or those of my near relations, who are mentioned in it, could be of any interest to the reader. It just occurred to me that the evolutionary progress in North India for the period (1903-82) as observed by me recorded in the form of an autobiography might be acceptable.

I owe a debt of gratitude to my parents who permitted me to open my eyes to the light of the day, and later gave me faith in life. Though my career was quite different from my successors, yet in my approach to life I was inspired by the ethics of my forefathers.

My life has relatively been carefree as I hardly had any burdens, and things came to me in fairly well defined outlines, with privileges of working and of feeling behind me a past that I was carrying forward, and being able to reckon even on the future. Life was never foggy, and being easy, I enjoyed my own importance which was both individual and collective. Even successes and failures of my humble life lost their charm and sting much sooner than one could imagine, I find it difficult to remember them in much detail. I did not play any great role of either destroying all to rebuild again, of making a clean slate of the past, of traditions, of creating a new personality for myself, a new universe, or a new God. Herein, I have therefore, tried to distract my thoughts from, rather than concentrate on, the contemplation of my own individuality. The theme is not based on an account of myself as related to events of the last eighty years or so, but in writing out a narrative of this kind it has been a difficult task as self-forgetfulness is quite out of place when the subject is my own life story.

When I see Sanjiv and Vipul, my grandsons who are in their fifteenth and ninth years, recollections of my childhood come to me more easily. Thus in writing about the stranger I the child, it became quite a pleasant task to live over again in thought, the days he lived. Some of the facts I have been able to testify or secure from my father whose mind was very alert even when he was over ninety five.

I am writing about the period I was young, I am not giving a record of my efforts, privations and savings for bringing up my children. I have also avoided to give an account of personal celebrations relating to birthdays, parties and marriages of relatives and friends or details of any funeral ceremonies in which I participated. Instead I have distributed the panorama which I witnessed during the period of my life. As I had neither tension, nor was I engaged in a headlong race, I found plenty of leisure to enjoy the company of my family. In fact, I had very few engagements outside of my own home. I accepted the life conditioned by my limitations and traditions and regulated my energy in line with them. I remained an observer of events or a humble actor in the drama in which I took part.

As I grew old I began to realise that my routine of life, which had aimed at producing adequate income to meet the needs of life, did not satisfy me. I joined the Bharat Sevak Samaj, in which organisation I came in contact with social workers and thinkers and with intellectuals who provided me with recipes based on their experiences and observations. I have ventured to bring them out in this narrative to some extent.

Very few people can be happy unless their way of life is accepted by their friends and relations. Although I did not imbibe all the prejudices, beliefs and customs of the community in which I lived, yet I did not have adequate courage to be hostile towards them. I acquiesced and joined hands when others practised them, to maintain their surroundings sympathetic. If I had a privileged life by having parents who allowed my freedom to have my own views on religion or politics or career, I in turn, did not interfere with the convictions that my own children developed although family heredity had its impact. The daughters-in-law that had been adopted into our family fold, had been nourished for their girlhood in somewhat different surroundings. Both of them have a university career – one M.A. in Hindi and the other M.A. in Psychology. After their marriage they were placed in the company of our family surroundings where lesser educated people occupied positions of privilege. If they retained in their behaviour respect for them, the people too, wonderfully compromised with them in allowing the young boys and girls to practise their own tastes and convictions. Absence of extreme hostility from the one set and tyranny from the other, by and large produced a congenial atmosphere.

VISHAV BHAVAN

Part 1: Kakrali

My Heritage

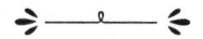

My grandfather was a well-to-do landlord in his day and age. He commanded great respect and held considerable sway over the people he came in contact with. In the village he was the supreme commander whose orders were obeyed and executed without question. His name was Lala Ram Chand but he was better known as Ram Shah – Ram, the King, or Ram, the Ruler. The solidarity of the family was built in and around Ram Shah, who was the head and the arbiter, who desperately wanted to maintain the joint family. According to him it was the only way to social security for all members of his family, who received what they needed out of the common pool.

The joint family discouraged incentives to progress in any direction but there was no alternative outlet. If any member felt disgruntled and desired to leave the family fold to try elsewhere for earning, he lacked both courage and assets. Ram Shah, himself, possessed initiative, enthusiasm and spirit of sacrifice. He was untiring, loved fatigue, and worked hard to earn a name and an adequate income for a comfortable living for himself and his dependents. He would stir up all prevailing peace for a life of activity as he was hardly ever upset by disturbing factors. He had thus earned his social rank and accepted all responsibilities that his social rank brought with it. His love for me (Bishambar, one of his grandsons) was greater than that bestowed on any other member in his whole family. I was the one and only person on whom he would not wish to enforce his will.

My father Mathra Das was the second son and third child among the family consisting of five brothers and four sisters. Mathra Das was married at the age of thirteen in 1891, his bride being two years his junior. Soon after his marriage he left school and began to take interest in mystic philosophy. He found a teacher -- a *sadhu*, Diwan Chand, who hailed from Jalalpur Jattan, the hometown of his wife, my mother. This sadhu was popularly known as *'bhagat'* or the devotee. Mathra Das became his devotee and thus he began to lose interest in home life, relatives and friends, and soon began to show signs that he would renounce worldly life and devote himself exclusively to the attainment of spiritual goals.

Ram Shah observed this change in Mathra Das and took the following course of action. He built a home for the teacher in his own orchard on the outskirts of the village of Kakrali and provided all necessary amenities for comfort. Time proved his wisdom as *Bhagatji* became a slave to Ram Shah. Mathra Das was persuaded to live in the family and receive his religious and philosophical lessons from his teacher. My mother was worried about my father's lack of interest in her home life but later her anxiety was diminished. A son was born on the tenth day of December 1903 in the early hours of the morning. My birth occurred after my parents had been married for twelve years. When a son is born in the village the whole population rejoices over the event and when the parents are sufficiently wealthy to be able to distribute sweets, the merry making takes the form of a village fair. This happened.

My mother had an instinctive faith and belief in religious

scriptures, parts of which she could narrate but could not write. She was never keen about her prayers. Ram Shah, my grandfather, however, would spare time every morning to read the Mahabharata, the great Hindu epic of which the Bhagavad Gita is a part. Even when I was a child I told him once that it was not much use reading the account of the battle between Pandavas and Kauravas at Kurukshetra fought thousands of years ago. He replied in a convincing manner that he did draw inspiration from the epic.

Our ancestral home was commodious but the rooms were unusually dark with no windows, and therefore used only when the weather would not permit our living in the open or on the verandah. Even guests were received and festivities held on the verandah. We also had a stable, fairly large though it was poorly built. This building had a central courtyard about sixty feet square and rooms on all sides about twelve feet wide and of varying lengths. These, too, were dark and lacked ventilation except for a few round holes about nine to ten inches diameter besides the doors. Its mud floors were daily stabilised with cow dung *lep* (applying a layer of dung). The roof was built of wooden beams and battens covered over by weeds and mud to provide a flat terrace. My parents and I were not the only people who lived in this stable besides the cattle and the horses, my grandfather also had his bedroom here. I passed the major part of my childhood in the rooms attached to the stable.

In all the rooms attached to the stable, there were rats far too numerous for any single cat to devour. Their abodes were either under the floor or in between the weeds of the roof. We often used traps but we failed to eliminate them. Either the rats were multiplying at a faster rate that we could catch and remove half a mile out of the village, or they returned. I disliked rats and would shriek every time one jumped on my bed. As rats are relished by snakes, the presence of rats also implies the presence of one or more reptiles. This knowledge made me live in constant dread of being bitten by a snake. I never disclosed this fear and as a matter of course I have endured this agony in silence.

Within six months of my birth my parents were advised that I should be vaccinated but the stupid story, which I was later told, prevented this from happening. Thus it went – the British Government through the practice of vaccination were trying to locate someone who was to destroy their Empire or drive them out from India. This person, from whose arm would ooze milk-white secretion from the prick would be the one who must be killed before he or she lived to strike. My grandfather had been warned by an astrologer that I was the likely child, therefore the government-employed inoculator was bribed and I remained without vaccination until I wished to leave for England in 1925. Gradually people learned about the advantage of vaccination and allowed the official inoculator to perform his task willingly.

I was born, like all of us, in a state of dependence – on all kinds of particular conditions, conditions of country, race, family, environment, health, brains, fortune, and in the course of our lives all of us depend on circumstances which are not easily foreseen nor can they be avoided. All of us must resolutely accept our dependence. But if we are, in one part of our life, dependent, another part of our life, on the contrary, depends on us. It is the latter task where our energy must come into play.

Having said so little about my mother so far I would add a little description of her. She was a woman of strong character, whatever anguish she suffered, she concealed. She saw shrewdly that the world is quickly bored by the recital of misfortune and willingly avoids the sight of distress. She was always anxious to listen to the troubles of others than to discuss her own. Whatever she spoke of her husband was with pride, although she guided him in all worldly matters. She loved me more than anything in this world. Her anxiety for me while she lived, and even at her deathbed was so great as almost to unbalance her reason. She would picture to herself terrible things that might befall me away from her side and if I came back late from my work, even when I was over thirty, she would be in a panic. She never punished me. She lived that way all her life.

The Setting

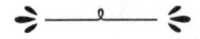

India is essentially a country of villages. The village of Kakrali in the district of Gujrat, Punjab (now West Punjab, Pakistan), where I was born, had a population of approximately three thousand souls in 1903. This was my *matri bhumi* (motherland) as it was then understood. The Muslims who were in preponderance consisted mainly of peasants, but had amongst them hereditary blacksmiths, weavers, cobblers, oilmen, barbers, tailors, washermen and the like. Hindus were either landlords or traders. This entire village community was well knit like the joint family tradition at the time. Muslims and Hindus lived amicably, and it was one economic ensemble. All worked happily and contentedly. Even the unemployed had his sustenance and lived contentedly with the prosperous among the community.

There was no technical mobility between the various occupations and all the groups practised their professions of heredity. The position of each group in the status scales of the community was with the nature of their occupation. It was largely a barter economy although the money economy existed side by side. If I needed a lock or desired to have shoes mended, the craftsman usually served without any monetary charge as my grandfather compensated them at the time of harvest with grain. It would be little surprise if under these conditions, I felt elated about the wonderful position our family occupied, or that I desired to follow my grandfather's occupation which gave him a position so successfully held by him.

With the relative stability of social life there was a considerable measure of cultural homogeneity not only in the village, but in the whole district. The lack of well developed roads restricted social contact and this introduced self dependence and conservatism in the community.

Traditional customs regulated the social life in the village. It mattered little to the people of the village who was the reigning monarch. The old saying was, *Dilli dur ast*, Delhi is a long way off, although in reality in 1903 the British had Calcutta as their capital of India, not Delhi. Calcutta was something like the other end of the world to the people of Kakrali. Hardly was anyone disengaged from his native ground and their motherland was their sacred village.

Kakrali had a central position which induced people of surrounding villages to visit it for buying edibles, clothing and other needs. Here they were able to purchase imported cloth manufactured in England. Long cloth, muslins and even velvets came to the village from Amritsar – a commercial city in East Punjab, and it fascinated many to purchase the fine materials in preference to the coarse cloth produced by the village weavers. I used to collect the coloured pictures which were found pasted to each piece of imported cloth. The village people were by no means rich but their needs were few and simple. There was, however, enough food and milk to go around.

The village commanded an influence over an area of one hundred square miles or more but my grandfather maintained his influence over a still larger area. The solidarity of the family was built in and around the worship of my grandfather which had more social than religious significance. The bonds which held together the social structure of the Hindus in that area were the innumerable bonds of family relationships so much so that the bonds of our own family and the bonds of the Hindus in that area were almost the same.

A peasant rural society based upon agricultural production did not need any collective organisation. The individual was free as long as he did not trespass the customs and traditions, and yet the entire village community had a cooperative life. By and large they were truthful, simple and had respect for one another. Education was almost a generation behind but it did not seem to matter as progressive change was slow everywhere. But, in social thought and behaviour the accent was on the common good, and the joint family was the best illustration of the attitude. The earnings of all individual members, whatever the size of the earnings, were credited to the common pool out of which were met the requirements of every member of the family.

The general economic standard of living in the village was low but the villager was contented, peaceful and law-abiding. The two predominant religions, namely Hinduism and Islam had not a little to do with his contentment, with blind faith in God and in His will. There were hardly a few people in the village who could read books and newspapers. The local priests whether Hindu or Muslim gave the people few rudiments of religious knowledge, and they did not encourage communal strife which became prominent with the advancement of education and political manoeuvres. Most of the village disputes were settled by recourse to arbitration and this was invariably entrusted to my grandfather.

Marriages, more often than not, were celebrated in spring, summer and early autumn. Guests of the marriage parties used to remain at the bride's place for two days and three nights and had to be provided with beds, lodging and board. If the weather was not cold, guests could sleep out of doors.

Occupations also formed a hierarchy. Butchery, for instance, was treated as a low profession because the butcher kills animals for a living. In our village only Muslims were butchers. It would not be true to say that Hindus did not kill animals like fowl, or do fishing, but they did not do it for a living. Working with leather was another low profession because handling hides is defiling and such defilement was related to the taking of life, and to the messiness of skinning and tanning. It may appear strange then that this profession was adopted by my uncle as an occupation decades later after India's Partition in 1947.

The work of barber and washerman involved handling one or the other kind of dirt and that made the occupation of both unclean. It was strange if not interesting that both the washerman and the barber refused to serve the sweeper. Hindus were extremely particular about purification through a bath after a haircut or shave by a barber.

Separation of the two principal communities namely the Hindus and Muslims was also achieved through restrictions on commensality. There was a concept of pollution in Hindus refusing to accept drinking water and cooked food from Muslims as the former did not regard the latter as equals. The womenfolk were more rigid about it. My father had an instinctive abhorrence with regard to such restrictions and he was able to quote from Hindu scriptures passages which run contrary to the practices of untouchability or of inequality between man and man. The Hindus and Muslims lived side by side in the village, but inter-communal marriages were unheard of, and none ever seemed worried about the barrier.

The villager's cottage, although built of mud walls, afforded according to the ideas of its people, comfortable shelter. The people did not have much clothing, but much was not wanted. They hardly suffered from the cold in winter. There was sufficient wheat, millet and pulses, vegetables and ghee and chillies which formed their food. There was as much sugar, sweetmeats and tobacco as they could afford to buy. Their womenfolk had ornaments either in silver or in gold or both depending on the family's hoarding capacity. However, from modern standards they were destitute of comforts and conveniences which are now considered essential to civilised life. But no one could say that they were devoid of simple pleasures and enjoyments as they celebrated their festivals and ceremonies both religious and social in ecstasy. They were, likely had to be, thrifty and frugal in their living and were self-reliant but acted and lived like a joint family to provide themselves with bare necessities. Both the landless and the landowner found support from the land, and it was the religious duty along with strength and sanctity of the ties of the family and caste, that the poor could safely rely on. Such was the setting and the surroundings of which I was a product.

Childhood Education

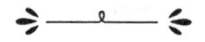

At the age of five I was sent to a school. The school building was almost similar in construction to the house occupied by my parents. I felt 'at home' because it all seemed familiar to me. I started with the Urdu alphabet under a teacher who believed that children could only be taught through the rod. The first primer containing sixteen pages possessed only one picture which was on the outer cover. This book was printed in litho, the only method then known for Urdu and the quality of the paper was such that we were compelled to have it bound to protect it from early destruction. We had no exercise books, these were unknown in the village school (*madrassah*). Every child used a wooden board about three quarters of an inch thick and measuring approximately nine inches by twelve inches long for writing. We would cover it on both sides with a thin layer of yellow clay paste which after drying gave a smooth surface. We would write on it with a quill – the quill being the stock of an aquatic weed shaped like a bold nib. The ink, too, was home made from black soot and gum. This mixture with a little water and a tiny piece of rag, was placed in a small earthen pot. The wooden plank and the quill were popularly known as *takhati* and *qalam*. I was equipped with a satchel and a slate on which I wrote and did my arithmetic. Lead pencils were yet unknown in the village so that we used small pieces of slate stone for writing on the slate.

No English, Hindi or Sanskrit was required of us. Urdu written in Arabic script from the right to left, was to be my language. Books were rare and money had much value. The children were taught that they must preserve the books as they passed from class to class; these could be left in good condition to those that followed. I received my quota of second hand books from my cousin Raghpat Rai Nanda, who gave me his companionship and assisted me with my lessons. I succeeded him year after year and invariably used his books as he preserved them well.

I was the youngest scholar in the class. The average age for admission to the village school was from seven although many students did not enter the school until the age of eleven or twelve. The bigger boys had hardly any advantage over me in the matter of learning but they were rowdy and could be a nuisance for the small boys. Had I not belonged to parents in a favoured position in the village, I should have received many beatings from these boys of whom I was afraid.

Being frail in my childhood I was not good at games. I lagged behind in every race and becoming conscious of my inferiority I refrained from taking part in any sport. My food was rich, plenty of milk and milk products, melons, sugarcane, raw sugar, meat, eggs and fresh vegetables which all we had in plenty. Roasted grain, wheat or maize was the common food every afternoon. Cash was to me a rare commodity and hard to obtain but everything considered worthwhile by my parents, was available. I was quite contented and happy. My rich food, with little exercise, rendered my figure bulky and I was nicknamed '*mota*' (fatty) and I had to reconcile myself to a considerable amount of teasing.

No girls were allowed to attend the *madrassah*. Their vocation in life was to help their mothers with household work and only very occasionally would they be allowed to play with boys of their age. Simple folk games were classified differently for each sex. Racing, wrestling, *kabaddi*, swimming and tree climbing were the most popular sports for the boys, whilst the girls played hide and seek, jumping the rope and various games played with a rubber ball. My parents were anxious that I should play with the girls and not with the boys for fear of my being hurt. I enjoyed playing with them but I was also not prepared to lose face with the boys. This state of affairs continued until I was ten, when I was taken out of their company to keep me out of mischief.

Most of the students thought that the school was for them a place where they could play for hours without interference. To be a student in those days and in a village school was a privilege not a right. If one missed attendance at school the teacher called at his residence to discover the reason for the student's absence. It was, however, not worthwhile to be absent from the school on working days, because if one missed one's lessons, the teacher would give the cane in reward. The teacher himself knew little and his general knowledge was poor. My parents being more resourceful were better informed and, therefore, I obtained more general knowledge from them than from my teacher.

I remember an occasion on which the teacher of the second primary class gave a lesson on the elephant. Learning that a government official had arrived in the village on an elephant he led us from the classroom to the roadside where the elephant was standing motionless without the *mahawat* (trainer). The teacher showed us four round wheels and the nicely cushioned seats inside for the *mahawat*. It was nothing other than a car. It was for him as much a novelty as an elephant could be. These circumstances caused this event to remain a great joke in the village for a long time and only after the death of the teacher did the story lose interest. With such limited material that the school possessed, I consider that we were reasonably well trained. Requisite education facilities were hardly available in the towns, the villages were ill provided and under the desperately discouraging circumstances only exceptional individuals were able to get over these embarrassments.

My father helped me considerably with my studies. Good handwriting was considered a qualification for a child. The Hindu boys usually proved to be progressive in arithmetic. As I was good at oral arithmetic, the elderly people in the village would put questions to me, and thus I became alert in memorising. My mother then began to ask me to count the utensils in the kitchen, clothes in the boxes. I now started counting anything and everything. Eventually I counted the chips of wood which lay about in the courtyard and the cow dung cakes in stock. Next I learned a number of theorems for which my father was the instructor. For a rupee in those days was equivalent to sixteen *annas*, and a *seer*[4] had sixteen *chhatanks*, and a yard sixteen *girahs*. From this relationship of measure I was told that the cost of a yard or a *seer* in rupees would be the same as the cost of one *girah* or one *chhatank* in *annas*. Such theorems proved useful for oral arithmetic tests.

My mother loved me immensely and I can be quite emphatic in stating that her love stood in good stead for my education and all round development. It brought reverence and a sense of transcendence about her in my devotion. This emotion continued with me as long as she was alive. I could be arrogant to a teacher, could be harsh towards an employee, resistant towards a boss, but always tame before my mother. She remained my master for long.

---

4   Unit of weight, equal to about 1.25 kg.

Childhood Education

I grew up from 'babyhood' to childhood with intelligence which my mother was never tired of announcing to all and sundry, although she never bothered to know how much I learned at school. She was much more inquisitive about my moral development. In my day, children, at least in the villages, were not given any mechanical toys although my girl playmates and I used to make dolls out of rags or occasionally provided with earthen toys or crude wooden ones.

I was not jealous by nature but I wanted the whole village to concern itself with me being the most beloved child of the man who ruled the village. My training too kept me away from jealousy. In spite of being the only child I was by no means a spoilt child, but I had a position among my age group, and I held that position as long as I lived in the village. This habit lasted with me and made me adopt a dictatorial attitude towards those who worked with me. When I was about twenty I formed a 'temple committee' in the village with the following of all who were between eighteen and thirty-five. I became its first president and took over charge of the entire temple property from the elders of the village. It happened that the village priest eloped with a young lass, I raised my voice against priesthood and arranged with Swami Sahajnanda, an ascetic living in the outskirts of the village, to impart religious education to the temple goers by his discourse on spiritual morality. Villagers accepted this and the arrangement was welcomed everywhere. I also appointed one of my father's cousins as acting president while I would be away for my studies in Lahore.

My mother was worried about my health because I was pale and languid. Whenever she broached the subject with the 'wisest old lady', my grandfather's only sister, she prescribed that my mother should give me a brother to play with. So, far from taking what the old lady said for granted, particularly when I had a whole hoard of girls and boys of my age to play with in the village, I was much inclined to go counter to her opinion. I never found the time heavy on me and even when I was not playing, my inner life was very active, which had been aroused in my childhood by my parents. Furthermore, by now I knew that little brothers, when they came, are usually quite tiny, know not how to walk, are incapable of conversation and offer no company.

So long as I was unable to read, newspapers, which were very uncommon things in the village, were very mysterious to me. When someone holding big sheets of paper covered all over with little black signs read aloud from them, news about deaths by plague or malaria, tidings about festivals and happenings in distant lands, my curiosity was aroused. Whenever there was an occasion to see magic being performed, I would not like to miss it and invariably if I could get hold of this *akhbar* (newspaper), I would spread it, and ape reading.

There is another memory gathered up amid the twilight of those far off days. One day – I cannot express myself with greater precision than that, my father and mother had left me in the house under care of a cousin sister for a whole week without my having known it. I felt very sad and ashamed at having allowed myself to be taken in, when there had been so many signs which could have conveyed to me what was afoot. The house looked cheerless and it sent a chill to my heart. To fill the void, my cousin sister was really too little. I loved my cousin immensely but she was not sufficient to take their place. The thought of living a whole week without seeing my parents reduced me to despair. I was told that my parents would bring nice things for me but I refused to be comforted on that day. But fortune took a different turn on the following day.

Servants

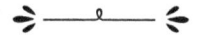

Ever since Partition of the country we had had a dozen or so servants, of whom the better ones departed as soon as they found that the salary was none too plentiful. Sometimes we had one who knew nothing of housework, but my wife thought that she would be able to train him. He spent six months or so and then took leave of us on one pretext or the other. We once had one who was off his head and with great difficulty we could get rid of him. Another servant who knew housekeeping and good cooking and was quite satisfied with his emoluments was always making trips to the army recruiting base until he found employment in the military service.

This is the general complaint from all middle class families, "You can't get servants anywhere. Things are not what they used to be when you could pick up a good, faithful, steady going servant without any trouble. Now things are quite different." Some people blamed Democracy, which, they said, had put all sorts of high notions into the heads of working classes and made them dissatisfied. But when were people not dissatisfied? The truth of the matter is that good masters and good servants are rare and almost always have been ever since the services were paid for in money.

I have but a scanty recollection of these early days when I had yet completed my fifth or sixth year that we had a number of servants in the house. Many of them were part-time and two of them lived in the house. None of them was paid in cash but rewarded in kind. There were three Mohammedans, one of them was an old lady, two or three Hindus and a Hindu Jat lady. They all belonged to the village. Of these I propose to describe three of them.

The old Muslim lady who shared our premises, was nearly of the same age as my grandfather and had been living with my grandparents and parents for years before I received her affection. Old age I liked, because it was beautiful, sometimes comic, and easy to make fun of; I had yet to learn that it was burdensome and sad. In fact, whenever I see my grandson mimicking old people I persuade him not to do so and even explain to him the plight from which the old people suffer when they reach an advanced age. 'Bibi' as she was called, I do not know to this day whether that was her real name or a nickname, was not frail in her body. She however, did not have the sharp memory of my aunt – my mother's sister who could relate things in good detail, of seventy years ago and could do so word for word even if it was repeated after years. Bibi was very fond of me. Was it instinctive or loyalty to my ancestors who had given her shelter and other basic needs, I was not able to analyse. My parents had full reliance on her that she would not leave me alone if they went out but they did not think it was safe for me to go about with her out of doors. I loved her in return and often clung to her bony arms and toil worn hands. It looks improper to call her a servant as she shared all the joys and sorrows of the family and even the diversity of her religion proved no barrier. In spite of all this nearness she was not allowed to enter our kitchen. When I look back on this aspect, I feel about our cruelty towards her, she who used to grind fresh wheat flour for us everyday.

The Hindu Jat lady whom I called 'Sister Haro' was a farmer. She owned land in the village and had her own house and a small family of her own. She was a widow and worked part time for us. Unlike Bibi, she was young and always neat in appearance without being gaudy. My father was like a parent to her and also her guru in the little metaphysics that she desired to learn. She swept our living rooms and the kitchen and very often cooked meals for us, on an average one meal every day. In her domestic activities with us she took on the character of some sort of confusion. While sweeping the floors she would say in resolute tones, "I have to cut the vegetables and cook them." What I mean is that while she looked ahead about her responsibilities, she continuously reminded herself about them. In her religious lessons I often sat next to her and I can say that my father spoke in such simple language that both of us could follow him. I remember her devotion during that period while my mind wavered from one thing to another. Sister Haro could not be called servant by any stretch of imagination although she performed as much work daily in our house as a normal servant would do in these days for forty-five rupees a month and his daily meals. Her affectionate disposition had led me to cultivate her society. But there were other considerations, less to my credit, that drew me closer to her. I thought her rather beneath me in intelligence as I could count and tell her tables in arithmetic of which she knew nothing. I greatly enjoyed correcting her whenever she made a mistake in her addition. I did my best to shine before her and she never felt small. She must have had her own assessment about these pranks of mine, but she was never angry with me.

Another part time worker was Satroo, not *shatroo* (which means enemy), but quite the opposite. He was a simpleton, rather a duffer as most of the elders called him. He looked after the animals – the horses, cows, buffaloes, a number of whom we had in the stable. As he had his own house not far away from ours, where he spent the night or middays in summer, he could be called a part time servant. He provided me with occasions for self glorification. Whether he acted or was genuinely foolish I cannot say. He was the only elderly person whom I did not call Uncle and was also never reprimanded for that lapse. Satroo had his upper hand when he was attending to his wards, the animals in the stable, and he gave me plenty of opportunities for being quizzical about animal life, their food and their habits.

Nanak was the cook who worked for us for a few years. He was the only outsider and I had my abhorrence for him, mainly because he had blue eyes and I had often heard that blue eyed persons were not trustworthy. As soon as I was old enough to have my say in small domestic affairs, I had him dismissed. He was substituted by a part-time local servant – a boy who was about six years my elder but a classmate in the school when I was in the first standard.

Masters and servants were all nearer to each other in the village. It looked to me very strange when my father's sister came to live with us from Simla with an *aya* to look after her children, and my aunt as well as the kids bossed over her. Naturally my feeling was that the townspeople were highly ill mannered. The *aya* was a specimen by herself. She was dark skinned. Never on any occasion had she been seen with her hair down, and a single hair out of place would have been a disgrace for her. She was so meticulous in preserving her unvarying mode of coiffure. As a contrast, our lady servants Bibi and Haro, rustic in life, liked their freedom in dress and style of hair. To me they were like a mother and a cousin.

My True Guide

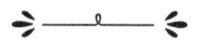

Hinduism is a heterogeneous combination of several philosophies regarding the creator and the soul. The individual is at liberty to believe in and practise any of them without infringing the tenets of religion. Stories from the Puranas such as the churning of the seas by the *devas* and the *asuras* to produce nectar had a religious impact on my mother. She also had explicit faith in the horrors of hell and the ecstasies of heaven and the need for prayers. My father, on the other hand, disbelieved, if not totally rejected, the value of routine religious prayers, in spite of the fact that he did not have the type of scientific education to replace instinctive faith. He had scientific temperament as far as his approach to religion was concerned. I learnt a few philosophical sayings of the type my father accepted, and he influenced my childhood more than did my mother whose faith differed from my father's. There was never any clash between them regarding religious matters and I learnt forbearance from them. With my father's guidance I learned to narrate Urdu verses and the whole village delighted in listening to my recitations.

My father was strongly opposed to the evils of caste and religious dogmas. In fact, he considered it a waste of breath to argue vociferously to establish any one religion. Men, he said, divide themselves into rival camps and fight for the mere words that appear to separate them although they confess common goals. He encouraged me to dine with all people of whatever caste and religion in spite of my mother's resistance, who to my knowledge would throw away bread if it had been touched by a Mohammedan. She strictly adhered to the habit. She believed that the bread, prepared with flour straight from the grindstone, kneaded with milk straight from the cow, ran no risk of pollution by low caste or Muslims. My father often read to me poems of Bulleh Shah – a Punjabi mystic and a poet who had preached the oneness of mankind and pantheistic philosophy. He helped me to have a disbelief in idols or demons. I remember to have committed to memory many '*kafis*' (couplets) of Bulleh Shah and one such couplet:

Kuchh dhane ke kuchh mane ke
Kuchh pahar wali rane ke
Kuchh Guru Nanak walon dekhde
Par aqal de andhe aplen walon nahin dekhde

Meaning that people of the world follow different faiths and prophets and become bigots. If the same people would concentrate on self improvement and better understanding they would discover the truth of oneness of human society. As soon as I was able to read Urdu well, my father bought a complete collection of poems by Bulleh Shah. However, this led to constant arguments between my parents regarding the type of education I should be given.

It is scarcely possible to overestimate the importance of training children to virtuous habits and of fellow-feeling, as in them they are easily formed, and then they last for life. My father led a very pious life and always tried to render service to the whole community of the village among whom he was living. It was both his counsel and his command that I should follow the dictates of my conscience. It matters little, he used to say, if a mean act is discovered or not by another person but it creates an uneasiness within oneself. The story of the lad, who did not pocket any sweets when no one was in the room to catch him as the boy himself was conscious of the wrong in that act always remained vivid to me. I had also committed to memory *Sarakutwali* (words of wisdom) under my father's advice. I was only nine years old at the time when it was considered that I should be taught many things which were difficult for me to understand. My grandfather had his way in making me commit to memory *Vishnu Sahasranamam*[5] in Sanskrit. All these were crammed into my young mind. I was able to forget most of them as soon as I had reached an age to do so. It took me less time to forget them than to remember.

I had no knowledge of what was implied by the word 'temperance' but I collected a number of books which were sold at give-away prices. They contained poems relating to the evils of smoking and drinking. My father was a great smoker of the hubble-bubble (*hukka*). Cigarettes were yet quite rare. He took great care about his *hukka* being clean and I often helped him fill the vessel with water through which the smoke would pass before being inhaled. Poems from the newly acquired books were read by me aloud, particularly those relating to the evils of smoking. This had its effect on my father. He vowed never to smoke and honoured his vow for the rest of his life. My children and I remained non-smokers although we do not raise objections to others smoking.

---

5   *Vishnu Sahasranaman*, the thousand names of Vishnu.

The doctrine of *ahimsa* (non-violence) which literally means non-killing was explained to me by my father at a very early age and long before it received publicity by its application to the Indian struggle for freedom under Gandhiji's leadership. It means that not only must one not offend anybody but one must not harbour even an uncharitable thought towards anyone. This is an ideal which cannot be reached but without this, a person's faith in God has no meaning. "*Yasmin sarvani bhutani atmaivabhut vijanantah,*" from the Gita.

A Muslim *hakim* (a doctor practising *Yunani* medicine) and my father were good friends. They often discussed about the oneness of mankind and the barriers that separated people into different groups. In fact, I can recollect that, at times, they felt such bitterness towards religious scriptures that they would, if they could, burn all of them. Their discourses had a certain amount of lasting influence on me. On one occasion I said to them if God considered it necessary to have so many religions then he could have distinguished one from the other with distinctive features and organs of the human body. I was patted on my back for it.

Once the Muslim *hakim* collected hundreds of '*bir bauhtis*' – insects having shining crimson velvety skin, about three-eighth inch long and one quarter inch wide bodies moving about on tiny legs which could be hardly visible. He imprisoned them in an earthen pot by sealing its top and left them in my charge. When he was gone I took the pot into the fields and released them. When he returned to collect them, I told him what I had done and expressed my indignation against his act of extreme cruelty. He loved me all the more for it, and recommended to my father that I should participate when they discuss vital subjects relating to human acts. There was a complete understanding, as far as I could see, between the *hakim* and my father.

Further there were the times when religious life dominated the minds of the people. Conditions changed with time – the less of God and the more of the creature. "Eat, drink and be merry, row well and discard this ferry-boat of life when wrecked." That is more acceptable as the aim of life, and if this be an expression of the divine will, as most of us would believe, in spite of modern materialistic age, then the divine will is named mainly in a negative sense. My grounding in religion was in the positive direction. Toleration for all religions and more for all branches of the Hindu philosophy, was the tenet given to me by my father. Respect for all faiths, and a conception of God above gods were my early lessons.

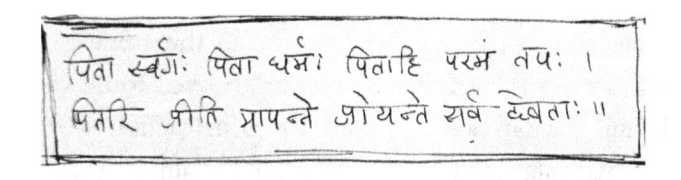

पिता स्वर्गः पिता धर्मः पिताहि परमं तपः ।
पितरि प्रीति प्राप्नते प्रीयन्ते सर्व देवताः ॥

Pita swargah pita dharmah pitahi paramam tapah
Pitari priti maapanne proyante sarva devatah

I was made quite familiar with Kabir's writings, some of which considerably influenced my thinking later in life.

Rangi ko narangi kahen, bane doodh ka khoya
Chalti ko gari kahen, dekh Kabira roya

The orange has a bright yellow colour, One could really call it *rangi* meaning coloured, but the word in use is *narangi* which would mean without colour. Kabir feels hurt, not because calling an orange colourless harms any individual but it indicates man's inherent leanings towards dishonesty. Kabir quotes two more instances in the same direction, namely, concentrated milk called as *khoya* (lost milk) or calling a moving transport as *gari* (motionless).

I have already said that my father made me commit to memory a few couplets from Bulleh Shah which never faded from my memory ever since I was three or four years old. It is difficult to be exact about my age for that matter but it is also immaterial. One that has often been quoted as being appropriate in relation to my life is

Itt kharke, dukar waje, te thand na hove - a - chulah
Aao faqiro kha kha jao, raji hove -a bullah

Come and eat, o traveller, the fire in the stove is always burning. Two-thirds of this couplet has proved to be very apt. Employing masons and *mazdoors* for construction works has been my main stay in life and our kitchen has almost always been kept going from an hour before day break to ten at night and even during six to seven hours in the night my father lights the fire or burner without fail twice or thrice during the period.

My father, who spent many valuable hours reflecting on the destiny of humankind, hardly ever devoted time to looking after his worldly affairs. Naturally, therefore, he was rich in sentiments. He gave alms to the needy, helped the poor with food and clothing. If my mother ever objected about these habits, he told her that the recipients always pray for my long life in return for the meagre material things that he offered them. She always felt satisfied with that explanation.

We had a beautiful mare, white in colour and with well developed muscles. My father knew every whim she had – of scraping the floor with her right forefoot when she wanted attention, of trotting a little faster when she was nearing the village on a return journey, of twitching her ears when she sensed danger in close proximity and the like. All the knowledge was given to me when I started to ride, which was quite at an early age. My father himself was not fond of the trot and guided me in the same direction.

My grandfather and my mother wanted me to go to the village temple every day both morning and evening, but my father, who was strictly secular and an exception in the whole family, influenced my thoughts at the tender age. While I often heard the too familiar version about the need for piety in life under fear that "God had a book in which he wrote down everything we did wrong," my father ridiculed it and I believed in him. When I grew up and came in contact with devout religious Muslims and Christians, I found that they too had identical faith in this belief and yet throughout my life my father's early teachings removed all traces of fear from Him. His own life was an open book for me, in which I could see his fervour for piety, zeal for charity, the enthusiasm for self renunciation without being wedded to his formal religion or attachment to temple. It has been difficult for me to reach his standards but he has guided my life.

Traditions

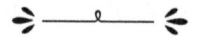

In the year 1912, I learnt that I was to have the sacred thread ceremony. I was scared about it as a year before I had seen a playmate of mine pass through this ordeal. I was not the sort of child who would try to resist or even try the patience of my elders. I, therefore, looked to the day with anxiety. Whilst the relations steadily arrived from far and near more than a week before the event. They brought no gifts. They feasted on simple foods and every day brought still more guests. On the auspicious day of my spiritual birth – the sacred thread ceremony – I was taken to the ancestral home that morning.

The setting was in a courtyard of the house with a red canopy about ten by ten feet fixed on wooden poles. I sat on a wooden platform raised a little from the floor – my mother on my left and a pretty cousin on my right. A barber was at the back of me and a *pandit,* facing me. Between the *pandit* and I there was some space on which were drawn geometrical forms resembling *swastika* rendered with white flour and turmeric. Folk songs relating to the occasion were being sung by the assembly watching the ceremony. When the songs ceased, the *pandit* uttered the religious *mantras* and later the barber was asked to shave all the hair from my head (*mundan*). The hair were collected and placed in a pan. I was then bathed and given white new garments to wear. Some boys and girls of my age threw lemons on my newly shaved head but they were soon prevented from annoying and hurting me.

I was now invested with the sacred thread which I ceremonially wore on my body after the bath. A turban was tied for the first time on my head. I had now become *dwij* (twice born), a true member of my caste according to Hindu traditions. I was told to recite short sacred words in Sanskrit thus taking a vow to defend the faith of my fathers and remain celibate to the age of twenty five years (in spite of the fact that I was later to be married at the early age of twenty two). The third vow was that I would devote most of my time in acquiring a sound education. These vows could never be taken seriously at that tender age. They had really been forced on me by codes based on customary practices. Hardly anybody was listening, least of all I could be serious, as I was feeling like a goat under a butcher's knife. The sacred thread remained on my body till my mother discovered some lice in its twines. I removed it and refused to wear another.

After the hair grew on my head, I was given a new pattern of haircut. I was not to allow my hair to grow beyond half an inch height at any time and the shorter the better, but I had to grow a tuft on the top of my head, and to give it prominence, the hair was shaved off every week around the tuft and farther towards the forehead for three to four inches and about an inch in width. I continued with this style of haircut for four to five years and then allowed the shaved portion freedom to grow. The amount of butter that must have been massaged into the shaved portion around the tuft daily by my mother would have sufficed for any person's meal every day. I presume this was to keep my head cool and to make my brain the great abode of intelligence.

Child marriage was not uncommon in those days. My own

forefathers regarded it as a good device for maintaining purity of their race. They assumed that if children were left free until they were twenty years or so, they would possibly have love affairs outside the *baradari* - a group of twelve castes. According to the then standards a boy of ten was a 'grown up' and so in 1913 I was betrothed, the word had no meaning for me but I enjoyed sweets that were given to me as if it were a festival. I presume that the little girl, about six years old and scarcely out of nursery, could know no more than I did regarding our engagement. It was merely an alliance between two families and we were not to marry for some years. There were no photographers in either of the two villages to which she and I belonged. My mother was extremely happy and often she talked to me of this little beautiful damsel whose father was rich and employed in the service of the British. In spite of my vow of celibacy at the sacred thread ceremony, my mother was looking forward to my early marriage. My childhood was not vanishing. My mother never refused me the pleasure of attending the marriage ceremonies that took place in the village. I watched them with a good deal of interest.

Performances of dancing girls were quite common at the marriage parties. I was told that I should not go to these assemblies, and although I never defied the restrictions placed on me, and for that matter I was looked upon as a well behaved lad, yet within me there was always a resentment. It was explained to me that dancing girls excite men to drink and gaiety, of which I understood very little. I was, however, interested in the amusement that the performance offered, particularly the exhibition of aristocracy by the amount of wealth the aristocrats could lavish on the dancing girls in public.

Traditions and customs largely controlled our social behaviour. Sacred sanctions, beliefs and superstitions had been passed on from generation to generation and the village people accepted them as a matter of course without questioning their meaning and validity. Because of this submissive attitude most of my elders maintained a fatalistic outlook on life. A cousin of my father became a widow. She was young and attractive. There was a great sympathy shown to her by our family as also by her in-laws. Customs did not permit widow remarriage amongst Hindus although it was not forbidden among Muslims. Thus she continued to live without a husband for quite a long time, because it was considered immoral and irreligious to remarry. It was considered sufficient for me to know that it had been ordained by God that no woman should be married to more than one husband and if he died she was doomed to perpetual widowhood. Some years later the custom began to show signs of cracks here and there and taking advantage of this my father's uncle secured his widowed daughter's remarriage within the 'marrying-in' group of twelve castes, to a widower. She lived thereafter, a happy life and had two daughters both of whom were well educated and nicely settled in their own married lives.

Marriages between boys and girls belonging to the village were taboo amongst the Hindus. Every boy, it was expected, would look upon every belle in the village, as his next cousin, and every elderly lady, as his aunt. The marriages normally took place in their young lives so early that at the age of puberty, most of them were leading a married life. As a result of this custom, coupled with a small population comprising a controlled society, the youngsters of the opposite sex remained almost all the time under rigid watch. There was a good deal of freedom when they met in one another's homes and public places, secret meetings would call for wrath from elders who were in those days, in command of the moral standards of the community.

The village *nayan* (barber's wife) was an institution unto herself as she was a medium of communications regarding all village ceremonies, their dates and appointed times. She even brought back the reaction of the invitees to a function (RSVP). She also carried the village gossip from one end to the other She looked forward to being adequately rewarded for her services, along with the washerman, the carpenter, the shoemaker, at times of marriage ceremonies of families whom they served. The rewards were not fixed as they, generally, depended on the status of the family and the importance of the occasion. They also never groused even if the rewards were not adequate.

Boys and girls were not allowed to marry outside their caste group. In fact, if their parents would stray outside the canons of society, they would have no friends in society. In spite of the rigidity the society appeared well knit, and allowed the various communities to protect themselves as units. This marriage aspect of the caste system was fundamental and could not be overlooked by my parents when in 1920 a proposal came from outside the caste group for my betrothal to the daughter of a well-to-do father and the girl possessing all the advanced accomplishments of education and sophistication. The codes and standards laid down by the elders of the family were respected.

Once the parents accepted the engagement for matrimony, society treated it with sanctity. It was considered in extremely bad form and a low act on the part of a family to raise objections for continuance of settled betrothal after the ceremony relating to it had been finalised. This practice was in vogue as far as the Hindu community was concerned. The Mohammedans, who more often than not, arranged marriages between very close kith and kin, did not follow the system of betrothals but proceeded with matrimony as soon as the parents decided to wed a couple of their choice. The couple was given a choice to reject or accept each other at the time of marriage by the Muslim priest who administered an oath of acceptance thrice by the couple at the time of the wedding. It was, however, not like the Christian priest making an announcement at the marriage service, "If any of you, here present know of any just cause or impediment why these two persons may not be joined together in Holy Matrimony, ye shall here declare it or else forever hold your peace." The Holy Matrimony could be objected to by those present at the ceremony but such a thing was not known in the village. There were no Christians there.

In 1915, my grandfather cancelled my engagement as my would-be father-in-law had entered into litigation with another relative of ours. I missed nothing and lost nothing, yet my mother looked very unhappy about it and in fact, she and I went to her maternal uncle where she could get over the distress.

According to village traditions, my grandfather lived for posterity. His whole life was not only tied up with the affairs of his own family including the grandchildren but with the group life of the village community particularly of the entire Hindu fold. Those, for instance, who were compulsorily without work could not be without food on that account. They had right to call on the share of others. A severe famine visited Punjab before I was born and I used to be told about its severity. My grandfather, who had stocks of cereals in his store, distributed rations freely so that the village community could tide over the calamity.

In those days, if I am not mistaken, there was gentleness about life, a certain air of good fellowship about people, an atmosphere of intimate and gracious charm more pronounced in rural life. There has been a continuous decline in that tradition over the years. People are not so near to one another now as they were then. It may also be that I was a child and tenderhearted that they all appeared to be very affectionate. Whether it was the sweeper, the washerman or the water carrier, or for that matter any servant, they made good servants and my parents good masters. As time went on this relationship became less emotional and more mundane. Both master and servants weigh mutual relationships on the basis of their rights and duties.

I was born in a family which was largely free from religious conventions. When I grew up, my upbringing was helpful in enabling me to ignore such traditions which were not amenable to reason. I was rarely afraid of any embarrassment from the community because of my family, my heredity, and my true guide in my early life. This was no personal merit. Religious fasting or *puja* on occasions like *Nagapanchami, Gangaur Vrat*, several *Ekadishis, Surya Shashti* and the like were completely dropped by my family for observance. Festivals like the *Baisakhi* (New Years Day), *Navratri*, twice in the year, *Basant Panchami* (beginning of February), *Lohri* (middle of January), *Holi* and *Diwali*, which were largely related to merry-making, were considered national and cultural, more than Hindu. Three festivals which were scrupulously observed in the village and in which all Hindus regardless of their status intermingled in the celebrations are described hereafter.

During the months of July and August, every year, the village people had a life of leisure and gaiety. They celebrated the 'Festival of Swings' but the 1917 festival is the first I remember so well. The festival is peculiar to Punjab rural life. It was not every day but the long weekends which were occupied by the festival. New clothes for the children and the young in multifarious colours, picnics under the trees to whose branches the rope swings were tied. The day would pass quickly away with swinging, singing and feasting. The young boys and girls returned in a gay and excited mood as if they were all drunk; as they were, but not with wine. I feel sure that the festival contributed its share in moulding the outlook on life of those who participated in it and experienced the joys of living. No one bothered to take cover under a roof, however hard it rained. Everyone loved being drenched as the light garments could be dried soon if the rain stopped. We always stayed out till after sunset and observed the beautiful hues of the setting sun during the monsoons. The elders often kept well away from us, probably pining for departed joys as I do now.

In August it was the festival of *Rakhi* – the festival of brothers and sisters. On this day, men of all ages visit their sisters and cousins if they are within town or village. This they did as the first task in the morning on this day. The sisters tie on the right wrist of their brothers a *rakhi*, a simple crimson thread or patterned silk flowers or some other ornamental pattern designed on a piece of thread. The brothers are given sweets and they offer cash or presents to the sisters. Both are dressed in their best. The festival has a significance, I was told early in life and I look upon it as true in conception, of the brothers taking a vow every year to assure protection to their sisters. I have no real sister but I have cousins and some adopted daughters of my father, all of whom I have taken to be my adopted sisters for the real ones and consequently I am not denied the pleasure of celebrating *Rakhi* every year.

This is followed by *Janam Ashtmi* -- the anniversary of Lord Krishna's birthday which falls on the declining quarter of the moon in August every year. It is a day of fasting but milk and fruits can be had. It is really fasting from cereals, and taking of fruits etc. does not take away the sanctity of the fast, which is broken when the moon is seen past midnight. The conch shells herald the time of Lord Krishna's birthday from the temples and the people who queue up for the *charan amrit* and *parshad* shout "*Krishna Maharaj ki Jai*" (Victory to Lord Krishna). They disperse as they receive the *parshad*.

Individual Existence

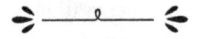

My grandfather was able, after much effort, to persuade my father to open a shop, in which I should assist him by devoting my time after school hours. My father had no confidence in himself to remain in trade. He lost part of his capital in his first venture. He stopped business. The discontinuance came to me as a great shock, as I had enjoyed my employment and felt that I was receiving training in business. It is interesting to look back at the fact that my father wanted to get out of that rotten business, and he deliberately gave extra weighings while serving his customers. It was not in his line and he could not advise me to become interested in trade. Next, my grandfather, in partnership with a cousin of his, installed a flour mill and put my father in charge of the organisation. I was asked to help him with simple accounts while dealing with customers. His main function was to supervise weighing operations. This time, as luck would have it, the new organisation made profits. It was, now being planned that I should leave school and apprentice myself in the operations of the mill. This did not succeed as the cousins quarrelled and my grandfather gave up his interest in the mill. My father seemed very pleased but I felt that after two dismissals I had no hope for a lifetime career. So I was back to my studies in earnest once more. I had only three months left in which to recover my deficiencies caused due to my experiments in the trade. In spite of this I excelled at the final examination.

The time had now come when I must leave the village in pursuit of further education. The nearest middle school was six miles away and my parents began to think seriously whether or not they should give consent to separation from home, of their only child. Personally too, I was unhappy at the thought of leaving my parents and my village for long spells at the middle school at Daulatnagar. My grandfather, who loved me dearly, was not satisfied with the standard of education I had acquired so far, although he considered that if I remained at home, my father was bound to enter into some trade to safeguard my future. In spite of all these undercurrents it was, at last, decided that I should apply for admission to the Vernacular Middle School, Daulatnagar. My grandfather felt very happy.

In March 1913, a roving dramatic company came to the village. It set up a small stage in the village bazaar with a simple wooden framework and gaudily painted cloth curtains. I was so much interested in the fabrication that I spent one whole day helping them in whatever way I could. The troupe employed no girls or women but instead young boys amongst them were dressed as girls for the performances that they staged during the fortnight they stayed in the village. Plays from Hindu history like *Ramayana*, *Raja Harishchandra*, and the like were staged and I desired to see every one of them although each performance meant four hours or so every evening. The actors were colourfully dressed and their features were well painted to represent the kings and common folk. They appeared very attractive on the stage and I met them invariably the following morning to convey to them my admiration. I was enthralled and even volunteered to join them and renounce my education. I was, however, severely reprimanded by my grandfather when he came to know about it. Those plays, which I attended for the first time, left a great impression on me, particularly the quotations uttered by the actors which they borrowed from the well known authors of these plays. The entire troupe was given free rations daily by the well-to-do in the village and at the end of the fortnight subscriptions were collected and paid to the company, who must have considered the collection as very good for they promised to return to the village the following year. Dussehra, which is a Hindu festival celebrated in October every year, was staged that year by the village amateur club, which came into being as a consequence of the visit of the troupe. I was selected to take part as an actor.

For admission to the Vernacular Middle School there were many applicants, more than the insufficient accommodation it had, therefore a competition test was set. My father accompanied me to Daulatnagar, where I was to sit for the test lasting for about two hours. The result was announced within an hour of the test and to my joy, I stood first and found myself in the position of a conquering hero as I came out from the school courtyard. However, I felt embarrassed when inhabitants of Daulatnagar, many of whom were known to my father, insisted on my receiving their congratulations. I was now convinced that as a result of this achievement my parents and grandfather would insist on continuation of my studies.

I was admitted, but in less than a week, I had an attack of typhoid. The verdict of the local doctor was that I must not journey back to my village. I was taken to the house of a relative in Daulatnagar where my mother came to nurse me back to health. She remained with me till the summer vacations when I returned home for two months' holiday. The vexed question of the continuance of my education again came up. Was it really worthwhile to allow me, still a child, to suffer the inconveniences of a hostel life. Now I strongly desired to acquire higher education and my voice was given a great weight. Vacations over, I returned to school at Daulatnagar.

The village of Daulatnagar was about the size of Kakrali but the presence of a middle school gave it greater prominence. The school was run by the Government and was equipped with two hostels, one for Muslims and the other for Hindu and Sikh students. The Hindu hostel could only accommodate twelve lads. Each boarder was given a bedstead, a stool and a wooden box within the two dormitories for shelter. Meals were cooked for boarders under an open shelter. Like all other students, I brought my share of wheat flour from home. This was examined and put in the pool. An account was kept by the superintendent of every *chapati* (flatbread) which each lad consumed and adjustment made against one's contribution of the wheat flour to the common pool. Each student had to declare three hours before each meal the number of *chapatis* he would eat at meal time. Each student had his own tin of *ghee* which he used as he desired, and had his own crockery consisting of a plate or *thali*, a bowl and a glass for his own use. Two meals were served, one at noon and the other just before sunset. The food consisted of the specified *chapatis, dal* and a glass of water. One could have more helpings with water only. No one bothered whether the boarders liked the food or not and no one complained for fear of the superintendent, who was proud that the monthly levy on the food never exceeded three quarters of a rupee for each student every month. This levy included the pro-rata expense of the food consumed by the cook who was a glutton. These conditions of life were so trying that I often thought of giving up on education there and going back to Kakrali to train myself for grandfather's vocation. It never matured.

I can recall to memory that necessities of life were available in the village at prices which could be hardly believable in the sixties. Wheat was sold at Rs. 1.50 per *maund*[6] and *ghee* at Rs. 30 per *maund*. There was no sugar scarcity. *Gur* (jaggery) was sold below the price of sugar and *meenja* sugar was available in abundance and sold at rates in between sugar and *gur* about Rs. 0.25 a *seer*. A pair of Indian shoes could be had at less than one rupee. The school fees ranged from one *anna* (six *paisa*) to four *annas* (25 *paisa*) in the primary classes and a reasonable raise in the upper classes. Businessmen, even the wholesale traders, hardly ever took to cornering wheat, rice or sugar to starve their countrymen. They stocked limited quantities and looked forward to limited profits. The so-called business magnates of today, the great speculators, can hoard and then sell at huge profits regardless of the consequences from which the consumer suffers. My father considered such practices as sheer nonsense, and would not care to become a businessman. He remained unworldly all his life and utterly indifferent to matters relating to money or material gains.

---

6   An Indian unit of weight. A *maund* is 40 seers, a *seer* is around 1.25 kg.

VISHAV BHAVAN

Part II: School Days

Education at Daulatnagar

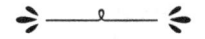

Each class in the Vernacular Middle School was under the charge of one teacher whose business it was to keep the boys fully occupied from 6-30 AM to 12 noon in summer and 10 AM to 16-30 hours in the winter months with one break of half an hour. Sundays were observed as holidays. The school did not provide any games either outdoor or indoor. There were hardly any extracurricular activities. Subjects like arts, music, civics, drawing were known by their absence in all classes. The curriculum consisted of Urdu, Persian, mathematics, history, geography and science. All subjects were taught in Urdu except Persian which had the identical script.

News was received that Mr. Wyatt, the divisional inspector of schools would inspect our school. Day after day the teachers met under the chairmanship of the headmaster to discuss ways and means of giving welcome to Mr. Wyatt. A plan was drawn up. All the students were instructed to wear a new shirt and a new *pyjama* or *dhoti* on the day of the inspector's visit. My curiosity, as probably that of many other students, was to see an Englishman for the first time – an experience by itself. Hours before his arrival the boys were posted along the route to convey the news as soon as someone observed a *pucca Sahib* – tall fair-skinned person wearing an English Sola hat, riding a maroon coloured horse, which he usually used. In the school premises, some two hundred boys who had been drilled for days on end for their performance before the inspector, stood in the courtyard, ready to sing to the glory of the English King as soon as the inspector entered the school. Everything went so far according to plan, but the teachers, too, did not have any experience of meeting a foreigner who could barely manage his *'hindustani'*[7]. Here are a couple of anecdotes which I remember from the occasion. The inspector asked the students if any one of us had seen an aeroplane. One of the students who was the oldest amongst the lot flung his hand into the air to suggest that he had seen an aeroplane. The inspector of schools interrogated further to find out where and how that village lad could have seen this most modern machine at the time. This class fellow of mine was not at all perturbed but on the other hand gave a very big surprise to the inspector, when he conveyed that he had a ride also in that machine. Questions and answers ultimately revealed that he had had a ride in a *tonga*[8], for the first time during his visit to the district headquarters. It gave the inspector and the whole class a hearty laugh when he explained that the machine was pulled by a horse along the road and the driver was shouting every now and then to the horse to pull his *hawaii jahaaj*, his aeroplane.

The teachers could hardly follow the Englishman's *hindustani*. When the inspector asked one of the teachers to bring a map of India, the teacher produced a small carpet. In fact, the boys, having understood what the inspector had asked for, were greatly amused at the embarrassment to which the teacher was put, and

---

7   Englishmen in India spoke an accented version of Hindi, referred to as *hindustani*.
8   Indian two-wheeled, horse-drawn carriage.

those of us who laughed received a beating from him after the inspector left the school. In passing, a reference to our science teacher may not be out of place, who, explained lightning among the clouds as the manifestation of God's own language, namely Arabic.

The greatest stress was on the learning of Urdu and arithmetic and anyone who excelled in these two subjects was considered best among the classmates. Urdu is a Turkish word meaning 'the army'. It was told to us that this was first introduced by the Mughal emperors in the military camps in which a common medium of conversation had to be introduced, and this language of the army was called Urdu. Another interpretation given for the same, was that this new language introduced by the Mughals contained words from an army of languages and like the army was a conglomeration of words from all the Indian languages. When written in Persian script with emphasis on Persian language, it was Urdu, and when written in Devnagri script with emphasis on Sanskrit, it was called Hindi. A common language called Hindustani was growing but the dispute with regard to common script for the whole of India remained unsolved between the Hindus and Muslims. Even after Independence, although Hindi was adopted by Bharat (India) as the national language, yet the antagonists of Hindi continued to claim an equal status for their regional languages. My language was Urdu – the language of my grandfather and my father, although we spoke in a dialect called Punjabi, which we never used in writing.

I was perpetually homesick and on the smallest pretext left Daulatnagar for my village even if I was to walk a whole distance of five miles or so. I was glad when the vacations came and I looked forward to spending a couple of months, days on end, with my people. It, however, happened that one of my father's sisters, who was already married, invited me to spend the vacations with her. My father agreed to take me to her home, which meant a journey by rail and by ferry boat as also a trolley ride along the canal bank. These, thus, came my way and I enjoyed every bit of this travel. One thing which has always remained a vivid memory is the 'forced prayer' under the directions of the boatman, which we continued to offer to God for our safe crossing across the stream. My aunt looked after me as her own child, she did not have one. Besides I felt much freer in her home and thus vacations were very well spent.

I returned to my school in September 1915, after vacations. The hostel was as uninteresting as it ever was but as luck would have it I could find a playmate this time in a nine year old Christian girl. Her father, who now lived next door to the hostel, was a very kindly person and his daughter, as also the rest of his family, were well-bred and well educated. They dressed in European style and looked different. This little girl knew English but was just attempting to learn Urdu. We became very fond of each other. She had a number of indoor games like Snakes and Ladders and Ludo which we often played together. She had quite a lot of stories to tell me from her English books of which I knew nothing, while I began to help her with Urdu and arithmetic. So long as we talked of stories or were busy with arithmetic, her father appeared quite happy but whenever he heard us talking about ourselves or about our career and future, his kindliness would disappear and he would ask me to return to the hostel. Once when I had sweets from home to augment my food at the hostel, I took some for my playmate. I gave them to her father who shouted for her to meet me and to enjoy these sweets together provided we did not play hide and seek. We both expressed our gratitude. While I did not mind eating from their table, the hostel superintendent did not like my doing it. He told me that the Christians are converts from low caste Hindus and remain polluted on the basis of Hindu tradition. I paid no heed to his advice.

One of the senior students, who had stayed too long in the eighth class, had grown to full manhood, was well built and could be disagreeable if one ignored his commands. He used me as a medium to exchange correspondence between him and the elder sister of my little friend, whose father found out and was able to secure the dismissal of that student from the school on the charge of misconduct. As a consequence, my entry to the house of that Christian neighbour was alas stopped forever. I felt a vacuum and to fill it I formed the company of a Muslim classfellow who held identical views, namely, pantheistic belief regarding the supernatural and contrary to the transcendent God of Islam. We both were conversant with the writings of Bulleh Shah. In spite of serious objections which were not abnormal from my Hindu class fellows, I did not hesitate to share his meals although he could not be permitted to enter the Hindu kitchen. However, I was not excluded from my caste and my *hukka-pani*[9] was not excluded. I could still have a pull at castefellow's pipe and drink from his vessel.

I loved Urdu poetry and had committed to memory select verses. It was common practice, as to be among the cultured class one needed a vocabulary of Urdu verses for punctuating one's conversation. Besides, I subscribed to an Urdu weekly named *Phool* (Flower). The school had no library so *Phool* was useful and a good acquisition. I could afford to buy books in addition to those relating to my studies. I took pride in that luxury when I possessed about a dozen books of my own. The headmaster was a very keen teacher and held night classes for those who cared

---

9   Literally, tobacco and water, but meaning social intercourse.

to attend. He was very keen that his pupils should do well at the final district board examination and bring him credit. He was also of the view that if he did not do so, the students were likely to while away time mostly in mischief making. I fully availed of this opportunity. I was obedient and submissive and in fact, according to my teachers and parents, a paragon of virtue. The headmaster had a nickname for most of the students. He used to call me *Damodar*[10] – I never understood the reason for this choice but one can wonder if he could foresee, as he was known for prophesising, that I would one day be a Special Officer of the Damodar Valley Corporation which was constituted by the Government of India after Independence for the development of the valley of the river Damodar – a tributary of the Ganges in Bihar and Bengal.

Maulvi[11] Nur-ud-din, the headmaster was thought to possess power by which he could foresee people's fortunes and could locate lost property through the medium of a magic paper. A student lost five rupees, who reported the matter to the headmaster. I was employed by the headmaster as the medium to concentrate on looking at his magic paper which was Kraft paper with about a nine inch circle painted black on a sheet of one and a half foot square. Whether I had any faith or not but I dared not reveal my convictions lest I be caned. I gazed at the black surface for several minutes, but when the *Maulvi sahib* explained to me what was expected, I nodded that I could see a large open space well lit by several lights and also affirmed that a chair had been placed and that a bearded fellow had occupied it. But when I queried for the information to be written down by the imaginary person about the lost money, I could not fabricate

---

10 It is likely that the nickname referred to his innocence. A simpleton.
11 Muslim priest.

an answer. I, therefore, told the headmaster that the seer had left the place and the chair had also been removed. *Maulvi sahib* was both annoyed and sorry but decided never to use me as a medium. It may be of interest to know that he was successful in tracing the lost note through his own administrative skill.

The teachers' monthly salaries varied from twelve rupees to twenty. They could hardly meet their needs, therefore they looked upon the students to subscribe to them things in kind such as wheat flour, butter, vegetables, etc. They did expect that kind of aid, but only from students whose parents were well off, and in turn, they paid greater attention towards the welfare and studies of their children. It did not interest me at that time whether it was a case of corruption or not.

On August 4, 1914, War was declared between England and Germany. The headmaster announced this in the classroom and asked us to pray for the victory of the British over the Germans. Within a few months, the Government publicised news of the War through the daily *Haq* in Urdu. It was compulsory for every school to display the news and promote the sale of *Haq*. I read it with enthusiasm in the beginning but soon lost interest in that publicity. One of my uncles brought fresh news, glorifying German achievements and its wartime machinery. When I grew old I realised that he was a past master in circulating gossip.

I had a cousin sister who was left an orphan. She was the daughter of one of my father's sisters. My mother had adopted her as her own child. Thus, she came to be my sister and in her friendship there was simple and frank sweetness – a sentiment I did not share with anyone else. We thought and felt alike although we did not spring from an absolute common origin but we were spending our childhood together like real brother and sister. She was my senior by four to five years. Even after her marriage, we maintained a close relationship till she died in 1955, and whenever we were together we called back memories of our childhood and inhaled again the perfume of the past.

I was now becoming conscious of my years. In order to bathe at a well it was now obligatory on me to wear a loincloth. Even for a massage of my body by my mother the same held good. I was no longer to be naked in public.

Some boys from the village were studying in Lahore after having passed matriculation examination of the Punjab University. When they were home for their summer vacations I was able to spend a good deal of time in their company. They inspired me and helped me with the courses I was at. My grandfather was also inspired with the hope that I will one day go to Lahore for my studies. Most of the boys after the holidays looked fit and well, whilst I had grown pale and weak with casual fever. My grandfather suggested and my mother gladly accepted to stay near me at Daulatnagar by taking a room with one of our relations there. Her care made it possible for me to continue attendance at school without detriment to my health. She returned to Kakrali only when I was normal again and could risk my board at the school hostel for a month or so before we had the Dussehra holidays.

It was 1916 Dussehra, when a magician visited Kakrali and he was our guest. Whilst he shared and explained some simple card tricks to me in the house, he revealed his mastery by a public performance in the village marketplace. There were no tickets and everyone from far and near was welcome to see the performance. Hundreds of people gathered and I can look back at the three tricks that baffled everyone. The magician was locked in a wooden box with hands and feet securely tied. A curtain was then drawn around the box and the magician came out of the box in a few seconds. He then went behind the curtain and again disappeared in a moment. The box was unlocked and the magician was found in it in the same posture as he was when the box was locked. In the second trick he produced a small dog from underneath a basket which contained nothing and when there was no sign of an animal in the neighbourhood of the stage. He then converted this little dog into a pigeon, appeared to kill it, cut it into parts and rejoined these bleeding parts into a living pigeon.

This was the final year in Daulatnagar and the examination was held at the district headquarters. Students of the 8th class from all Vernacular Schools of the district appeared for a common test in March. Every day, as I entered the centre for examinations, my father waited for me outside the hall. It is difficult to say today as to the effect it had on me while writing answers to the question papers, but having secured first division, I may draw the conclusion that my father's presence gave me a presence of mind to do well. I went to Daulatnagar to collect my school leaving certificate. I received congratulations from my teachers and friends, and my Christian friend and her father were overjoyed with the news. I assured them that I would lose no opportunity to see them whenever I pass through Daulatnagar. This gentleman gave me a copy of the Bible translated in Urdu. Prejudiced as I was against Christianity under the influence of my own religion, I did not care to take the present home.

At the District Headquarters

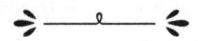

⇒——☙——⇐

The district town of Gujrat (now in Punjab, Pakistan) had a population of approximately fifty thousand persons. It was an historical place being once a battleground between the English and the Sikhs some time in the year 1849. The town presented features of both old and new civilizations as in parts of it looked rural and in others fully urbanised. Whilst in the village, food, clothing and other basic needs of life were more or less for all sections of the population, it was not so in this town where the various groups of community appeared distinct from one another. The senior district officials, lawyers, doctors formed a class which had already isolated itself from the poorer sections of the community and the contrast in their living standards was prominently visible.

By the third week of April 1917, I had joined the Government High School at Gujrat for Junior Special Class for a course in English. The Headmaster as also the Second Master dressed themselves in European style, while most of the other teachers were not particular about western trousers but regularly used coats tailored to European style with *pyjamas*. All of them used the English pattern of shoes. I abandoned *dhoti* for a *pyjama* but I did not use a coat and was quite happy with only a shirt.

Later I started using a waistcoat over my shirt. I had my hair cut according to fashion in the town and also began to have my clothes ironed frequently. Thus I had begun to change from my rural standards to urban fashions and mannerisms.

I purchased a pair of English shoes which was a luxury possessed by no other child in our village. I liked them immensely and became very proud of them. However, I soon discovered that they were badly made as they lasted for less than two months and also learnt that their soles were only painted cardboard and not leather. Everyone who saw them so quickly worn out condemned them in particular, and all English shoes in general, and considered them as poor substitutes for the local shoes which were well made and would last easily for a year. This was my first experience of national pride as I used to tell all the villagers that the English shoes are no good, not knowing that to call that shoe an English shoe was a misnomer. It was only a cheap copy of the shape and style of an English shoe. Anyway, I gave up using shoes of that shape till the year 1921 when I joined the University of Lahore.

The life at the school was full of interest. Although the hours of study here were the same as at the middle school, but we could have a gossip with our classmates, even remain away from the class without being observed. One could spend time in the school library and borrow books for study at home. The school had a canteen catering light refreshments, which we enjoyed during the interval of recess. Outdoor games were played after school hours, although I was generally hesitant to participate in them.

I had many relatives in town, some of whom were senior Government officials and others lawyers. I spent many evenings with them as also all holidays when I was in town, but for any long vacation most of my cousins who had their maternal connections joined me to go to Kakrali, where we had a life of leisure and plenty. In town I lived in the hostel in a dormitory which had a commodious verandah attached to it on a sunny side. It had a kitchen and the verandah where the boarders would dine. The hostel was equipped with bathrooms and lavatories, which conveniences were denied to me at Daulatnagar. Further students of many different ages were living in the hostel and I was able to find a number of my own age group. The Superintendent of the hostel who was also the Second Master permitted me to visit his house, his family and play with his children.

A bazaar in a small town in Punjab.

The main life of the town of Gujrat centred around the bazaar, where sweetmeat sellers displayed their sticky viands. Chandler's shops, booksellers, clothiers and shoe shops attracted crowds of people, particularly those who visited the headquarters from villages. They all moved under the shade of deep awnings, which were generally improvised for the summer season. District Courts, which were not distant from the school, had large numbers of litigants visiting them and it was fun how they were called to the judge's court by a peon shouting for 'X' and in the absence of quick response, 'X' was prefixed with undesirable names. Such seemed to have been a custom to which no one objected. Lawyers had, I was sure, a flourishing business as almost all of them had very large houses in which they lived, had their own libraries, consulting rooms, and accommodation for their clients. Religious festivals of both Hindus and Muslims were celebrated with guests.

The town had a railway station, which was on the main line of the Western Railway. The centre of gravity of the town's businesses was already shifting from the old city to the new bazaar coming into being near the railway station. Between this bazaar and the town was an octroi post where all goods going into town were taxed and this gave the new bazaar an added advantage to sell imported materials at rates lower than those prevailing in town. This octroi tax was not only resented by the people, but people made efforts to evade it.

There were in the town three high schools preparing boys for the matriculation examination – Government, Christian Mission and a Muslim Zamindara. They held inter-school matches in cricket, football, hockey and sports. These came about in autumn (October to December) and they attracted not only the student population but all shades of people from the town. At the close of the season, just before Christmas, a prize distribution was organised invariably under the patronage of the District Commissioner. Personally I was not fond of games, leave aside winning a prize, but I enjoyed the entire season of sport.

In the year 1917, before the commencement of the season of sport there was a heavy downpour all over Punjab and the Punjab hills in September. The town was flooded. It damaged houses and crops. The school grounds had knee-deep water. We moved about on planks when we could find one. The hostel dormitory having a high plinth was not affected but as the water did not completely recede for three days, we were put to a lot of inconvenience. Various religious organisations and individuals rendered help to those in distress but the Government of the day was callous. It did not seem to be any concern of the Government and one was forced to accept the viewpoint of the agitators that the foreign Government is quite indifferent to our national problems whether they be small or large.

After passing my Junior Special examination from the Government School, I joined the Zamindari School for the Senior Special in which I had to devote, as in my Junior Special, almost the whole time to the study of English. Here, I received a couple of lectures every week on improving agricultural production. Attached to the school was a boarding house, once the Royal Rest House of Maharaja Ranjit Singh, the ruler of Punjab before its annexation by the British. Here I was a boarder and lodger in the building that had housed a powerful man.

Close to the hostel there lived a *faqir*[12] who was renowned for his prophesising. Whenever he hurled abuses it meant to the seeker, his accord with the wishes of the seeker. Besides this he spoke very little. Crowds of people visited him and had faith in his spiritual attainments. In any Western country he may easily have been deposited in a mental hospital. Later in life too I came across fortune tellers, but I have always reckoned them as close relatives of the magicians who surprise us with unbelievable magical performances such as I have narrated in the previous chapter. In the town of Gujrat lived a small community and I believe they still exist as a distinct set of people styled as '*Shah Dola's* rats'. They are generally all dwarfs with heads almost one

---

12 A religious mendicant.

quarter of the normal size. How they came to possess these peculiar features, I have never discovered.

I have always felt very sorry for having taken two years longer than the students from the town to join them in the ninth class after passing my Senior Special in 1919. It proved to be of no advantage to have two years of concentrated learning in English as I always felt the lapse in my standard of the English language against those who studied it for eight years. For the next course I joined Kidar Nath High School – a new school started by a local philanthropist. It was merged with Sanatan Dharm School after a year. That, too, was also an addition to schools in town.

A Digression

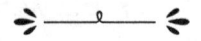

I have already used up a good deal of paper with the recollection of my early days, but I have just found tucked away in a corner of my memory, a couple of incidents my mother said about me when I was a little boy. One day she was going to take me for participation in a marriage ceremony to a nearby village and she spent what seemed to me an eternity in collecting a few odds and ends which she had to carry with her. When at last she was ready to go looking so gay and nicely dressed, I glanced at her sullenly (so at least she told me), and I declared that I will not go for any such occasion, and that I renounce all pleasures and all good things of this world from that day forth for evermore. My mother said that she felt quite astonished about my attitude which she had never expected. This episode vividly came to my mind when I witnessed an almost identical situation in my grandson's behaviour vis-a-vis his parents. He insisted to be left behind so he could play with his mates rather than visit his mother's relations in town. My son demanded an explanation from my grandson for his change of mind. He found it difficult to offer it and agreed to go, and made no extreme pronouncements like those of renunciation such as I had made more than sixty years ago. For the first time in life I began to brood over the past and analyse why I was not gentle on that occasion when I was normally considered and known as a placid child. There must have been some reason – reason which exercised a potent sway over me from my earliest years. In spite of being the only child I was by no means considered a spoiled kid, but without intending any boast on my part, I can say, maybe due to inborn heredity, that I was endowed with a larger share of reason than most of my kind in the village. Whether I understood the meaning of reason then I know not, but I take it to mean today is the noun of the adjective 'reasonable'. The reasonable man is who, observing the lack of order that exists in the natural world, and the folly of mankind, does not persist in talking of the order of the one and the wisdom of the other.

One morning, accompanying Bibi, our Muslim lady servant about whom I have already given some account, in her room I examined with great attention the quilt which she used for herself. I did not know or understand modern art then, in fact I have made no effort to know it even in my sixties. The quilt if I recollect too well, looked printed in all sorts of colours in small but unidentical patches, and I must have stood by it in curiosity for quite a time when Bibi upbraided me for wasting my time on silly things, and explained to me that there was nothing there to admire about the old thing which had been patched over and over again. She was a poor lady and that she could not afford a new one. This aroused my interest in a different direction and I stated my observations and her explanation about the quilt to my mother, who gave Bibi a new quilt. Later in years I often witnessed how my father often helped the needy out of his own meagre ancestral income which had dwindled with years. I must confess that he is much richer than I in this particular aspect as I began to look after my own comforts and provide still more when earnings increased and I shared very little with the poor and consoled myself by saying that it is the function of the State to look after the depressed people and classes.

The Reign of Terror and After

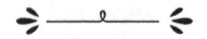

⇒———€

The human world had come out of a four year's terrible purgatory in 1918. Eleventh of November, 1918, brought the Treaty of Versailles, when two minutes of silence was observed at 11 AM as a mark of homage to those who lost their lives in that human catastrophe. I was too young at the time to know why the War was fought but it was considered enough for me to be told that Germans, who were aggressors, had lost and the Allies, who included the British, won the War. Later I learnt that India had fought side by side with the British in the theatre of War and because of this participation, the British had promised to introduce reforms to the extent of making India a British Dominion after the hostilities had ceased, and that they had gone back on their promises. Early in March 1919, it was openly talked that the British had not only refused to stand by the commitments in favour of our people but had hurled an insult by infusing the Rowlatt Act – more popularly known as the Black Act. I made no efforts to find its provisions, but there was resistance in every town and that the Nation was astir and determined to shake off the British yoke. The expression of indignation gave rise to sporadic rising disrespect for the rulers and their laws. One could hear, for the first time at least in my life, *Inqlab Zindabad* (Long Live Revolution) from large crowds in procession and in one voice. It was spontaneous and without plan, there it was, without control. Government buildings like railway stations, offices, post offices, courts etc. were damaged and burnt hoping that by this the whole Government machinery would get a severe jolt and the Government would be bound to come to terms. The Government, realising the gravity of the situation, armed themselves by imposing Martial Law in place of the Civil Administration. Curfew was imposed on movements of people. And the army was empowered to 'shoot at sight' anyone who disregarded the authority and limitations imposed under the Martial Law.

It is a long history as to what happened all over the country but I restrict myself to a realistic account of the punishment school students in which I am included, had received at the hands of a mighty Government that inflicted a reign of terror on the lawbreakers and the innocent alike. School boys of all the schools in the town from the sixth class to the tenth class numbering six to seven hundred were ordered to assemble each morning at six in the parade ground. They stood in files and each boy in his turn had to walk a small distance from his position to the saluting base where the 'Union Jack' the British flag was fluttering in the air at the top of the flag post, salute, and then turn and walk back to his position. It usually took three hours to complete the process. Students then marched either to a hostel or the school whichever was nearer to them from the parade ground. Teaching had been abandoned altogether as the students hardly had an hours' rest before they were back to the parade ground for repetition of what they did from six to nine. The second time they stood under the burning midday sun, its scorching heat for another three hours, and then returned for a meal and just a small respite before they returned for a third round to the parade ground. No umbrellas were allowed to be used even when the temperature recorded in the shade was near 110 degrees Fahrenheit. This kind of punishment was carried out for a fortnight. Once, as I approached the flag post, I smiled at the 'Tommies' – two Tommies, one tall and the other short guarding the flag. This was considered enough outrage or disloyalty to the Crown for inflicting me with six canes. I certainly grew embittered although I did not revolt for fear of Martial Law and of greater punishment. Many of the boys fell sick, but the Martial Law refused to show any mercy, as we had been told that any one could absent himself only if one of his relations offered himself as a substitute.

Later the method of this drill changed as the number of those who fell sick increased substantially and substitutes started to take their places. A whole class of one school, instead of one student at a time, was ordered to march in file to the saluting base and this went on for another fortnight. This was followed by the combined march of the students of one school at a time and then ultimately this was relaxed and substituted by having the Union Jack in the compound of each school and students had to offer a mass salute to the flag every morning before classes started each day. A military officer was always present in the school yard at the time.

The All-India agitation against the Rowlatt Act had created the atmosphere for Mahatma Gandhi's leadership. India demonstrated her national disgust over the Government Acts and the Government retaliated by resorting to brutality and indiscriminate atrocities on the innocent. Besides, what has been stated in the preceding paragraphs, the ruthless firing at Jallianwala Bagh at Amritsar, under the orders of General Dyer, remained the ugliest mark on the British Administration in this country and left the Indians embittered, whose leaders always quoted that reign of terror in order to arouse the feeling of the masses against foreign rule.

Another factor after the First World War, namely the part played by the British in the defeat of Turkey and the dismemberment of the Turkish Empire aroused the Indian Muslims. They too joined the political upsurge under the Indian National Congress to ventilate their grievances against the British under a movement called *Khilafat* (Opposition) led by two Ali brothers – Mohammad Ali and Shuakat Ali. This *Khilafat* Movement started in the wake of Martial Law and in fact, it brought about fraternisation between Hindus and Muslims and laid the foundation of secularisation in India. The ill wind of the Marital Law brought about a great deal of good in awakening the whole of India for the struggle for political freedom.

My uncle, Lala Mool Raj Uppal, a prominent member of the local Bar at Gujrat was one of those who were sentenced to life long imprisonment. These punishments were inflicted without trial under Martial Law. Later, however, these terms of imprisonment were either relaxed or these alleged criminals were declared innocent.

The Martial Law, even before its lapse, was coupled by an epidemic – till then unknown to the medical profession. It took a large toll of human lives. I survived in spite of a severe attack. I still remember that this was known as 'black fever' which meant that it was imported from Africa during the First World War. My tracheal canal was so choked by some kind of inflammation that I had almost lost my voice, and it took over a fortnight before I recovered from the acute illness. This happened when I was at school eighteen miles away from my home sweet home, and my parents. I sent no information about it to my parents as the Martial Law as it stood, had cut us off from our kith and kin. The summer vacation was very welcome that year as I could go back to my village for peace and tranquillity. But when I narrated all that I had suffered from both at the hands of the Government and the black fever my mother exclaimed, "Why have I survived to hear the woeful tales of the reign of terror, and the near death ailment!"

Surprisingly, however, this reign of terror was followed by the Government of India Act of 1919, the important feature of this Act was the partial establishment of responsible governments in the provinces. It introduced 'dyarchy' or dual government. It must not be concluded that it was compensation for the horrible acts committed during the Martial Law but it was prudence of the rulers that they recognized and considered it imperative to enlist new forces on the side of the executive to place a share of the responsibilities of the executive Government on its critics.

The reign of terror of the Martial Law regime controlled by gangsters did not produce servility but reduced considerably the awe with which the white man was regarded before 1919. The Martial Law gave birth to fearlessness in the Nation. The fear with which an Indian used to regard the white man in the second decade of the twentieth century can hardly be fully understood by the present generation. The white man was considered as being endowed with supernatural powers over the forces of nature and a being to be trembled before and implicitly obeyed. By disobeying the Rowlatt Act and deliberately ignoring Martial Law even at pain of death, collectively or individually, enabled the coming generations to look at the white man in the face undismayed. Ten years later Nationalist India effectively demonstrated the triumph of fearlessness when thousands courted imprisonment and faced all kinds of brutalities with courage bringing moral renaissance to the people of our country. Again it was the enforced humiliation

The Reign of Terror and After

which gave birth to Gandhiji's *Satyagraha*[13] movement and later still to the 'Quit India' movement of 1942. The evolution of free India, it could be said, started with the upsurge of 1919, which terminated on 15th August, 1947.

---

13   Literally *satya* (truth) + *agraha* (insistence), *satyagraha* was a word coined by Mahatma Gandhi for his policy of passive political resistance as a tool to demand *swaraj* (self rule) or Independence from British occupation.

The Arya Samaj

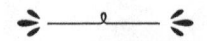

The educated classes of the urban population being prepared to adopt new social ideas in the Hindu society and yet maintain their roots in Vedic philosophy accepted the doctrines preached by Swami Dayanand, a religious reformer, and the sect named Arya Samaj founded by him. Besides preaching belief in one Supreme Being and the doctrine of successive rebirths or transmigration, it extended its opposition to pilgrimages, idol worship, bathing in sacred streams, which were practised in Punjab by all Hindus. The Arya Samaj, in fact, decried all religions and claimed *Vedas* to be the repository of truth. On occasion it advanced its movement by active participation in politics. Its missionaries appealed to the Indian national sentiment and therefore the number of Arya Samajists increased rapidly in Punjab.

The Government held that the disturbances of 1919 were mainly organised and led by Arya Samaj and as a result the largest number among the arrested and punished under the Martial Law belonged to the Arya Samaj. It had centres in all district headquarters. It worked particularly against Christianity which was busy in proselytising activities. One noted example of self-sacrificing personality who combined religious, social and political activities of the Arya Samaj was Swami Shradhanandaji.

The Arya Samaj

After the Jallianwala Bagh Massacre in Amritsar during the notorious Martial Law he left Gurukul Kangri for helping the orphans, the widows of the carnage. When the *Satyagraha* of 'Guru Ka Bagh' was going on, Swamiji helped the Akali Sikhs and as a consequence was thrown into jail. Swamiji founded and established Gurukul Kangri, now a *Vishwavidyalaya* (university) for the revival of Vedic learning and national pride.

In Gujrat town the Arya Samaj was quite active. My uncle Mool Raj Uppal was a very staunch Arya Samajist who I accompanied to listen to discourses of leading Arya Samajists in the local Arya Mandir. I can well recollect the great fervour with which the Samaj organised '*shastrarth*' (intellectual debate) with religious heads of other religions to show the superiority of the Vedic religion over all other religions that came into existence before and after the *Vedas*. The attack was more severe against Christianity and Islam but it did not spare the Hindu Sanatan Dharma. Christians also poured abuse against Hindu Dharma.

The doctrine '*Aryavrat* for the Aryans' was also being pushed forward which brought the Samaj into clash with the Government and other religious sects and later the *Shuddhi* (or Purification) movement which meant reconversion or bringing back into Hindu fold those who had embraced other religions, created an antipathy between Muslims and Arya Samajists. The Samaj worked for removal of untouchability from the Hindu society simultaneously with participating in the National liberation movement. It advocated *Swadeshi* (indigenously produced) cult and austere living. My father, who believed in universal love, did not accept the Arya Samaj and its stress on picking up holes in the scriptures of other faiths but was of the view that it should find out the good points from all scriptures and assimilate them in our own beliefs. My father's younger brother Shiv Nath was a staunch follower of Dayanand and he was the secretary of the

Arya Samaj which he established at Jaranwala, Lyallpur District. He addressed congregations from the Arya Samaj platforms. I remained devoted to the views held by my father.

Under the advice of my uncle, I joined the D.A.V. College Lahore in 1921. Lala Sain Das was the principal. His eldest son Dev Raj Mehta was my classfellow. Lalaji was also my relative and this nearness brought me closer to him. I visited him often to seek advice. He was goodness personified and austere in his living. He affected the lives of many students by his sincerity and devotion towards religious life, free of lust and engrossed in his work as a sacred duty. He gave me one advice to which I have adhered all my life – never to beg from anyone for personal gains but to hold the beggars bowl out without hesitation for the benefit of the community. Here I also had the privilege to have a few meetings with Mahatma Hans Raj ji, the then accredited leader of the Arya Samaj (College Section), and a personification of extreme selflessness. The Samaj was also the forebearer in spreading literacy in Punjab along with socio-religious activities for creating a climate of hope and confidence in the Hindu fold.

I was already refusing to accept any of the 'stock' ideas and traditions which were being practised in the village. They often did not appeal to reason and here I felt to be quite near the Arya Samaj, but I never accepted the Persian *'Pidram Sultan Bood'*, my father is king. How would it help me if I was not, and to maintain my kingdom I must be flexible in adopting the power of all the latest scientific progress than harp on the past. Back to the *Vedas* can be a political strategy but is against the process of evolution, and any edicts which prohibit doubts and questions makes the growth of the community virtually impossible. The straight line backward movement is no solution for the Hindu fold, which must adapt itself with the times and revolutionise its socio-religious problems with the inherited wisdom.

The Arya Samaj had two sections, in fact it still has those, namely, the College Section and the *Gurukul*[14] Section. One desired to propagate a literal curriculum and the other demanded a higher moral tone and emphasis on religious education. Thus the College Section viewed the growing utilitarianism in society with favour and took upon itself to impart scientific and technical education along with a smattering of theology while the other section was in favour of revivalism and devoted its energies in turning out religious missionaries. It was also said that the College Section (*Maas* or 'Meat' Party) favoured non-vegetarianism while the other (*Ghas* or 'Grass' Party) tabooed meat eating. But how far meat eating had any religious sanction with the College Section, nothing could be said with certainty. By and large, the Samajists were not in favour of meat as a diet. The D.A.V. College, for that matter, did not have a single one among its scores of messes in the college hostel serving meat. The Samaj was primarily involved in making their schools and colleges places for imparting *Vedic* education along with more modern subjects. The teaching of Hindi was compulsory in schools, while at the college level the students were persuaded to acquire Hindi. I avoided learning Hindi.

When I was studying at the D.A.V. College Lahore in 1921-23, I felt much freer to participate in the Congress movement. It would be rank ingratitude to forget the services rendered by the Arya Samaj to the cause of Independence. In fact, the work of reformation in the Hindu society, the intelligent and sustained work in connection with austere living, the removal of

---

14 *Gurukul* is the traditional Hindu education system, where the students (*shishyas*) literally live as family members (*kul*) of the teacher, the *guru*. In this case, the *Gurukul* Section refers to a traditional curriculum, versus the College Section, to a more Western curriculum.

untouchability, *Swadeshi*-ism and promotion of pride for Indian culture, made possible the emergence of the subsequent mass movement under the Indian National Congress, which eclipsed the slow moving programme of the Arya Samaj in Punjab. The Government of the day knew very well the part played by this socio-religious organisation in arousing the masses against the Alien *Raj* and did, under one pretext or the other, try to crush it either by charging some of its leaders with criminal acts or through some of the Indian Princes who acted under the behest of the Viceroy in arresting the leading Arya Samajists in their territory.

The College Section of the Arya Samaj controlled many D.A.V. schools and through them it created the requisite psychology in the coming generation for sacrifice. I feel convinced that the strength of devotion compelling to sacrifice for the ideals of *Dharma* or nationality owes nothing to the inborn heredity of the individuals but entirely to the collective heredity or to the bringing up by training and example imposed on the rising generation under the influence of emotion of the ideal. In the political upsurge against the Alien Government, the Congress was largely able to draw upon the youth trained in national schools whether controlled by the Arya Samaj or the Khalsa Panth in Punjab and this must have been equally true and applicable to other parts of the country.

A surprisingly large number of people who had adopted the teachings of the Arya Samaj as their faith were carrying on its mission with dedication and zeal in the twenties of the present century. I can confidently say from my recollections that this Samaj had aroused among its followers an appetite for religion such as the Hindus have not had in the nineteenth century. Till the Arya Samaj came in Hindus could be converted to Christianity and Islam and there was no return for them.

Similarly, if a Hindu married a girl from another faith, he had to adopt his wife's religion and if a Hindu girl married a lad from another faith, she had to be converted to the other faith. Thus, there was a constant drain on the Hindu fold. Arya Samj removed this religious disability and made it possible for Hindus to accommodate people of other faiths through conversion.

The *Gurukul* Section, before the pre-Independence period was not looked upon favourably by the bureaucracy as the *Gurukul* institution was a symbol of Hindu tradition – the teachers and the taught alike used cap, *kurta* and *dhoti* as their dress and were prepared as missionaries to put up with inconveniences of living and to suffer for the promotion of *Dharma* of their forefathers and the country. Things have now changed. My wife and I, during one of my trips, visited Gurukul Kangri in 1965 and came back with a feeling that the old sources of inspiration had dried up. Students of all kinds had entered this *Vishwavidyalaya* as they do in any other university, with their eyes on finding suitable services after they attain their degrees. Although we saw a mixture of old and modern cultures at the centre, I felt convinced that many a student showed by their modernity that they had entered the sphere of forbidden delights.

Some Random Childhood Reminiscences

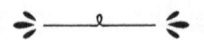

Habit is, in a way, an accidental precipitation, and hence becomes a limitation if it forms an instinct. Some experiences of childhood or boyhood produce a persistent emotional bias in one's later life, although individual habits based on these may not move down to the next generation. I have random reminiscences of a number of such accidents which have been responsible for creating a lasting fear. I narrate them as illustrations.

A joy which was forbidden to me was to bathe in the pond. The village had two ponds which were used for a dip in summer by villagers and their cattle alike. One day I made up my mind to break away from the imposition and joined my playmates. I was further encouraged by a friend who promised to give me lessons in swimming. I got into the pond along with him and when I failed to keep my body afloat, he did save me from drowning, but I got such a dread for my life that I have never tried to learn swimming or have the pleasure of bathing in rivers or sea or even in a deep pool. Similarly, I once had a camel ride and I received several injuries as a result of a fall from its back. Somehow, maybe through my own inefficiency or lack of encouragement and training, most of these exploits went wrong. I thus developed a habit, amounting to fear – no more camel rides, no swimming, no tree climbing.

One of my teachers in Zamindara School, Gujrat, impressed me immensely with his intelligence. He was strict in using the cane when students made mistakes. One day he told his class that he had quarrelled with his wife and that instead of being harsh towards her, he was going to appease his wrath by caning the students for the mistakes that they are likely to make in dictation in English. He dictated and found that I made no mistake in spelling, but had overwritten one word. Having finished beating all my class fellows, he turned to me to give me a slight stroke with his cane. I protested and when his eyes grew red with rage, I ran away as if for my life. He followed me, but by this time I was out of his reach. When I returned to school the next day he was in a different mood. Lucky me.

In the following year I had joined the Kidar Nath High School, which was started only that year (1919) by a local philanthropist. The school was well equipped both with staff and apparatus from the very beginning. With a likelihood of entering the medical profession I became interested in science, hygiene, physiology as my special subjects besides English, geography, history and mathematics. I was the top student in the ninth class, at least I thought so. This made me careless, I devoted more time to gossip, social, political and religious assemblies in the town. Having been advised by my parents at home and by teachers alike I was becoming proud and arrogant in school. If I was not aware of this, very few among the elders were aware of this change in my nature. Once when the science master wanted to cane me for my insolence, I left the Kidar Nath School to take my matriculation as a private external student instead of accepting the whims of the school teacher. Some time later I realised how foolishly I had acted in not taking account of my own limitations and lack of tuition facilities at Kakrali. I humbly returned to the school to seek re-entry and to my astonishment every teacher including the science master welcomed me back.

I had never worn a coat until I crossed my fifteenth year, when I felt I needed one so that I could appear as smartly dressed as many of my class fellows. I spent thirty-five rupees in getting a coal made to my measurements of fairly expensive Kashmir woollen material. When the news of the acquisition reached my village, it became the centre of conversation there for weeks, and I was informed that it met their disapproval. I was declared extravagant and I was advised by my parents not to wear it whilst I was at home for the holidays. In Kakrali, no one would think of donning a suit tailored in European style but there was one solitary exception. He was my father's cousin who would also refuse to use a *charpai*, a cot for sitting on, in public and would demand a chair and if he did not get one he would keep standing. These habits, he felt, made up for his literary, rather educational, deficiencies, not having gone beyond the ability to recognize black print over white paper. I was told that a pastoral woman once requested him to read a letter for her. Although he felt puzzled about what to say, he enquired of the lady from where she had expected the letter. When, in reply, she said that it could be from Lahore, he returned the letter expressing his regret for his inability to read, because he had no opportunity to go to Lahore.

I forget the year but it was in winter that 'bubonic plague' known as 'black death' broke out in severity. I have faint recollections that the entire Hindu population of the village left their homes and lived in improvised camps on the outskirts, while the Muslims stayed where they were living. The Muslims believed that those who were destined to die, would die with or without the plague. The deaths occurred in the village by scores daily among the Muslims, and not a single Hindu would dare visit the village to mourn the dead and neither would he welcome any of those left behind to visit the Hindu camps. The community life had abruptly come to an end. This state of affairs had continued for about six weeks and then the daily deaths abated not because the epidemic was brought under control by any medical treatment or by measures to check its spread but mainly because lesser and lesser people were left to be attacked and the weather too turned warmer. The Hindus returned to their homes. I, now, missed many of the old faces but the majority of those among the Muslims who loved me, survived, and I was delighted to meet them again. Later in life I learnt that the rats, man's bitterest enemies, were the carriers of the 'plague infected lice' which attacked both human beings and rodents. If the rats could be eliminated, the lice would not survive, but rats being prolific animals averaging 3 to 6 litters a year and about ten young to each litter, are a big menace. If all the offspring would survive, one pair could produce, theoretically, over three crore (thirty million) descendents in three years on the basis of five litters annually. Their population, I understand, is ten times the human population in the country, and one rat eats about 13 kilos of cereals annually and spoils our food stocks by its droppings.

During the summer holidays of 1916, I had a severe attack of typhoid. Medicine was in the hands of quacks and mystics, and villagers hardly had any faith in allopathy. When I was still invalid, a quack prescribed grapes as a nourishing food which alone could bring me back to normal health. Grapes were in those days a very rare commodity, available only in very small quantities in district towns. They were sold packed in small wooden boxes in which the grapes lay between two layers of cotton. My grandfather, after a great deal of effort, was able to buy about two dozen wooden packages with their contents and he felt that properly rationed, they would last a fortnight. The quack took charge of this stock saying that he would administer these to me in a regulated diet. No one suspected his *bona fides*, but when it was found out that he had enjoyed the bulk of the grapes himself and there were none left after three days, this so-called doctor had a real beating.

I developed a skin disease after the typhoid. It was an itch – an all time itch on the scalp. Medical aid failed to give me relief. I was cured by the application of some wood ashes given to me by a hermit living in the mountains. It happened that way, it is quite true, but I don't believe it today. Having been cured I hardly had guts to bring reason into the picture with my parents.

One morning a lady brought her daughter aged twelve to our house. The girl was walking very badly with her limbs flopping around lacking control. She had a vacant look on her face but did not appear to be suffering actual pain. I have no idea what the disease was – epilepsy or polio. The child was laid on a bed and a *Sadhu* priest was called for treatment. Several *mantras* were chanted and hymns sung. As this ceremony continued, the girl slowly fell to sleep. The body was then covered with a white sheet and we, all in silence, left the room. The *Sadhu* stayed in the courtyard for several days. As far as I remember, no food was given to the patient. The girl was still sleeping and the *Sadhu* asked us to recite the *mantras* after him and sing hymns. The *Sadhu* then uncovered the feet and pressed his hands slowly. She regained consciousness, rose and was given nourishment.

I stood first in the third primary class. My grandfather found immense joy in boasting to one and all of my success and for a prize he bought me a cap glittering with imitation golden thread work on satin. In relating this I am not so much concerned about the prize but its fate. I put on the cap and moved along the marketplace and then out into the open along the stream which flowed along the outskirts of the village. It was running full because of some rains in the hills some time earlier in the day. On all such occasions village folk clustered along its bank to watch the fury of the flood. Here I was skitting along a few paces in front of a cousin of mine of my own age group. When we walked well away from the crowd he asked me to take off my cap. I regarded his request as unreasonable, beyond that I could not analyse whether he disliked it or felt small in the presence of my prize cap. I simply did not reply and trodded along my way. I had unsuspecting trust in his friendship and therefore thought no more about it. He asked to remove the cap and hold it in my hand and told me that it was very ugly. I thought that he was jesting but he came nearer and tried to pull it off. I resisted his attempt and pressed my cap down on my head with care and every further attempt on his part made me press the cap further down. He seemed to drop the idea of pressing his demand and we walked hand in hand when all of a sudden he made a dash, laid hold of the cap, took it off and sent it flying into the running stream. For a time he did not seem to realise what he had done, but when he saw me in tears he became nervous about the treatment he may get from his own father. He did not have to wait long for the reception he expected. This came from those who observed his criminal deed. I would not infer any conclusion from the event.

Maternal Uncles

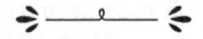

My father's maternal uncle was a *zamindar* (landlord). He had his own land, which he ploughed himself. He lived in the village of Jalalpur Sobtian and was a Sobti himself by subcaste. This village was about eight to ten miles from Kakrali. I visited him often in April at the time of the *Baisakhi Mela* (New Year Fair) and lost interest in it when I was thirteen years old.

He lived an austere life for our standards and I can recall from memory that he was accustomed to living on very little, but felt for his sons, whom he wanted to be well placed in life. He had nicknames for all of them. The eldest was called 'Judge', the second son named 'Deputy', the third '*Tehsildar*' and so on. In spite of the material difficulties which had increased his suffering, he maintained an ever ready wit, which would be uncommon in these circumstances. Whenever I visited him during the *Mela* day, he catered lavishly and ungrudgingly.

Mr. Sobti often talked to my father about the multitudinous memories connected with his land which was his forefathers', and in doing so he always felt happy. He always showed courage to live and hoped that 'Judge', 'Deputy' and the others would one day bring back his glory. I never learnt the story related to his ruin and his being under debt. In fact, I had no interest in the subject.

My interest in him lay in his titbit stories. Some of them remain fresh in my memory as they are meaningful. One of them runs like this. Mela Ram owed Amin Chand some money which the former would never pay. In desperation Amin Chand threatened legal action. One morning Mela Ram turned up before his creditors house with a heavy bag over his back. He unloaded it and shouted for Amin Chand, "Come on with the accounts. I will settle with interest." He pushed the bag into Amin Chand's *baithak* (drawing room), and emptied its contents. A heap of tamarind seeds covered the floor. He then told Amin Chand to sow the seeds on his own land and they would produce a thousand trees in the land that is lying waste, and that each tree would in due course of time produce a couple of *maunds* of tamarind which would pay Amin Chand more than he was owed after the very first crop and the subsequent crops would be his permanent gain and free bonus. Amin Chand stood stupefied while Mela Ram felt satisfied that he had settled the debts for good.

Another story related to Parvati and her two sons Kartik and Ganesh. The one was a prince, dynamic and ever alert, while the other with an elephant face was always static and immobile. The two brothers were deeply jealous of their mother's affection. An opportunity arose for them to put themselves on trial. Pavati asked both of them to go on a race circumnavigating the universe. When the mother said "Go", Kartik mounted his peacock and flew away out of sight. Ganesh kept on sitting by the side of the mother, who asked him to move as otherwise he would lose the race. Ganesh got up from his seat, walked once around his mother in a small circle and then stood before her saying that he had arrived and won the race.

My mother's maternal uncle was a petty shopkeeper. He lived in the village of Kotla only one mile away from Kakrali. He often visited us, and every time he came down, he had so much to talk to my mother that I wondered what it was all about. As I began to take interest in their conversation I observed that they generally talked about relations and matrimonial engagements which he could sponsor. I was greatly encouraged by my mother to spend a holiday with him and his daughter who was about four years older than myself. They had a parrot which was in an iron cage which housed a perch in it. The bird swung to and fro on it but was not free to fly out. The parrot trilled forth snatches of some religious couplets and was called 'Ganga Ram' probably for that performance. Without claiming to read what things were in his mind but he seemed delighted in his strength – the deep incisions he could make in a mango or a guava whenever served to him, tearing to shreds even a piece of wood with his beak after closing his grey claws around the victim in less than no time. I was very fond of this bird and just for seeing him I would go to Kotla as often as I felt could. I was still a little boy when I walked up to the cage and stretched my fingers to touch his eyes that blazed like rubies but I could not reach them. My mother's uncle shouted at me "Bishambara, leave the creature alone. He might bite your finger." I disregarded his sage warning and I had reason to regret it.

Gandhiji

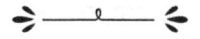

The man who fought the biggest Empire and won, I saw him for the first time when he visited the town of Gujrat in 1919. He could speak Hindi only with a great effort and yet there was pin drop silence when he addressed the people on Hindu-Muslim unity and on the creed of nonviolence. I cannot remember exactly what he said, but from the simplicity of his attire and his manner I felt conscious of my personal devotion towards him. This has lasted over the years. I accepted everything he said and I accept all that even now when he is no longer amongst us to maintain the education of his tenets. At the time, however, I was still under the spell of indignation at the treatment meted out to me during the period, the reign of terror, at the parade ground in the city, and therefore I seemed to lack completely, the ability to understand the seeming conflict between hatred and love.

Mahatmaji's statements and writings became headlines in the Indian Press, more particularly in the vernacular dailies. *Swaraj* (Self-rule), *Swadeshi* (Indigenous), and *Satyagraha* (Gandhiji's coinage for nonviolent resistance) were words that appeared almost daily and these became the talk of the town. His camp followers and the country's politicians elaborated his message in a language which would appeal and excite the masses against the Alien Raj, boycott of English goods, and non-violent non-cooperation with the rulers. I can look back and see that I had heard or read about Gandhiji's commands which could not have been uttered by him. Local Congress leaders once told us, "Gandhiji asks you to refrain from using cloth manufactured in England or other English goods as only through their trade do the Britishers enjoy their present prosperity and they will come down to their knees for a compromise with the Indian people for fear of their own starvation." Later in life when I learnt more about him and became his devotee I said to myself, "Could he have said those words even in 1919? No."

I subscribed to an Urdu daily so that I could keep up-to-date with the current events and affairs of my country. The political agitation was growing in intensity. My constant reading was affecting my daily thoughts and I felt like uttering the lines from an English poem in the poetry book I was reading in school – "Mine not to reason why – mine but to do and die," I now developed the habit of reading loudly to a small crowd the prominent news from my daily and when I went home for my vacation, I carried that habit. The villagers who were still influenced by the events in the town felt amazed that I could express forcefully what was intended to be conveyed to them. Although I often stressed that they were all now soldiers in the struggle for the Country's Freedom, they looked unmoved. Mahatmaji was destined to command the country's political stage till Independence.

The villagers did not understand his social inventions such as revival of hand-cording, hand-spinning and hand-weaving of textiles and the revival of handicrafts. They did not decry them as the people in the West did, or Indians educated in the Western and urban modes, because ruralites had blind faith in his wisdom. They, however, understood that he wanted to use their idle time to spin and weave their own cloth by which they could augment their income. As industrialization had not made much advancement in the country, the people had at large, an open mind. Regarding Gandhiji's politics, no diplomacy or statesmanship was involved. I always felt that he commended the cause of our country to the British people as something beyond the stature of a political agitator. To me, he was a saint – the Saint of Sabarmati as he was known. He had full faith that the British would withdraw from India by the method of *Satyagraha*, as in his own words, "In the application of the method of non-violence, one must believe in the possibility of every person, however depraved, being reformed under humane and skilled treatment."

During the Second World War when the rulers felt that they had just about finished the pranks of the 'Naked *Faqir*', the latter issued an ultimatum – 'Quit India'. The rulers and the counterpart of the ruling race sharpened their batons and widened the entrance to the jail gates. What happened in 1942 after Gandhiji's arrest and of other leaders is a part of Indian history now, India moved considerably near to complete freedom. The British rulers seemed convinced that India had a determination, under Gandhiji's leadership, to make all sacrifices to achieve their freedom. Within five years India succeeded. Freedom was a reality. The fetters fell off.

Gandhiji was against the division of India, but the country was divided by carving out a new country – Pakistan. It produced an ill will and hatred between Hindus and Muslims and the division led to the calamity of the mass exodus of non-Muslims from Pakistan and of a large Muslim population from the parent country. The blood and tears that wetted the soil along the long trail, with aged mothers pining for martyred sons, with wives without husbands, and tens of thousands left orphaned by the battle for freedom, inflicted immense pain on Gandhiji. He mourned and almost wept every day and expressed utter grief at every prayer meeting against the human insanity that played havoc in both countries.

It was good luck to have been born and grown in a period when the energy of the Indian character asserted itself on the minds of the country's youth. We were under the spell of those who worked untiringly and with devotion for the country's freedom and upliftment and always laid the greatest emphasis on improvement of social and moral standards of the people.

Whether it was my school days or later in life, Gandhiji influenced my whole outlook on life. If I took to *khadi* (handloom cloth) for my clothes, I paid no attention to its cost but the fact, that I wore the articles spun by the village women in their spare time and woven by the rural weavers who stood in need of work, was strong enough urge to keep to *swadeshi* clothes. I deviated from this path for a few years, but soon returned to my faith. Both capitalism and socialism of the Western type, being based identically on the ideal of material welfare, wasted their energy on the amassing of wealth for the material comforts either for the few rich people or for the whole Nation. Gandhiji did not like his countrymen to follow in their footsteps, but to develop an economy which would develop a happy mental condition. That is why he held that our mental and moral development is dependent on our physical work and as a consequence brought out a scheme for basic education, which was worked out in greater detail by Dr. Zakir Hussain, the present President of India. In the non-violent society of Gandhiji's conception there could be no room for any exploitation of humanity. The English proverb, 'work is worship' meant to us basic education.

The history of the world is the chronicle of the cross-currents that the persons, who had implicit faith in what they professed and worked at, and who were martyred for being serious about their job, left behind them. Gandhiji lived and died for secularism and brotherhood of mankind. One of those who shouted "Gandhiji *ki Jai*" (Long live Gandhiji) for his victory in the battle of freedom, murdered the Father of the Nation on 30th January 1948, for Gandhiji refused to join in the chorus of 'a tooth for a tooth, an eye for an eye' which millions shouted in post-Independence period since 1947. Gandhiji still lives through his death.

VISHAV BHAVAN

Part III: My Youth

Two Indias (Urban and Rural)

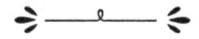

I have incidentally mentioned 'the village community' and have described it as a self-contained society, having its group of cultivators, its field labourers, its village artisans, its grain dealers, its grocers, and its moneylenders. This community had wonderful power of survival in troubled times and it had lasted in Kakrali as probably elsewhere in spite of the tumbling down of one dynasty of rulers after another. It was visible that even the political upsurge in the country had no effect on the community. People talked of Sikh *Raj* and of English *Raj* but the village life had remained unchanged. In times of trouble they would fortify themselves. There was political unrest in the towns and cities, but our village looked least concerned and it considered itself a small state. What was true about Kakrali was equally applicable to other rural areas. Whatever may be the reason, apathy, illiteracy, fatalism, it was in a high degree conducive to their happiness and to the enjoyment of a great portion of freedom and independence.

The district headquarters, the town of Gujrat was in a transitional stage between Kakrali and Lahore with greater leanings towards urban life. The characteristic of the archaic economy of isolation and independence of the village was disappearing and was giving place to Western urban civilization. Many of my relatives in town were products of both rural and urban life. They loved the village life for a change but were proud to belong to a town. I had no occasion to feel small in the town but later when I joined the university in Lahore I was just nobody in the great multitude of the city. In my beloved village I was their hope, the future hope of the entire village community, but they feared that I might go the same way as few others did after college education – never to return to them. They were familiar with that one way traffic from rural to urban India which had commenced, but they still hoped that I would maintain my moorings in the village.

The city of Lahore held many attractions, movies and theatres. Charlie Chaplin and Harry Lloyd as comedians, Ronald Coleman and Douglas Fairbanks for adventure, Lon Chaney as character actor, and Mary Astor and Clara Bow as famous actresses on the screen. They attracted college students. I very occasionally visited picture houses, but I was keen to stage performances, which were enacted in Urdu, which to my knowledge was a storehouse for literature, culture and wisdom. It was in very chaste Urdu that the playwrights produced the plays, and the drama somehow always left some lasting impressions on my knowledge of Urdu. It was mainly for this that I was hardly ever deterred by the inconvenience of spending six hours in seeing the performance – the six hours being equally divided on each side of midnight.

The city of Lahore had a most varied picture, many kinds of dresses, great contrasts in a teeming population, crowds of people sitting and lying on the open ground were seen outside the city walls and in the shade of buildings amidst noise and movement. There was also a haphazard mixture of poor and wealthy areas, overpopulated and deserted areas, which gave an impression of disorder. The Civil Lines with government buildings, colleges, university and courts presented a different picture to the rest of the city. The Anglo-Indian buildings were dwarfed by the architecture of earlier periods. Here the contrast between the rich and the poor was scarcely possible, particularly in the Civil Lines where there were no real neighbours. I had relations in the city and I lived with them on and off. They lived with their neighbours as if mutually they were strangers and I could discern the contrast with our community life in the village, where families lived near one another and toiled together for generations.

Looking back upon the traditions of family life from the distance of time I feel that even in cities home life had a kind of sanctity which no longer seems to be the case. The austere tradition of a healthy middle class family life has gradually been replaced by sensuous, genial and fibreless society. Women in the urban areas are becoming more and more like men, even encouraged to stand alone and are occupying themselves with pursuits hitherto regarded as masculine.

The townsman had a very poor knowledge of God's earth. An occasional picnic in a park or by the riverside could never compensate for nature which was shut out to lakhs of people in the city of Lahore. They could, however, boast about electricity with which most homes and shops were lit every evening. There were still some who used storm lamps or oil lamps. The shops did not close till late in the city. Diwali, known as the festival of lights and which in the North marks the anniversary of the coronation of Rama after his triumphant return from Lanka, was made gay since the advent of electricity. Although the festival was celebrated in the village with great gusto, Lahore did it with electricity and as such great crowds were attracted to the city for Diwali.

Modern India exists only in large cities and even there partially. There is a growing tendency to go 'modern'. It was under check when the country was fighting its struggle for freedom but ever since Independence not only the cult of *Swadeshi* received a setback but the leanings to ape the west in style, cosmetics, furnishings, dress etc. had gathered force in all urban areas and is now infiltrating into rural areas. Gandhi's influence on Indian thought and politics is on the wane although political leaders often take shelter even for their wrongs by misquoting him, or when they desire to improve their eloquence.

The roots of Indian civilization are in the villages. The people of my village, like so many other villages, were rich in basic traits like goodwill, neighbourliness, fair play, courage, tolerance etc. and even though the urban influences have tried to kill the goose that laid golden eggs for them, the human quality of villages has not badly deteriorated. Whenever and wherever I lived in villages after having settled in urban areas, during the last thirty to fifty years, I have seen simplicity and truthfulness well maintained as also cooperative life. Every human being in the village is a part of the whole, weddings and festivals still celebrated by the whole village community. It is a pity that townspeople occupying positions of power in the administration do not encourage village people to evolve schemes for their own betterment.

I did not go back to my village and everyone of us who crossed his matriculation felt that his best chances of employment and enjoyment were in great cities. The elders could not dissuade and did not, in fact, like to keep back from their young educated progeny, what seemed sure gain. Those of us who entered trade like my uncle, found great opportunities of amassing wealth. They did not care to remain landlords, who were despised and discriminately treated by government legislation. The growth of large towns has therefore gone on at the expense of the villages.

Must that process continue? My uncle who, after Partition, settled down in Sadar Bazar area in Delhi, although admires the town of Chandigarh as ideal for living, yet gets bored with its quiet life. He does not find the hum of Sadar Bazar in this new town and has become a confirmed Delhi*wala* and loves to watch the full tide of life from the window of his house overlooking the West End Cinema on Phoota Road, Delhi. Meantime in my village as in any other, the peasant continues holding the plough which tracks along the trail of scratched furrows and shouting at the drooping animals and sometimes swearing at them for not pulling fast and hard enough. By midday he plods back home, unharnesses the animals and reclines himself on a *charpai* and has his *hukka* (hubble-bubble) for a digression.

Unless the countryside can offer to the youth some satisfactory food for the soul as well as body, it will fail to hold its population and they will go to the overcrowded towns. This process results in lessening of rural production which in turn affects urban population adversely. It is more a human problem than an economic one. It is one of the illusions of modern materialistic thought to suppose that as high a quality of life is not possible in a village as in a great city, and it might, and therefore should be the aims of our planners and administrators to dissipate this fallacy and to show that it is possible to bring about comfort enough to satisfy any reasonable person to create a society where there will be intellectual life and human interests in the countryside. The rural areas will then hold their own, tug for tug, with the towns.

The townsmen have a little veneer of Western education and consider the villagers to be crude and rustic. Maybe I have a bias for the country people in considering them superior to their urban counterparts. Physically they have some magnificent specimens and morally they have higher standards of integrity, austere living and a happy way of life. Urbanisation has, however, come to stay. It is only necessary for the townsmen to know that they cannot flourish by the exploitation of their own counterparts in the rural areas.

In my village there was no electricity, not even in 1947 when I migrated to our new homeland after Partition of the country. When I built the power house at Nilokheri, a small refugee township built in Karnal district in Haryana and then extended the use of electricity, the invincible power from heavens, the whole outlook of the refugees changed without much pressure from the administration. The refugees were themselves very keen to start industries, cottage and small scale. They were transformed. What was applicable to the displaced persons in one refugee centre, was applicable to the whole of rural India.

The villages of India have provided the urban areas with food even at the cost of starving themselves. This occupation alone has so far been inadequate to give them ample work. When Gandhiji used to lay stress on *Swadeshi* cult, his whole emphasis was that the consumer goods, both for themselves and the urban population should be produced by the villagers which form the bulk of the people of our country. Although I understood this at a very early age, yet even when I adopted *Swadeshi*-ism, it was not cent percent.

Ours had been a race with an unbroken record in the world that gave but never asked back, that embraced but never repelled and that culture still persists both in rural and urban India, although more pronounced in the former and in spite of the vicissitude of centuries past. If a stranger visited a poor peasant's house, he will receive all attention and so will his children, the food in the kitchen whatever he has will be placed at the service of the *atithi* (guest), the family contenting itself with the left over after the *narayan* (the guest as god) has been served. It is still

Two Indias (Urban and Rural)

commonplace for a poor man in tattered rags, while driving his cart, to sing on the freezing winter mornings – *"Ram bhaje ja, Kam kare ja, Phir kiska dar hai, Is nagri mein sabhi musafir, yeh kiska ghar hai?"* Chant the name of God, Work hard, Then you have nothing to fear. We are all travellers on this Earth, It is nobody's home.

The old social order is being rent to pieces now and something new is taking its place but it is a continuous process. Its pace can be slow or fast. There can be no finality, which means death, about any one particular system or social order. What is obvious today cannot be the final picture. This process is applicable to all parts of the country – not only true in large cities and towns where evolution has been faster over the past three decades, but marked change is now visible in the countryside where apathy, it is said, reigned for long.

The new methods of cultivation for increased production and the changed method of winnowing for speedy recovery of grain, the introduction of hybrid varieties of maize and wheat will materially help and bring about change in their static mind. But what is happening is that the villagers are depending more and more on mill made articles rather than maintaining an emphasis on indigenous products. Within my own life I have seen how we have battled against very difficult problems, the solution of which was essential for the Nation. I am convinced beyond doubt that no slogans on socialism would bring about the requisite transformation if we do not encourage the purchase of articles of food, clothing, implements, soaps, and many other goods of our daily use which the villagers produce even if their products may be crude. This process will induce them to improve their workmanship and assist in bringing about social change. Urban India must save rural India where its roots lie.

We had an ancient tree in our garden at Kakrali. Its foliage covered a huge area under which nothing else would grow. My grandfather had the tree felled and the whole of its visible trunk was also removed. To excavate and dig out the underground stump and roots was considered an unnecessary and costly affair. With the passage of time it threw up new shoots from the left-over stump, but its roots sprouted at several places over a large area and if left in position, we would have had many more trees of the same species. The removal of the trunk had meant nothing to the tree, which survived our onslaught as its roots were well protected in the ground and were capable of revival of what appeared to have been destroyed. Our Nation and its culture have survived the ravages of time because its roots are spread over a large area – in rural areas.

The villagers, it has been my experience, desire to improve their lot, and the ways they go about it are the main forces that will shape the future business and politics of any region during the present time of evolution or change. The eventual balanced economy of the whole country – rural and urban, would call for a special treatment of rural India – a total war against unemployment, seasonal or total, and against wants and poverty for mitigating the privations and hardships of the community's less favoured sections.

In the year 1962, when I was working with the Bharat Sevak Samaj, the organisation under the guidance of Shri D.K. Mehta – a nature cure specialist of Bombay, and President (servant) of the Society of the Servants of God, passed a resolution adopting the 'Five Needs of Life Movement' as its programme. This movement did not aim at providing the *minimum* needs of life but the *optimum* requirements for the healthy growth of human beings. Among the two Indias – rural and urban, its emphasis would have been the former. Those, including myself, who adopted this movement, did not accept it as practical, and therefore, it did not make much headway.

My Grandfather's Death

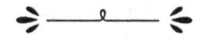

My parents sent a messenger to the town to convey the news of serious illness which had overtaken my grandfather. Tears rolled down my cheeks as I accompanied him to the village. Eighteen miles seemed endless. To imagine my grandfather ill was a strain on my imagination. I prayed all the way that he might be well by the time I reached home. It was too late. He died before I arrived. He had always been very kind to the poor and a guide for the joint family that he left behind. I saw my grandfather's face which had enhanced dignity. People came in and out of the room where his body lay. Women cried and men wept. I stood motionless. My mother's touch was helpful as I broke down and wept and cried. I was about fifteen. The sense of this loss swept over me in all its intensity and I could feel the end of my future education, as he alone loved to see me have the highest scholastic attainment.

My mind was mostly modelled on my father's. My father did not believe in death of the soul which according to him was immortal and did not have any identity distinct from God. The body, he always said, was just a shadow and just visible like it. These rigid beliefs rendered him an optimist. He was hardly ever gloomy or grave. He, even at the time of the death of his father, was not taken over by any pessimism in spite of the fact that he was exclusively dependent on his father for his material needs. My mother was too prone to emotion and was melancholy over what happened. These are the recollections I have within the chambers of my memory.

My grandfather had a friend who was a Muslim weaver. He was of his age, although infirm, but proud of his generation. He was bald except for a few straggling grey hairs. He was a simpleton and it is still fresh in my memory, an anecdote showing his simplicity and faith in his friend, my grandfather. This weaver, once when he was suffering from fever, asked for my grandfather's advice, which was rendered in the form of a prescription written on a piece of paper. Besides, he was verbally told to grind it fine in a mortar, mix some water and drink. The old man recovered from his illness within a day or two and reported to my grandfather about the efficacy of the ink and the paper he had given him, as he ground the paper in the mortar and used it as medicine. He lamented most bitterly of all the death of his dear friend. He wanted to die in his place.

An old *brahman* (upper caste but destitute) widow used to share my grandfather's bedroom. Her devotion to my grandfather was one of a servant to his master. She did not have to cook her own meals as she was given the requisite food for every meal from the joint family kitchen. Besides, on all festivities, the villagers (Hindus) bestowed her with sweets and small presents. Thus, she was quite well off, and in fact, she had quite a bit of left-over sweets which she used to store. I, often, went to her for sweets and invariably she told me that she had none. Although she conveyed emphatically her reply to be final, but relying on my own past experiences, I assured her on all occasions that she had them in one or the other earthen pitchers that she used for storage. I always succeeded in the long run. After the death of my grandfather she never refused but on the other hand was too willing to part with the sweets. She hardly survived the shock and died within twelve months of the death of Ram Shah.

My grandfather always felt concerned about my father's indifference towards money and looking back I can also testify that my father has never known the value of money or I had better say that he knows it too well when I see that money is the cause of all these ills that afflict our social order. Whenever he is given cash, he is keen to part with it as soon as he possibly can. My uncle Shiv Nath began to share what he earned with my father who had lost the financial umbrella provided for him by my grandfather.

My grandfather had five brothers and a sister. All the brothers lived in the village and had the same vocation in life. The eldest had died about two years ahead of my grandfather who took his turn in October 1919. The dear sister lived at Daulatnagar and the announcement of her coming to Kakrali was always received with great enthusiasm by one and all among the Nanda-fold. She was a very domineering personality because her six brothers were heads of their own joint families and she was their darling sister. I do not know when she lost her husband, she had three sons. She was younger than my grandfather, her brother, but she appeared a great deal older than she really was. I felt quite at ease in her company and my stay in Daulatnagar resulting in greater nearness than the other children, her arrival caused me joy. Every time she came to stay with us, she examined me with greater attention than on any previous occasion and then submitted the report to her brother. Whatever evils she found in me, she explained that they arose from the fact that I was the only child of my parents. Two months after grandfather's death, my mother gave birth to another son.

"A brother was born" was the news conveyed to me at

Gujrat. I longed to see him and by the Christmas vacation he was a few days old when I lifted him in my arms. He was bestowed on me as the closest friend by nature but he did not live long. Four years later another was born but he too lived for one year. Thereafter I remained brotherless and the only child. Even the good news of the birth of a son to my uncle Shiv Nath conveyed to me did not last long. The child died before I returned home from England.

My grandfather's concern for my welfare was very prominent in his life. He was charged with discrimination in my favour by interested parties when they felt safe in making such remarks. I was not yet seven that is certain, but was I six and a half? That is what I cannot be sure, and now there is no one left who could throw any light on this point. However, I can console myself with the reflection that more important lacunae present themselves in the history of the Nation. I have said all this because the event that I am going to relate is such that it has well lasted in my memory. It was getting really dark when I returned home after my play in the evening. I found my parents, and more particularly, my grandfather feverishly excited and the old man in tears. They thought I had been kidnapped by gypsies who were living in the improvised tents outside the village or I may have lost my way in a maze of paths in the thick *Shisham* forest a mile or so away from the village. They had already been to find out whether I was at the house of any of my playmates. They were now getting ready to go to the forest with storm lamps when I made my appearance. My grandfather was the first person to look at me very carefully all over, touched my forehead and found it moist and saw that I had soiled clothes. Where had I been, was the inquiry. Nervously I recounted my adventure having accompanied a Muslim lady whom I always addressed as 'aunty', to climb on the mango trees for collecting some fruit for her and that while climbing was not so difficult, but getting down became dangerous. The old man was enraged as he could not think that the Muslim lady could dare keep his grandson out after sunset and utilise him on such a risky errand without his permission. My father, who appeared to be calm, desired to forget and forgive, but my grandfather sent for the old lady. She was trembling all over as she walked into the courtyard. This time the old *brahman* lady in the house came to her rescue by saying that my grandfather should put it down to ignorance of the Muslim lady who was otherwise a good soul. She, herself, reprimanded the culprit and made her apologise. The whole village now knew the event and it became quite embarrassing for me for days on end to move without being asked by someone as to what happened on that particular evening.

The sorrow which had overtaken the family after the death of my grandfather was very deep, but realising that none of us could conquer death and death is inevitable, everyone had to console and bring strength to bear it. Those who did not know that the old man had a fall from an eight foot height in the dead of night while on a visit to a dying villager, were keen to hear that repeated about their loved one, from some witness of the accident that proved fatal. They admired both the sacrifice and his courage to continue his mission, and everyone seemed to repeat, "God willed it so. We do not understand His plans."

My Uncle Shiv Nath

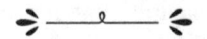

Among the five sons my grandfather had, Shiv Nath was the central figure. He had passed his matriculation examination before I was born. It was then considered a scholastic achievement. He preferred to join Government service in preference to joining his father's vocation in spite of the fact that his job was not well paid. He got married when I was a wee little baby and he along with his wife settled down away from the village and gradually removed themselves away from the joint family fold. He was my uncle, about whom I knew very little during my babyhood, but as I grew in years he started taking interest in me. He had no son. He showered his attention towards me as his own child and as the years passed he grew very fond of me. By marrying his wife's niece to me in 1925, he established another close relationship. He planned a future for me when he arranged to send me abroad for higher education.

My uncle left Government service after the death of my grandfather in 1918. His death brought about a partial dismemberment of the joint family as the entire property both moveable and immoveable was divided between his sons. My father and my uncle Shiv Nath pooled their respective shares but it gave rise to a new problem. My uncle, who was still a

Government servant at Jaranwala, had, collaborating with one of his personal friends, a businessman, entered wholesale trade in cereals, cotton and oilseeds. Someone was needed to represent him in this trade while he would continue in service. His choice fell on me but my mother disagreed with him and persuaded him to allow me to continue my studies. Ultimately it was decided that he would leave Government service himself and look after business while my father would see to the affairs related to our common landed property.

In early 1923, my uncle expanded his business by opening a branch at Lalamusa, only about twelve miles away from Kakrali. He urgently needed assistance upon which he could rely. It appeared to him that it might be wise for me to abandon my educational career and join him in business. This time I pleaded with him to allow me two more years at the college. He agreed. But I realised that any new circumstance would change my uncle's opinion about my future and that I was, like most of us, a creature of the environment in which I lived and grew. I could see that I was not the master of my fate.

My uncle, whenever there was a suitable audience, grew rhetorical about me. "My nephew will do this and that …," he would say. All that did not seem real and it gave me a vague sense of discomfort and even at times humiliation. He eulogised me in my presence but it gave me satisfaction that he was now looking ahead for my advanced education which was not going to end abruptly after graduation. Soon after I left for England in 1925, my aunt gave birth to a son. She already had five daughters, all of whom I had adopted as my sisters and not as cousins. When I received the tidings of the newcomer my joy found no bounds and I wrote back to my parents and uncle how happy I was once again to know that nature had been kind to give me a brother (not a cousin). Unfortunately the lad died in the middle of 1928 before I returned home.

It was not without regret when he left his Government service, and as he has often narrated to me, that he could count on a bright future if he had continued in his post, but he did not like to travel along a road, a vocation, which failed to provide an impetus to speculative life, one full of interest. He planned to become a trader and a commission agent. He did successfully for several years until in 1927, when I was abroad, he lost heavily, amounting to financial ruin. He did not lose heart but conveyed to me the serious implications involved including the loss of mercenary help from him in England. It was a shock for me but I succeeded in earning money for myself by resorting to translation work from English to Urdu for some British firms exporting medicines and cosmetic products to India. I carried on this work for a whole year, by which time my uncle recovered his position to an extent that he was able to send me passage money for my journey homeward after passing my B.Sc. Honours (London). I owe a great deal of gratitude to him.

My father's younger brother, my uncle Shiv Nath.

Boyhood Anecdotes

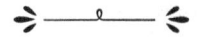

From Gujrat I shifted to Victoria Diamond Jubilee High School at Wazirabad, another twenty miles towards Lahore. This school had a reputation for securing a substantial number of university scholarships every year. It had a new atmosphere to which I was not accustomed. At Gujrat I always found myself as intelligent as many others in the class but I now discovered that unless I worked hard, I would be a back bencher. But as luck would have it, I started with my pre-matriculation year in the company of those who were not all serious about their studies. I was a boarder in the school hostel, where I was in a common dormitory with that group of students. The headmaster, realising that I could be saved for the school and myself, ordered me to leave the hostel and hire a flat as near to the school as possible, so that he could conveniently keep vigilance over my efforts. This was done as desired.

I now had a room to myself and hardly had I settled down in it, that I observed a dancing girl living just across the road opposite my flat. When the headmaster saw the situation, he scolded me for my indiscretion but later cooled down when he realised that there was no other flat available and that I had neither the money nor the inclination to waste myself in her company. The room was on the first floor with a projecting balcony under which on the ground floor some blind beggars assembled every night for shelter. They often talked about their daily collections and how they utilised their charity. It was always amusing to listen to them – how many cigarettes they smoked, the type and quantity of intoxicants they enjoyed each day. Soon after sunrise they used to disperse on their daily errand.

Living in a flat provided greater digression from studies and wider contrasts with people in the town. It did not mean lesser attention to my lessons in the class or to my home task, but instead of gossip and playing cards of the hostel days, my leisure was now utilised making friends with persons older than myself and those engaged in trade, politics and industry. Once, not very far from my flat, a fire broke out. Many people rushed to help put the fire out. I happened to be among them. We brought buckets and formed up in a line. The buckets were passed to and fro. The wind was blowing the flames and smoke in our direction but everyone was doing his best to deliver water to the point where it was needed most. Gradually the fire came under control and to embers still glowing. At this juncture, a man, his name I don't remember, with his hubble-bubble in his hand came to the spot and enquired of the owner, whose property had been reduced to ashes, if he could use the smouldering wood for his tobacco. How awful! It has never faded in my memory that men could be so spiteful.

It was the pre-matriculation year and I was expected by my parents and teachers to work hard in order to secure a distinction and a university scholarship. Unfortunately I fell a victim to typhoid – a disease by which I suffered many a time in my early life. I lost weight and vitality to such an extent that my survival was considered a miracle. After a long absence I returned to school more zealous for participation in the political movement than in my studies. The headmaster once again came to my rescue. His threat to evict me from the school had a good effect on me. I promised to work at my courses assiduously and acted accordingly. I secured first division in the final examination but was unable to earn a scholarship.

For the matriculation examination Wazirabad did not have a centre but all the students had to go to district headquarters at Gujranwala. Arrangements for our food and lodging were made for us by the school authorities daily close to the centre. Communication facilities in those days were scarce and only *tongas* were the means of conveyance between the town of Gujranwala and the examination centre at the Government school situated on its outskirts. Those could hardly be relied upon for carrying about one hundred and fifty students of our school appearing in that exam that year.

When I was taking the examination for practical science, the examiner-in-charge, while I was busy, enquired of me if I was betrothed. After I replied in the negative he became exceedingly inquisitive regarding my ancestry, my father's vocation and many like questions. I objected by saying that it was inopportune to waste my time in attending to his queries, none of which had any relationship to the duty in hand. You shall not be the loser, he said, as he was to award the marks for the tests in practical science on the spot. I could understand what he was aiming at. I was quite well rewarded for my obedience. The incident may be quite trivial but it reveals how examinations can be unfairly conducted by personal considerations of the examiners.

After finishing the examination I did not go back to Kakrali but reported to the headmaster to whom I was extremely indebted. As he asked me to assist him for a couple of months by working as a teacher under him for the junior classes, I accepted the same. It was during this period that I developed a devotion towards him as he influenced me by his life of austerity and piety, which stood me in good stead after I joined the college in Lahore.

I have failed to mention that I had two very close relations living at Gujranwala. I should have normally stayed with them when I was taking up the university examination, but the risk of losing time in discussing matters relating to mutual relationships, as also the likelihood of being late for the examination, I stayed with the whole class. Now that I was free, I found an occasion to proceed to Gujranwala for a week's holiday. I left Wazirabad by train but on the way I fell fast asleep. Not only that I passed over Gujranwala while asleep but the train was nearing Lahore where I spent a couple of days with my aunt about whom I have stated elsewhere that she was a widow remarried.

In 1921 I joined the Dayanand Anglo Vedic (D.A.V.) College in Lahore for university education. I selected Inter Science (Medical) for my subjects. The college catered for education up to M.A. and had more than fifteen hundred students on its roll. Not less than half the students came from *mofussil*[15] villages and towns, who lived in the hostel attached to the college. I lived in a room shared by four boarders, and luckily all of us were villagers. I had no suit or a necktie and I had never worn a collar and neither did I know how to knot a necktie. Only a small number of my class fellows used western style clothes and they did not receive any merit for donning them.

I had not used a wrist watch and in fact I purchased one in 1925 when I was preparing for going abroad. It did not come to me as a gift from friends or from my father-in-law as has now become quite common practice. In this matter of the wrist watch I am reminded of a college friend who used to wear one on each

---

15   Urdu word for rural districts.

wrist, also one in each pocket – four in all. The reason for this, he explained, was to compete with his cousins, each of whom had possessed a wrist watch for twenty years. His arithmetic was that in seven years he would have 4x7 equal to twenty-eight watch years while any of his cousins would have 1x27 or twenty-seven watch years. He thus hoped to beat them in seven years. This strange theory impressed me in quite a different way, that is, if a person has been denied 'a way of life' which he desired, he is bound, where opportunity arises, to live intensely the way life which was in the past taboo.

The summer vacations, whether from high school or college used to be pretty long, and were invariably spent in my own village in the company of my parents. I always looked forward to the vacations and it was a sad occasion the day I had to return to school. My mother used to prepare my favourite dishes for a whole week before the holidays ended and also some sweets were packed which would last me a month or so for augmenting the relatively frugal meals which were catered in the hostels. On one occasion, I believe it was in 1921, when I was in D.A.V. College for my studies that my roommates sensed possession of these sweets, or they may have observed me taking out a small portion of them from my box and eating the same. They raided my box when I was not in the room and finished the whole lot of the sweets. In fact, they told me that they were distributed to many other boarders living in the adjoining rooms. I had no other course but to acquiesce against the robbery.

By 1919, I was considered to be of sufficient age to decide small matters for myself. Without prior sanction of my parents, I left the school hostel and moved to a room in a friend's house which was very close to the school. Living in the hostel and walking nearly a mile twice daily was not only inconvenient but not free from danger of being manhandled by some ruffian of which there was no dearth in the district town of Gujrat. This room was a part of a very large house and a Sikh Gurdwara and it had an independent door opening in a street besides the one connecting it with other rooms in which my friend and his wife lived. My friend was also my class fellow and he had already been married two years at the age of fourteen. He was also the father of one child. From the window of the room which opened on a side street I used to observe a young girl nearly of my own age going past my room every day. She lived in the adjoining house. My curiosity was aroused and gradually hers too, until we became familiar. I once admitted her into my room by the external door, but coincidentally my friend opened his interconnecting door and walked into mine. The girl slipped away at once and my friend called his wife in. I was told that it was not becoming of me and that if I liked her, she could meet the girl's parents and secure a matrimonial alliance. So far nothing of the kind had occurred in my mind and it was too big a question on which I could take a decision myself. My friend's wife, however, knew that such an alliance would not be easily brought about in those days. I belonged to a Kshatriya sect and she to an Arora sect. My friend, therefore, saw that our meetings were discontinued as his wife thought that I had been indiscreet.

The Influences of Political Upsurge

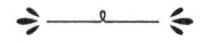

The years 1920-21 can be said to be historic in the struggle for India's freedom from foreign yoke. The Indian National Congress resolved to accentuate its programme of non-cooperation under Gandhiji's leadership. A wave of civil disobedience was visible everywhere.

Bal Gangadhar Tilak, a veteran national leader whose reputation was equal to that of Gandhiji, died in August 1920, and later that year a country-wide appeal was made for a Tilak Memorial Fund of one million rupees. A Congress volunteer visited the Victoria Diamond Jubilee School in connection with the fund for collection of subscriptions from school boys, but the headmaster disallowed his entry into the school, rather, ordered a forced exit from the premises. My indignation against the action of the headmaster found responsive cooperation from my classmates, who walked out of the classroom as a body, shouted slogans against the headmaster's highhandedness, and called for a day's strike from the school. More than half the boys from all other classes followed to join in a meeting announced for the purpose. Tempers ran high and under the advice of a senior student it was resolved to demand from the headmaster for the recall of the local Congress volunteer to the school for collection and to induce the students for liberal contributions. I led the delegation to meet the headmaster, who readily agreed to our demands.

A week later, we were told by the headmaster that the Duke of Connaught or Marlborough was visiting India on behalf of the British King and that he was likely to come to our institution. The ceremony, it was announced, would include the distribution of metallic medals to be pinned to our garments, followed by sweets. The whole function was in the memory of our Lost Soldiers in the First World War. After school hours we devised a plan for its boycott but somehow it had leaked out, the headmaster, therefore, had all the outer doors locked on the day so that none of us could go out. We too had come to know about it, and instantaneously formed a different plan for non-cooperation.

The school authorities, realising the gravity of the situation, became tactful. The Second Master entered our classroom and himself raised the slogan of "*Vande Matram*" (I bow to thee my motherland) and we joined him. He repeated it a number of times and aroused our national sentiments and then explained to us why it was befitting on our part to wear the medals in commemoration of those who laid there lives in the cause of righteousness and he quoted Sanskrit *shlokas* (verses) from the Bhagavad Gita in support of his argument. In spite of all this he failed to influence the students. When the Second Master handed a medal to the first boy, he returned it to the giver, who immediately left the room and the boys now began to shout "*Vande Matram*." The headmaster declared a holiday and how he handled the situation *vis-a-vis* the Government administration never came to light. We left the school in a triumphant mood.

Before the close of 1920 the railwaymen declared a general strike over the entire North Western Railways, the only Government controlled railway at the time in India. This was organised under the personal guidance of Mr. Miller, an Anglo-Indian ex-railway guard. The strike ended ultimately in a victory for the railwaymen who were given increased wages. I met Mr. Miller some twenty years later at Quetta, where I was the President of the Railwaymen's Federation, Quetta division of the North Western Railways. 'Miller's Whistle' was even then as powerful as it was twenty years earlier, but he no longer occupied that dictatorial position as he did then. The Indian political upsurge was his greatest ally in those days of unrest. The railways had lost considerable revenue as ticketless travel flourished during the strikes. Travellers walked in and out of the station platforms as if they were public roads. A few trains were kept running by the Government, and those too gave unsatisfactory service. The whole atmosphere was charged with the spirit of non-cooperation after Gandhiji had asked his countrymen to return all Government titles, to boycott law courts and educational institutions, to resign from Government services and to not take part in the newly constituted legislatures. But the greatest response came to his call for a boycott of English goods. I took to wearing handspun and handwoven coarse *khadi* for my clothing. I did not understand how spinning over a *charkha* could be a means of winning freedom from a foreign yoke. Furthermore, handspinning appeared outdated in a machine age. I refused to waste my time in spinning, and many of my class fellows laughed the idea to scorn and said it was going backward. We were too young to understand that if an advanced technology did not benefit a considerable population, it was more appropriate to augment technology that could improve their economic condition. Gandhiji wanted to bring simple machinery to an unused reservoir of manpower, the unemployed agriculturists in particular. Our national leaders took to spinning and weaving as a symbol for the promotion of the idea underlying Gandhiji's plan.

The first elections, based on limited franchise and separate electorates, were held in 1921 after the introduction of the Mont-Ford Reforms. The Indian National Congress boycotted participation and did not put up any candidates, but here and there it supported candidates to defeat *'Toady Bacha'* candidates in order to show the strength of the popular will or display its hold on the masses. I remember that Shri Uttam Chand, a barber, was able to defeat a prominent well-placed royalist. It was often said by Congressmen in those days that it could secure a victory even for a dumb driven animal for a seat in the assembly against any human rival at the polls. This held fairly true even during the first elections after Independence, and as a result many fools and crooks found places of respect in the State Assemblies.

In the month of June 1921, the leaders appealed to the people for a bonfire of their such personal clothes as were made of foreign cloth. I was in the D.A.V. College Lahore at the time. Emotions ran high and the clothes continued to pour into the collecting stations. A bamboo skeleton shaped in the form of a sea going vessel was created along the banks of the river Ravi which flows on the outskirts of the city. This skeleton ship was draped with the various coloured garments. On the appointed day for the bonfire people flowed from all directions and it was a surging mass of humanity, there may have been three hundred thousand people that watched the draped ship. Lala Lajpat Rai, styled as the 'Lion of Punjab' made a soul stirring speech just about the time when the sun was setting in the west and thereafter set fire to the improvised ship. Many people had carried their personal clothes or other foreign goods, approached the fire and threw in their bundles. Fear did, however, lurk within me that the Government through its watchdogs, the police, would deliver some form of punishment for our offences.

Up until then Indian political leaders were busy driving the British rulers out through speeches from wide platforms. Rhetorics had reached a new level of excellence. The vehemence notwithstanding, the British officers continued, undisturbed, their afternoon tennis and their evening *'chhota peg'*[16] even when Gandhiji issued an ultimatum that they should give India the substance of Home Rule or he would order civil disobedience and have a complete boycott of English goods. Whether in amusement, the cynical rulers may have had an extra *'chhota'*, but within a year of the ultimatum, Manchester had to close many of her textile mills.

Communal trouble in our country was the reverse of non-violence and although our countrymen – particularly the educated – understood the machinations of malevolent religio-political Indian leaders and the diplomacy of the Alien Government, yet they seemed helpless. Both among the Muslims and the Hindus, the so-called custodians of religion failed to see common human interests and each tried to profit at the expense of the other and this feeling was fully taken advantage of by the British. For instance, in 1906-07, a Muslim delegation led by Agha Khan obtained from the British Government in India a promise that Muslims should vote separately for their own candidates for the representative assemblies that were to be created. As the freedom struggle grew in size, the anti-national and communal forces created an atmosphere of mutual hatred and suspicion between the principal communities terminating in the division

---

16 A single shot of whiskey.

of India, rendering millions homeless. August 1947 brought freedom to the country with chaos and misery to many both in Pakistan and India.

During the spring and summer of 1924, Hindu-Muslim tension had grown in an alarming degree, partly as a result of *Shuddhi* (Purity) Movement which had been led by Swami Shraddhanand among the non-Muslims in the neighbourhood of Delhi and partly by the machinations of the British Government in India whose strategy of 'Divide and Rule' worked havoc with communal understanding. It was a cause of the deepest distress to National India but for Gandhiji it was so unbearable that he felt himself called to undertake a fast for twenty-one days of penance. Every effort was made to induce him to abandon his fast, but he remained adamant. His fast commenced on the 18th September, 1924. Nearly three hundred persons including both political and religious leaders of the two principal communities and also a few from other sections met at a joint conference to bring about a change of heart between the communities. Political arguments, obvious and cogent, had completely failed before the fast, which introduced new emotions for bringing about unity in order to save the life of one whom they held in deep and affectionate esteem. On the eleventh day when Gandhiji's condition became somewhat serious, there appeared unanimity among the leaders to practise mutual toleration. I do not recall the exact way by which they convinced Gandhiji about the positive change of heart, but he gave up his fast. Even the student community was equally affected both before and after the fast. My neighbour roommate, who was a Muslim, was friendly to me because of my religious views, grew indifferent during the communal disturbances but returned to his normal self when I returned to the hostel after the vacations early in October.

Religions have, in their heyday, discouraged examination of

even their dogmatic elements and have forbidden their followers to be critical about them. On the other hand, they allow their followers to be intolerant. The only solution of such a state of affairs is the spread of scientific education and training and this, the country, was very much lacking. But, even during the frenzy of communal disturbances, examples of high morality of individuals in protecting the lives of those professing a different religion, may have exceeded those of bigotry which plays havoc during communal upheavals. The mischief-mongers always play upon the baser human feelings and arouse their co-religionists to hatred for the rest of the society. The obligations of morality and religion, which is not always easy to distinguish from one another, largely influence conduct of the communities. A process of evolution was visible and circumstances are bound to change. When people will begin to feel happy or miserable through their own character and conduct, then the tendency would be to limit the influence of religion or religious prayers only to spiritual aspirations. Once the people would not mix religion with politics, it will reduce fanaticism and promote the spirit of co-existence of communities. Unfortunately every community has good as well as bad elements and it is the latter who are provoked by an alien power for throwing blame by one religious group on the other. This process of 'Divide and Rule' was well mastered by the British.

The devotion of society, determination to face hardships and austerity was however, growing side by side with occasional communal outbursts. The termination of British rule on 15th August 1947 brought an end to the freedom struggle and an initiation of a new line of constitutional development – the Republic of India – with a Parliamentary Government based on adult franchise. The 26th of January 1952 marked the passing away of one epoch and the emergence of a new one.

The struggle for freedom had given new value to suffering. The jails, which were places for internment and torture used by the State (an Alien Government) for the criminals only before the political awakening, were now used for large numbers of political prisoners under the wrath of their rulers. Anciently, there was no glory connected with jail going, but Gandhiji and his followers made jails as places of pilgrimage. The glory in jail-going was not in the jail itself but was derived solely from our leaders who suffered privations for our sake.

VISHAV BHAVAN

Part IV: College Days

Lahore and University Life

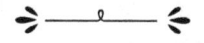

The majority of university students seek education for securing a lucrative career and this has always been true in our own country. 'Knowledge for its own sake' is easier said than done. In the days when the British ruled the country they needed for the services, men who would have working knowledge of the English language and trained in various other subjects through the medium of English. While recruiting graduates for the requisite posts, the selection was made on the basis of merit, way of living and even modes of attire of the applicants. Communal considerations came in after the Mont-Ford Reforms at the expense of merit. Western dress had already made an inroad among university boys. I, too, was influenced to a small extent but the simultaneous political upsurge in the country for Independence was constantly causing me hesitation. Such were the conflicting forces around me at that immature age.

It is difficult to analyse today why I had given up the idea of distinguishing myself in the class, and from the day I left the high school I set about getting what distraction I could out of the city life. And so, on the first day after admission I was conscious of a desire to escape from my environment – the college and the hostel. The college I had entered did not encourage games or sports, and I was also not keen on them, thus I remained away from the playfield. During the period I was at Daulatnagar, the school had acquired about one hundred acres of land for having its own building. This land was being used for outdoor games in which I began to participate. Soon after, I received a number of injuries on the field. My parents begged of me to discontinue playing both cricket and hockey and in deference to their wishes I observed this pledge throughout my life.

The hostel attached to the college had more than twenty messes, each being controlled by a manager nominated by the Superintendent who was also the Vice Principal of the college. The food was poor in quality in the mess in which I and a number of others shared. We asked the manager to do something about it but he ignored our request. This gave me an opportunity for distraction by raising the banner of revolt against the manager. All the boarders did leave that mess on my persuasion and ate their meals in other places. I was taken to task, reprimanded by the Superintendent. I was not to be deterred or be repentant for the course taken by my colleagues who were firm as a team. This brought forth a change of attitude of the hostel Superintendent who nominated a new manager. We celebrated the victory in the old mess which was reestablished.

The college authorities had engaged a professional coach for wrestling. I was persuaded by a friend of mine to take to this exercise and accordingly one morning I went to the wrestling ground. My first and last lesson in wrestling was like this – the coach picked me up, dropped me on the loosened earth of the *Akhara* with my belly down and sat over my back, commanded me to lift him up, throw him aside and relieve myself. He must have weighed much more than a quintal[17] and I was yet

---

17   A quintal is 100 kg.

tender in body and even muscles not fully developed. I tried the impossible, perspired and finally requested him to be relieved from his captivity. I left the wrestling ground never to return to it. My body ached badly for a week.

The country was under the spell of the National struggle when I started my university career. I had joined D.A.V. College Lahore. For several months I brooded over the usefulness or otherwise of the choice I had made of university education. I obtained access to Lala Lajpat Rai through Bharati, his nephew and my classmate, expressed all my doubts to Lalaji and asked for his advice which he willingly gave. I no longer cherished the idea that I should give up my studies in order to join the National movement but I was told to keep abreast of the changing times. I continued to read the newspapers for news and views, and this I did, at times loudly for the benefit of my classmates.

Here I was in Lahore, a very different place from my village. I have said elsewhere that heterogeneity seemed to have overtaken the city as distinct from the uniformity in village life. If one went around in a shirt and *dhoti*, another had only a loincloth and still another a European suit. I made my choice, a turban, a shirt and a *salwar* and an English type of shoe and a closed collar coat for winter. This remained my attire until I left for London in 1925. All my clothes were made of *khadi* except the coat which was Kashmir tweed. The city was the centre of various types of activities, social, religious, educational, sports, political, commercial and industrial. My own interest largely lay in education and the political movement but the institution to which I was now attached, laid emphasis on social reformation and *Vedic* religion. The Dayanand Anglo-Vedic College was run by the Arya Samaj, which was very zealous about the elimination of the curse of untouchability from amongst the Hindu fold. The so-called depressed classes were excluded from Hindu shrines, were not allowed to draw water from the same wells from which caste Hindus did. This was considered by the Arya Samaj to be highly detrimental to the Hindu community in not accepting this low caste Hindu population as their own part. This work took the shape of a social movement styled as *Shuddhi* – purification of the untouchables.

The Arya Samaj organised community dinners between the high and low castes. It was in a way a process for reconversion as many untouchables even dropped their colloquial names for the most fastidious Sanskrit personal names. The *Shuddhi* Movement began to spread but it was also meeting with opposition both from caste Hindus and other religious groups. It so happened that caste Hindus of Jammu – a province of Jammu and Kashmir state, killed a *Shuddhi* volunteer worker who was an Arya Samajist. To express indignation against the outrage the Lahore Arya Samaj organised and took out a procession through the streets of Lahore. I was among the processionists shouting slogans against caste Hindus.

The D.A.V. College had as part of the education the inculcation of the spiritual values of life. They, thereby, attempted to draw the minds of students away from Western influence. As religion and science (*gyan* and *vigyan*) were complementary in the Hindu philosophy, Western scientific discoveries were not treated as heresies but it was stressed that all scientific knowledge is contained in the *Vedas*. Not knowing Sanskrit, the language of the *Vedas*, and having facilities to learn science from books in English, our regard grew for the West and its scientific advancement. The college insisted on compulsory religious education with four periods a week. I found no interest in those lectures and absented myself from them as often as I could.

The college had no place for Urdu but I continued my studies in Urdu literature on my own. I could write well in Urdu and made use of it for fun and expansion of my political views on current topics as also conveyance of protests on behalf of students for any mismanagement by the college hostel authorities. Not far from the room in which I lived, we had community bathrooms where hundreds of boys bathed daily in the morning. While waiting for their turn at bath, they had ample time for gossip and seeing a number of notices indicating time and date of group meetings, advertisements and other posters. Over the night I wrote in free hand and secretly posted the manuscript over the outer walls of the community baths for the students to read. I continued to do this daily over two months and watched from a distance my victims with a good deal of interest. No one knew the unknown hand that placed on the walls, a new subject almost every morning. I do not remember why I gave up that habit.

Leadership was a matter of interest to me – be it at even a small group of people. I formed an association of sixty or seventy boys from the district of Gujrat to which I belonged. I became its secretary and continued in that office till I left for Great Britain. The association aimed at close contacts between the students hailing from my district and studying in various colleges in Lahore. Together we had picnics by the riverside where we made use of boats provided by the college for rowing for exercise and fun.

The year 1921 was already drawing to its close. I was now familiar with my new surroundings and gradually began to drop some of my acquaintances who produced mental conflicts for me. The political atmosphere was still explosive, but by now I had finally decided not to actively participate because it meant less interest in my studies, although I had simultaneously accepted that they were least important if the National status did not change. My uncle, who at one time was only interested in the termination of my scholastic career, was now only too keen to insist that I must receive advanced education in any subject that I would choose for my career. He did not know that I was losing ground in my studies and by the close of 1922 my friends felt that if I did not work hard I might easily fail in the final. I accepted their advice and recovered the lost ground with the result that I secured a first class in the Intermediate (Science). This enabled me to secure admission in the King George Medical College Lahore, but I was compelled to change my course from Medicine to Arts subjects and later to Engineering.

My parents felt that a Medical degree, which meant five to six years at the university, may involve expenses beyond their means, as my father had, for lack of interest, reduced the material wealth left in his charge after the death of my grandfather. The family business of 'landlordism' had gradually dwindled to an extent that it had become unremunerative.

I, now, received admission in Government College Lahore with English, mathematics and physics as my choice of subjects. Here the atmosphere was quite different to the D.A.V. College. Instead of life member teachers who led an austere life, I had English or anglicised professors drawing fat salaries and living a life of pomp and show. Here most of the students wore European-cut suits and often conversed in English but in spite of these influences I continued to use my *khadi* clothes. I never felt embarrassed in spite of being a solitary person wearing *swadeshi*, handspun and handwoven, clothes. My classmates often persuaded me to change my attire but I stuck to my own apparel which to me was now a symbol of our National struggle for freedom.

The college was built in Gothic style of architecture, resembling a church from outside. It had two hostels, the Quadrangle (old hostel) and the New Hostel. I was given a furnished cubicle in the latter for my first year in the Government College. It was usual with the boarders that they stuck wall paper below the wall pegs from which clothes could be hung. The following year I lived in the Quadrangle. In each of the hostels were three kitchens but the D.A.V. College hostels had twenty kitchens. Each mess was controlled by a manager elected or nominated from among the participants.

In the D.A.V. College only vegetarian food was provided for board. Being fond of meat dishes I along with others of the same cult visited restaurants for food. We found a vendor who was known for meat dishes. His place was dark, full of flies, and had a long wooden bench for customers to sit on – no comfort whatsoever. The place was smoky, our throats used to get itchy, eyes smarted, and yet we made no protest. The proprietor was least interested in making improvements.

In the year 1924, a theatrical company widely advertised a show – a drama named *Zulm - ul - Zulm*. Many students reserved their seats well in advance. Soon after the commencement of the performance it became obvious that we had been duped by a group of swindlers. Even the stage trimmings were exceedingly poor. The college students had their revenge. Never, I should think, I saw a more imposing shower of bricklets hurled on the stage. The attitude of the whole audience took the same turn. The actors ran away for their lives. The furniture was broken to pieces.

It was about the middle of 1921 when I formed the habit of a weekly shave by a barber. A year later I purchased a Gillette safety razor, quite an expensive one for a college student. I resorted to shaving my own beard and cancelled the contract with the barber. This outfit journeyed abroad and moved about in my kit for several years and wherever I went. After many years of honest service its locking arrangement is still in order, and the two containers of the blades are still glittering nickel. Only the outer case is revealing brass at places below the nickel plating. When mass evacuation took place in East and West Punjab after Partition of the country, it was salvaged along with a few other things and this complete set is still in my posession.

During August 1921 my mother gave birth to a male child who died within a couple of months. I felt that God did not allow me the joy of having a brother. I had, therefore, to adopt others to be my brothers and sisters as I went along in life. One of such friends, whom I adopted, was my classmate who lived in a room adjoining my own in the D.A.V. College hostel. His name was Surindro Nath Chopra, now Dr. S.N. Chopra, a leading surgeon and health office, Brynmore, South Wales.

It was the period of Dussehra holidays, 1921, when I visited the home of Surindro in Gujranwala (now in Pakistan). I did not accompany him but had requested him to meet me at the Railway Station, Gujranwala. I was feeling feverish when I arrived there. I was taken to his place in his transport. His mother straightaway put me to bed and his parents showed extreme kindness. I felt that all the thoughtful service given to me during my illness for a week or so was nothing other than parental care and this produced in me a sense of intense gratitude to them and a brotherly affection towards Surindro. On return to college Surindro began to address me as *'Bhra ji'* meaning his elder brother. Later, however, it became my nickname by which almost every boarder in the hostel began to call me. Both of us had entered for our Inter Science (Medical) course. He was definite in his intention to become a doctor but for me it was merely a course of education with which I might or might not work for a medical degree.

Both of us were now united by a strong friendship. I had thrown into the relationship the tender indulgence of an elder brother, he had the warm admiration of a younger one. We gave to it the dignity that distinguishes brotherly love and by degrees we had drawn from it an incentive to nobler feelings. It also gave us that peace which is born of mutual trust and similarity of nature and tastes.

He went to England for his studies two years after I had gone over for my course in Engineering and when I left London in 1928, he came down from Edinburgh to see me off and spend some time with me. He confided in me about his relationship, rather intimacy, with a Scotch girl whom he later married. He has now three children and I do know how many grandchildren he has.

Influences of an Ascetic

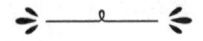

Swami Sahajanand, who was a native of my village, who had renounced the world and its pleasures for a hard life of an ascetic, had wandered over the country in search of truth. His original name was Lakhi Chand but since his renunciation he had adopted the name of Swami Sahajanand. He had, now, made salvation the only end in life. I often spent an hour or two a day in his company whenever I was home for holidays. He also lent me books in Urdu dealing with Hindu philosophy and spirituality, which developed my intellect to the extent that I was somewhat able to talk on spirituality. I owe him gratitude for the new knowledge which diverted my attention from reading cheap novels and obscene printed matter. Swamiji was among the well read in this particular direction, but he did not possess the power of transmitting spiritual impulses which I was told, his Guru had done when he sat at his Guru's feet. Later in life I met many *sadhus* and *swamis* and I found our country full of them. They were themselves beggars for truth, yet they claimed to give gifts to others. Probably I have made no effort to find a Guru.

It would be incorrect to say that Swami Sahajanand's company did not influence me in any way. I often turned to Swamiji with my doubts on religious dogmas. If he was not always able to solve them in a way acceptable to me, it was not his fault but my basic knowledge of his religion based on his self-realisation. He was a seer whose business was to see and not meddle himself with God-eclipsing activities which make seeing impossible. I had, therefore, an explicit faith in his advice.

Our village folk did not love him or listen to him. They seemed to have prejudice, which at times amounted to hate against him because he insisted to possess his share of his ancestral property which his brothers were unwilling to part with. Why should he have needed it was beyond my comprehension, after having renounced these material belongings for several years.

Having spent over ten years practising *bhakti sadhana* (meditation) during which period he rarely had real rest and had what may be called an apology for sleeping for an hour or two in the sitting position, he told me, he was freed to change his conviction about truth-realisation. According to him, many sincere aspirants belonging to different sects, having attained the state of *samadhi*, retain their respective sectarian notions about the nature of truth. Decades later, after his death in 1926, when I was abroad, the same experiences were passed to me by another *sadhak*, to whom truth-realisation was visualisation of his own conceit and individualistic in character. This often aroused doubt about the efficacy of *bhakti* for realisation. The attainment of concentration in thought through the *sadhanas* could hardly be denied and that it would help to control one's natural impulses, propensities and feelings, and to regulate one's thoughts, speech and actions. By such self discipline one could achieve comparative purity and peace of mind, he often told me, but he would, by no means, be master of his fate.

He gave, occasionally, religious discourse, mainly from the Gita. As a boy I could hardly understand and grasp the wisdom of Krishna. Later in life, I had the occasion to know more about the philosophy contained in the Gita from my own father. It had always perplexed me how Gandhiji, a great devotee of Krishna's sermon to Arjun at the battleground of Kurukshetra, could be a pacifist. Swamiji, having renounced mundane life, did not come across the aggression of exploiters where he would have to choose between self suffering and the destruction of the evil doer.

Swamiji's vow of *brahmacharya*[18] was never put to test. He did not have material possessions to be drawn to lusts of worldly life. He was not married. He did not permit females to enter his *ashram*. His food was cooked by his *chela* (disciple), a vegetarian diet without spices. He used milk and milk products in adequate quantities. I never saw him taking exercise but he had long walks both morning and evening. I never saw him in agony with any physical ailment, but I was told that he died of heart failure in 1926 when I was abroad. Why did he have a heart attack?

Either I did not believe in any vow for myself or maybe I was incapable of adhering to any restrictions, I had generally felt that it closed the door to free choice or free thinking. Looking back over the last fifty years I can recollect only one occasion when sometime in 1951 I put on yellow undervest as a constant reminder for the vow I quietly took to practise *brahmacharya* from then onward. Within a month I realised that the hidden yellow robe was of no avail.

A few days before I left for England for my studies in Engineering, late in 1925, my playmates in the village gave me a farewell party. A number of meat preparations were served and vegetables were kept out of the menu. My friends knew my weaknesses for meat dishes, but after spending a year or so

---

18 Pure and austere living, resisting sensual pleasures.

in England I became averse to meat diet and became a strict vegetarian without taking a vow. Again when I left London for tramping in Europe enroute to India, I returned to a mixed diet as a free choice. Once again in 1945 I imposed upon myself strict vegetarianism under the influence of some friends and my family. I maintained this choice for nearly six years.

My father was a vegetarian ever since I can remember but what surprised me most had been his lack of control of his palate, and yet at no stage could he be tempted to a meat diet. I do not remember his ever having mentioned to me about a vow in this regard. It has been his free choice. He loved and still relishes in delicious eatables – sweetmeats, pudding, fruits, spiced pickles, well cooked vegetables and fruits. This may be one of the reasons which has tied him down to mundane life in preference to asceticism, although the major cause has been his keen sense and desire of service towards his fellow beings. It is his conviction that it can be best rendered by participation in the life of the family and the community.

Swami Sahajanand, to whom I conveyed the news of the golden opportunity, which was offered by my uncle in order that I might have a fuller technical education abroad, did not give approval. He had never visited England or any other country, nor known the ways of English people. In spite of this fact he explained the different outlook on life between the East and the West. He made no impression on me. I was seeing information from other quarters. He had his own apprehensions regarding my ability to refuse the acceptance of temptations. In spite of his repeated warnings I was determined to grasp this opportunity. I felt that the time had come for me to seek wider interests in pastures new. Swamiji compromised but asked me not to marry before going to England but here my parents thought otherwise. My mother was of the opinion that the very difficulties which marriage or married love would encounter in separation, would bring with it an understanding of life and responsibilities, in general.

I loved my people and my village. I had the influences of my father, Swamiji, and Gandhiji to sustain me. One thing I had learnt by now was that my doings, howsoever important they may appear, were really of common occurrence and other people were least interested in them. It was going to be still truer when I shall be living in freedom in a country where I would not be hedged and I could follow Walt Whitman:

I think I could turn and live with the animals, they are so placid and self contained,
I stand and look at them long and long
They do not sweat and whine about their condition,
They do not lie awake in the dark and weep for their sins,
They do not make me sick discussing their duty to God,
No one is dissatisfied, not one is demented with the mania of owning things,
Not one kneels to another, nor to his kind that lived thousands of years ago,
Not one is responsible or unhappy over the whole Earth.

– Walt Whitman

The Survival of the Fittest (Random Thoughts)

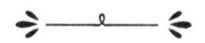

For centuries, we in India, particularly the Hindus, had existed and believed in the religion of subordination and renunciation. Even in politics under Gandhiji's leadership the motive force was non-violence and passive resistance to the authority engaged in exploitation and keeping our people under its yoke by the use of force, to which it seemed wedded. The faith (Christianity) to which the ruling nation belonged had passed away from the mind of authority and instead the doctrine of force had taken its place. The Darwinian thesis seemed to affect their minds, and presented to them a conception of the world which they rendered exclusively in terms of force and struggle. Darwin's presentation of the evolution of the world as the product of natural selection in never ceasing war – as a product, that is to say, of a struggle in which the individual, efficient in the fight for his own interests, was always the winning type – touched the profoundest depths of the psychology of the ruling races. The doctrine of survival of the fittest in the war for existence had come to prevail in business, commerce, politics, social existence and war preparations.

I remember that when Dean Inge spoke from the pulpit of St. Paul's Cathedral in London during the period I was in England, about the theory of evolution, someone from the congregation got up from his seat, reached close to him and then hit Dean Inge with a stick. The news flashed across the press and a controversy started whether Dean Inge, had or had not, the right to speak on a subject which on the face of it clashed with the Christian faith. Believers in the Bible who accept mankind as descendants of Eve and Adam, could not take pride in monkeys being their ancestors at any stage of the creation. Personally I find no scientific reason to believe that any one of the human beings ever have had monkey great great grandparents. I may just jot down my recollection that Dean Inge was downgraded to the office of Dean of Birmingham. The Dean of Canterbury gave his verdict that the Dean of St. Paul's Cathedral had no right to speak on Darwin's theory from the Church.

The law of survival of the fittest, that is to say, "If A was able to kill B before B killed A, then A survived." And the race became a race of A's, inheriting A's qualities. This would mean subordination of the individuals in the social world of civilization, but the history of the human race is indeed nothing else than the progressive history of the sacrifice of the individual efficient for himself, for collective efficiency which is being organised gradually, merging in the universal. Instead might has become superior to all interests of the individual, the group or the State, resting on the successful application of force.

Darwinism is strictly the science only of evolution of the individual. It is not the science of evolution of society, which is not inborn heredity but social heredity and is acquired by the individual from without or imposed upon him by society. When I studied biology for my Intermediate examination I was given to understand that the vast difference between positions in the world of advanced and less advanced races was due to corresponding differences in their inborn qualities. Whether it was true or not I accepted it to mean that the theory supported the belief held by Hindus and particularly the Arya Samajists that the Hindu society with its ancient culture was far more advanced than the ruling nation. Later, when the Nazis rose to power in Germany, they propagated the belief among the German people that they had an advanced inborn heredity, and this resulted in the Second World War in 1939-45. But what the Second World War proves is that it is not the inborn heredity of the individual, which is almost identical for all races of the world, but the collective social heredity which is transmitted through the culture, that is the master principle of power.

From time immemorial human beings have struggled, on the one hand, for their survival, and on the other, given serious thought to the purpose and end of human life. Two extreme ideologies have evolved in regard to the 'struggle for existence', namely an unbridled licence to the individual acquisition of wealth, and annihilation of the individual for identification with the giant State. Both seem to have failed in finding a solution to the human struggle of 'survival of the fittest'. If power creates lust and greed for accumulation of wealth, the latter maintains an unsatiated desire for political power and status in the community. Both these approaches have failed to inculcate the spirit of cooperation among the members of any unit of human community, leave aside the World Society. A visible symbol of cooperation, as opposed to the theory of the survival of the fittest, has been the Hindu joint family which offers social and economic security to all members, young and old of the family, eliminating the ill-effects of the extreme ideologies stated above.

Another type of struggle in life is produced by the fear of public opinion and this mainly arises in youth. If one is lucky enough to secure a career and surrounding congenial circumstances for oneself, then he or she can escape social persecution, but while one is struggling to become independent financially, one may be at the mercy of the ignorant people who consider themselves capable of judging your actions. If one has to struggle against this kind of repression for a long time, the possibilities are that one's energy may be impaired and in the end he or she may be embittered for a lifetime and the damage done may be irreparable. One should, while struggling in young age, generally accept public opinion, but not to the extent of voluntary submission to any unnecessary tyranny. There is no need to become eccentric or antisocial, but one should be natural in one's behaviour towards conventions.

Recuperation of Health

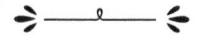

Within one week of my joining the Government College I had a very severe attack of dysentery. The Medical Officer of the college gave me treatment. He alternated a dysentery mixture with a dose of castor oil for no stools on one day and a purge the following day. It may have been the right treatment but I was getting no relief, and in addition started running a temperature. I was in bed for over a month and lost almost six pounds in my body weight. I applied for long sick leave so that I could go home where I could have greater care and nursing. The leave was not granted. The principal failed to realise how I felt about my illness fearing that damage to my health was already beyond repair. In fact, while lying in bed all by myself during college hours I composed Urdu verses relating to my nearing end. Prakash Chand Agarwal, a friend of mine who nursed me the most, advised me to proceed to my native place regardless of the consequences which might ensue in the absence of sanctioned leave. I accepted his advice. At home I recovered more speedily than I had imagined. Whether it was the change of station, food or what, which helped in the recovery, it is difficult to say. My parents, when I was back on my legs, planned for me a holiday in Kashmir so that I may recuperate in health during the summer vacation – three months stay in the charming climate of Kashmir to make me fit as a fiddle. What a wonderful feeling from one of despondency, to one of love for life, and according to a Persian couplet, I was visiting heaven on earth for a wonderful holiday there. The couplet runs as *Gar Firdos bar ruh-e-zaminast, haminast haminast.* O Firdaus (the poet's name) if there is heaven on earth, it is here, it is here (in Kashmir).

Of all the natural phenomena which make a lasting impression on the mind, mountains rank easily first. Particularly, this is true in the village communities, to whom I belonged, and to whom Kashmir is the land of Hindu sages where the *Vedas* had been composed. I travelled by rail to Rawalpindi and then by omnibus through sixty miles of British India and almost one hundred and forty miles into the territory of Kashmir which was a princely state then. It took us just over thirty-six hours before the bus entered the city of Srinagar at dusk. We had a night's rest while half way in the journey.

I was expecting Srinagar to be a modern city which was visited by large numbers of tourists every year but its ramshackle hovels just on its outskirts gave me a shock and a rude awakening. We were chugging along to the bus terminus at Amira Kadal, 'the first bridge'. My host was a police officer in charge of transport. I could therefore experience no difficulty in discovering his house. For a day or so, I was assisted by his children in going around the city, but having been accustomed to finding my own way, even in a much larger city, the city of Lahore, it never alarmed me if I temporarily lost my way in the town. The Jhelum river, which more or less bisected the town, was my best guide. During a short interval I came across many strangers who were out for a holiday and met old friends who had chosen Kashmir for spending their summer vacations. Among these I found two persons who were my teachers in Kidar Nath High School, Gujrat. They soon proved to be good company and together we planned our stay at Ganderbal in a houseboat, and within a couple of days found ourselves there.

At Ganderbal, a small village by the side of a tributary of the Jhelum, one could see three different social groups, the Europeans mostly British, the Indian visitors from the plains, and the local Kashmiris. All suffered from different 'complexes' which were sufficiently strong to keep them apart. Their division, one would say, was more pronounced than the Manu's *varn ashrams*.[19] Among the Hindus it was possible for a *vaish* to become a *kshatri* by a change in one's profession, but these three communities had at the time, allocated to themselves rigid forms of social status, the ruling class, the Indian gentry and the natives.

We three played indoor games and also had long walks. My companions were prolific readers. One loved English literature and the other was fond of history while I felt that a knowledge of current National upsurge through study of dailies was the right way of spending time. Later, however, I considered that foolish on my part as I was out in Kashmir for pleasure. Together we decided to spend much less time on books and news. Although I lived happily with them on the surface, I had become absurdly introspective. At night I would often lie awake, tracing back and back the particular circumstances which changed my thoughts and my career in life. I alternated between scientific reasoning and continuous upsurging of my emotions regarding a political career for myself.

We took our meals together. The dining table was laid for us by the owners of the houseboat at every meal. Neither of

---

19 The separation of the population into classes based on profession: *brahmin*, scholars and teachers; *kshatri*, rulers and warriors; *vaish*, farmers and merchants; *sudra*, artisans and servants.

us was accustomed to the use of European cutlery therefore none of us felt embarrassed to have the same removed from the table. The *hanjis* (owners of houseboats) provided furnishings and equipment, largely needed by their European visitors every summer. In another houseboat moored nearby there lived an Indian doctor working in the army hospitals. He joined us invariably to make a foursome for 'auction bridge' at cards which was the most popular game of cards in those days.

I was very inquisitive to know about the English people who lived at this holiday resort. I had no idea, then, that I would be visiting England within a year or so, but I had just desired to know how and where they were different from our people. My companions were equally shy, but the doctor, having been educated abroad, was quite at home with most of them. The doctor allowed me to go for a stroll with him occasionally and thus I started to join him in saying good morning or good evening, as the occasion permitted, to his European acquaintances. I went only thus far and no more. Kashmiris, who were my countrymen and even spoke Hindustani without much difficulty, appeared equally distant as I was not able to make any inroads amongst them. I remained equally stranger to them just as the English were from us.

I could hardly know at the time that I should one day return to Kashmir as an officer of the state administration with which I was later associated for six years. Thus, what I missed in those days, became familiar to me later in life, both in respect of the English people and the Kashmiris. I will leave all that account for subsequent chapters.

After spending nearly three months in Kashmir and visiting most of the popular holiday resorts, I returned to my village. I had put on weight and looked well although my mother still felt that I was too lean and that she would feed me and look after me during the fortnight that I was going to be with her before my return to college.

Mother was not quite sure if I had fully recovered from my ailment and therefore did not like the idea of my departure for Lahore during September. She wanted me to stay another month but it would have meant a loss of a whole year before I graduated. The motive for getting a degree, to secure a career and to earn a reasonable livelihood through Government service, was uppermost in my mind. I returned to Lahore looking forward to devotion towards my studies, in which I had lagged on account of my illness.

Simultaneous Hectic Activity

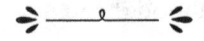

It was in those days, common practice to agree to the engagement of their children provided they were within the 'marrying-in' group, but it was not considered necessary to obtain the consent of the would-be couples. There existed a well-recognized fable of precedence among the Punjabi kshatriya castes under which one was permitted to take his wife from a subcaste below his own on the precedence list but could not without loss of social esteem, give his daughter even to a kshatriya of lower subcaste. This system prevented marriages of Hindu women with men of castes of so-called lower degree. Western methods of courtship between couples before marriage was almost unknown and unheard. I had been engaged in accordance with this custom.

My parents were very keen that I should be married before I left for England for my advanced studies. They were, therefore, very busy in finalising the details of my marriage. The village priest had the sanction of the community to fix the day and time most auspicious for the marriage to take place. He could dictate, in spite of his lack of intelligence, and my parents accepted 29th of September, 1925, as the date of my marriage. In later years, the hold of that priest disappeared as the dates for marriage of my cousins and my children were determined by me on the basis of convenience for friends and relatives who had to partake in the ceremonies.

Marriage is said by cynics to be a lottery in which we all hope to win a prize. Whether these marriages are contracted by our own free choice, or arranged for us by the choice of our parents or relatives, or accepted by us as a result of the force of circumstances, or as so often happens in the West when our thoughts are turned to the wonder and beauty of all the romance which has brought men and women together in a communion of love, some of us must win and some must lose. Marriage among the Hindus, though not strictly monogamous by law, was enforced by custom to preserve monogamy with a large amount of success. Divorce was not permissible in those days and the Hindu code bill and the Hindu Marriage Acts of post-Independence periods had no place. The matrimonial customary restrictions bound the couple for life with a spirit of compromise, of give and take resulting in reasonable companionship and mutual understanding. Those who accepted the customs, won the game.

For nearly a month before the date of my marriage my people seemed busily concerned with preparation for the festivities. Sweets were being made on a vast scale for distribution to friends and relatives. Gradually relatives were pouring in from villages and towns for merry making and feasting. As the day grew nearer, the gaiety increased all around in the village and there was another excitement besides my wedding in a few days' time – my departure to a foreign land. In fact, I was placed in an unusual position of leaving my wife behind in India for three years within a week of my marriage. While my parents were busy making requisite arrangements for the ceremonies connected with my marriage, those appeared to me at the time unimportant side issues not requiring my attention.

The formalities of obtaining an Indian passport were many and troublesome. Local police officials were asked to report concerning my political leanings and activities by the Deputy Commissioner. The report had to contain an account of the activities of the family to which I belonged, particularly whether we were loyal to the Rulers. My mind remained disturbed on this account till I obtained my passport. Then I proceeded to Lahore to meet the people who had been abroad and also stayed with my friend at Gujranwala in order to seek his father's guidance. His father was highly delighted that I was proceeding to London for Engineering and gave me advice regarding the wardrobe suitable for my journey and about the life of a paying guest in an English family. He estimated that I would need Rs. 15,000/= for three years' course inclusive of my passage both ways. He calculated Rs. 2500/= as immediate need.

I had never donned European type clothes so far, never worn a collar or a necktie, nor ever used a wrist watch. As clothes had to be tailored and purchases made, I returned to Lahore. I was still engaged in getting the OK regarding admission to the University of London which I was able to obtain hardly a fortnight before my marriage. This alone kept me in the horns of a dilemma which I did not share with my people. At times I felt miserable about this delay and sometimes about my ability to travel happily by myself to England. But having accepted the help so gladly from my uncle both for my journey and my stay in England, coupled with my ambition to be of greater service to my people and my homeland upon my return, I crushed those fears.

Regarding my marriage, invitations along with sweets were now being sent in accordance with the customs of the area through our family water carrier who carried the sweets in place of water, and moved from village to village walking miles and miles on end with heavy load of slabs of sugar (*gandoras*) – ten slabs each of over a kilogram in weight for near relations and probably five slabs each for distant ones. Five to six quintals of sugar were utilised in this shape for such distribution. The carrier was well received everywhere and in fact this was 'hay time'. My father, as I have said, had a charitable disposition. He found this occasion on which to help the poor and the needy with food and clothing.

A few of my father's cousins had grievances against the parents of my wife-to-be, they were reluctant to participate. But my mother and my uncle ably handled the situation so that they willingly came around and the celebrations commenced on a grand scale. My parents were prepared to spend their all and even to go under debt if necessary to satisfy their pride. My mother was particularly anxious to secure the admiration of friends and relations. I was her only son and this was 'the event of her life'. The village did not have a local musical band, so one was engaged from Daulatnagar for a few days before, for accompanying the marriage party. There was a variety of musical instruments, brass horns, the highlander's bagpipes and flutes and drums. Besides, a well known singer was engaged for entertaining the guests and the villagers, as it was no longer accepted as honourable to engage dancing girls. The village now looked gay and happy and a 'hustle-bustle' reigned there till the marriage party left to wed the bridegroom.

The marriage party left for the bride's village Chopala after an early morning meal. It comprised of men and boys as no females were to join the marriage party in those days. Besides Hindu friends and relatives, a number of Mohammadan *zamindars* joined us, although it was not quite usual. Several servants, fireworks attendants, the members of the band and the family barber were included in the party, altogether numbering over one hundred.

Most of them were on horses, but the servants and other menials walked all the way, a distance of about twenty-five miles. Although the September sun was not quite strong, the absence of breeze made the journey unbearable, passing through millet and maize crops standing six to eight feet high on both sides of the narrow track which meandered from one village to another on the way. All of us perspired freely and were thankful each time we emerged into an open space devoid of crops. Those on horses had to halt at several places on our way in order to allow time for the weary stragglers to be with the party, and at every halt we had some light refreshments. After we had all refreshed we set forth again. We took the last lap of our journey more leisurely and had so arranged our programme that we arrived about five in the afternoon just outside the bride's village, where we were greeted by the bride's relations. We were escorted to a resting place in the open under a banyan tree where they had spread carpets for us. They took great care to look after us for the duration we had to stay there for tea and change to new clothes before we got into the village. I wore a new *khaddar* shirt, a new *salwar* and tied a dark silken turban, then a small ceremony when the priest tied a *sehra* of silken and golden threads with flowers both artificial and natural hanging down from my headgear to my chest. Over these a tiara in silver was tied around my turban so that all this provided dignity and prominence to the bridegroom.

I mounted my favourite white steed that was dressed up for the occasion with brocade, and a servant carrying a large decorated umbrella approached me and held it a few feet above my head. The steed moved slowly along the walking party, all the rest of the horses having been sent to a stable in the village for rest and feed. The party was led by the receptionists and the band towards the village. I was in the rear on horseback followed by servants and the lads of the village. When we entered the narrow lane of the village the procession became single file. The village women were occupying every available space along the edge of the terraced roofs of the house on both sides of the lane, most of them singing songs of the rituals of marriage, or talking to one another or discussing whether or not they considered me to be a worthy match for the bride. The party was soon led to the school building, the school having been closed for three days in order to make the building available for our stay.

After a few preliminaries related to the marriage ceremonies, soon after sunset, the marriage party, headed by the band with improvised lights provided by burning oiled torches carried by servants on both sides, the single file moved slowly towards the bride's home, which was ablaze with lights from open burning fires consuming cotton seeds soaked in oil. At the entrance to the house the *milni* (introduction) ceremony was performed. Those introduced, embraced their counterparts on the bride's side and garlanded each other. After this the party was taken to the dining room for dinner after which they returned for rest to the school building. When most of the people, after the day long journey and a heavy meal at dinner, had just gone to sleep, they were awakened to have milk. No one seemed to mind it.

The actual marriage ceremony took place soon after five in the morning of the 30th September, 1925, and it took nearly two hours to complete the function which was held in a courtyard and under an improvised canopy. Floor coverings had been spread for guests while two raised seats were provided for the bride and bridegroom. The bride was wrapped around by a richly embroidered shawl-like garment covering her whole body and the wedding garments. The priest lighted the sacred fire and *havan* performed by chanting of the *ved mantras* in Sanskrit. The relatives sitting close to the fire, my bride and I, and the priests kept the fire burning all the time by adding *ghee* or purified butter and incense at the termination of each hymn. It rendered the whole place aromatic. I had a strange feeling of excitement coupled with thoughtfulness. For the first time I realised that the lady by my side was to become my wife and my life long companion. The thought uppermost in my mind was "would this union bring us joy or sorrow." Both my bride and I were asked to narrate the hymns after the priests, particularly those relating to the pledges. I was emotionally awakened by the aroma of incense and realised the solemnity of those pledges which I had to honour all my life. My voice, while stating the vows, must have been heard by all who cared to listen, but what she said inaudibly none knew, but the priests explained that she understood. The vows between the couple did not appear to receive a great deal of attention as they were uttered in Sanskrit which was not understood by many either on or off the stage.

One corner of the bride's shawl-like garment was tied to the bottom edge of my long shirt and then I led her seven times around the sacred fire. She was now my wife and I her husband. Contributions were made to various social and religious institutions by both the families. My wife was escorted to her parent's rooms from the *mandap*, and I met her relatives both young and old in the courtyard in a formal way. Then back to my resting place to get ready for breakfast, emotions surged within me, but I revealed nothing neither expressed excitement nor one sign of melancholy.

After breakfast it rained heavily and by mid-day the approach to my wife's home had become exceedingly slippery, making it inconvenient for the party to reach there for the luncheon. Food was therefore served at our lodging. By afternoon, the weather had cleared and the streets were soon dry which enabled us to exhibit the *wari* (clothes and jewellery for the bride) through the streets. Embroidered silk clothes and ornaments were placed on

Simultaneous Hectic Activity

large metal plates and carried through the streets on shoulders. The procession was led by the band. Banarsi *saris*, shirts, *dupattas* or *chunnis*, *salwars* were all embroidered with golden thread and sequins. It was tailored for my wife, to her measure and so were the ornaments – jewellery for the head, forehead, ears, nose, neck, wrists, fingers, ankles, feet and toes. All these gifts were presented to my wife by my parents. She received presents from her own relatives besides '*dowry*' from her parents consisting of clothes, jewellery, cash, furniture and household equipment sufficient for a small household.

It is my belief that the *dowry* system must have had its beginnings amongst aristocratic families, whose numbers being limited would have found it difficult to secure satisfactory husbands for their daughters and this necessitated some sort of financial competition in securing a suitable match as a son-in-law. Parents, who either had no daughter, or a predominance of sons, would have found themselves in a strong position to demand high value for their sons for matrimony. Lower ranks of society are apt to ape the rich and the higher castes, thus the system developed informally into the present form and custom of *dowry*.

We had another day of rejoicing before the marriage party planned to leave for Kakrali. Members of our party had an early meal and then gathered outside the village where my wife was escorted by her relatives. It was an ordeal for her to part with those with whom she had been associated for the past sixteen years. A decorated palanquin (*doli*) was already placed there in which she entered after certain rites. The packed *wari* and *dowry* had been loaded on the backs of camels. The *doli* was now lifted by her brother and three male cousins for a few yards and then by other male relatives for another few yards thus conveying to her that they all wished her well. Four out of the six hired men then lifted the *doli*, the two relief men walked alongside. A *nayan* (wife of the local barber) accompanied this party as a chaperone for her. She also walked along. I was on horseback, keeping its pace in consonance with the walking men and those carrying the *doli*. The rest of the party moved well in advance and reached Kakrali hours before we did. It was about sunset and the people of our village were anxiously waiting for our arrival. The *doli* was parked in one of our own orchards just outside the village and not very far from the village temple to which she was escorted by my mother and many other ladies with the band in front of them. Then from the temple to my home where she was welcomed formally by my mother by pouring sweet oil on the door sill of the entrance door and then the crowd of ladies that had assembled in our courtyard burst into singing the songs of welcome.

I had accepted that my parents had chosen alright, my life long companion. We had entered into an indissoluble bond. This mutual contract could only be fulfilled by devotion towards each other and by taboo to extra-marital love. I knew more than she did that a scholastic gulf existed between us and the same was going to become bigger after I received higher scientific education abroad. This, I explained to her before I left for England with a view that she would use the two or three years that I would be away, in accomplishing herself with as much education as she could. She was modest and shy. Probably it was natural for her to be. She did not appear to be excited and I had been trained to self control and restraint, while she scarcely spoke and looked nervous. We had been married for more than thirty-six hours and yet my persuasion did not make her talk much. I felt that we had very little time together because by sunrise visitors would begin to call and then we would remain separated for another twelve hours. Normally, after two days' stay in our home, I should have taken her back to her parents where both of us would have stayed for a few days. This formality had to be cancelled as there was very little time with us before I left for my journey abroad. This helped to bring us closer and it became obvious that she had been moulded in a religion of implicit obedience to my wishes. Even when I returned from England after three years' stay there, she was still in the same cast.

At the time of my departure it looked as if the whole village had gathered outside our house. Everyone wanted to bid farewell. My mother was in a passive mood. My wife was not near me. I touched the feet of my mother to obtain her blessings and advice. She kissed me and in a choked voice said, "There are certain laws of nature which are universal all over the world, for instance butter must melt if it is anywhere near the fire." I understood what she desired to convey and she also told me that I should make my stay abroad as short as it could be. She then led me to my wife, who spoke nothing. She looked wonderfully fair and I carried that picture of hers in my memory. I, too, could hardly speak much. It was an occasion when our expressions conveyed to one another what each had to say.

Having paid my respects to elders and a handshake with my mates in the village I mounted my horse, which was escorted some distance by a relative and still quite a crowd moved along to see me off beyond the last village hut. While my mother appeared sad and she could not get rid of that feeling, my father showed no signs of emotion. My wife stood at a distance. She was still shy, her eyelashes shading the downcast eyes.

On October 11, 1925, I reached Lahore where I spent two to three days in hectic activity mostly in the company of my classmates. Bakht Singh accompanied me to Bombay where too we spent some time making purchases and sightseeing. We tried to remain happy in spite of the approaching separation. Bakht told me that he would make every effort to join me the following year.

Bakht and I were such fast friends that we could try vainly to enjoy our breakfast before my departure and in that touching, our fruitless effort brought about deeper sadness. We knew that I was going away and had to catch my boat that very morning. Whenever our mutual conversation languished, none of us thought of taking it up again.

Journey Westward

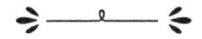

On the morning of October 17, 1925 I sailed for England on P&O Ship S.S. Mooltan. It was anchored in the Bombay harbour having arrived earlier from Sydney, Australia, to refuel and embark fresh passengers. Bakht, who had accompanied me from Lahore, remained at the quayside as the ship moved out. I saw him wiping his tears at my departure for London. When the boat was well out to sea, I left the balustrade on the deck for my cabin, where to my extreme delight I found another Indian student – Autar Singh, as my cabin mate for the journey.

We heard the gong strike conveying to us that lunch was going to be served in the dining room. We went to have a meal but finding that our place was reserved in a corner and at a distance from other passengers, we left the dining room as a mark of our protest. The steward was informed that unless we were given positions alongside the European travellers, we would not eat there. The Chief Steward saw us in our cabin, apologised and promised to meet our wishes. That particular meal was, however, served to us in the cabin.

We were the only two Indians on board. Autar was very shy and had no intention to mix with the white people – maybe he had an inferiority complex to a greater degree. I soon befriended several Australians and by paying half a crown as subscription for games I entered in the field of sport. Some of the games needed a female companion for playing and I was able to persuade a French girl to be my partner for mixed games.

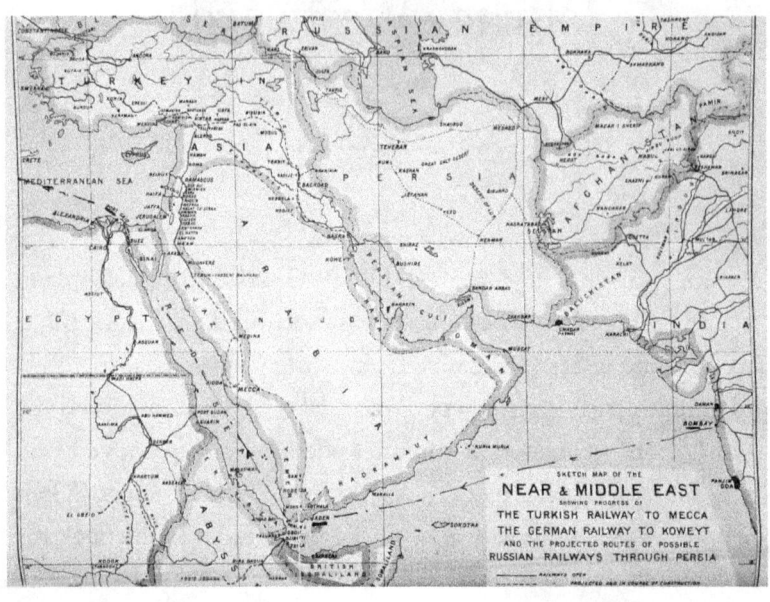

SKETCH MAP OF THE
NEAR & MIDDLE EAST
SHOWING PROGRESS OF
THE TURKISH RAILWAY TO MECCA
THE GERMAN RAILWAY TO KOWEYT
AND THE PROJECTED ROUTES OF POSSIBLE
RUSSIAN RAILWAYS THROUGH PERSIA

In the Indian Ocean, The Mooltan had to encounter prolonged rough weather that the passengers became restive and had a feeling of giddiness and vomiting. They would not like to eat and most of them lay in bed. Racial differences vanished for the time being and anyone who was well enough to do nursing was acceptable. The ship rocked and rolled with the striking white horses. It was out of question for anyone to remain on the deck.

The weather was not unbearably hot. I weathered the journey through the Indian Ocean quite well. Not having ever seen the sea, this itself was an exciting experience, but I must have missed things worth seeing. We reached Aden, which I had connected with the Biblical Garden of Eden. I had expected to see a rose garden along the seafront but it was a complete disappointment and the place was melancholy beyond description. Our ship was soon surrounded by small fishing boats which were laden with so-called Oriental goods – beads, necklaces, engraved articles and embroidered garments. The Arab merchants dressed in their national attire attracted the attention of the passengers on the ship. Only some selected were allowed to come to the ship's deck to show their goods. I needed nothing and bought nothing. Those who were familiar with their trade could be seen haggling on prices and at times even one quarter of the price asked for initially, was accepted by them.

A number of Arab lads were seen almost floating in the sea, waiting patiently for coins to be dropped by the passengers in the sea for them to dive, catch and retain them in their mouth under the tongue. It was exceedingly clever but no one would deny that extreme poverty made them take this work as a profession.

We were allowed time to get down and spend an hour or so. We hired a taxi to see Aden and its near suburbs but I did not go far and there seemed nothing which could interest me. I treated myself with a box of dates and came back to the ship for luncheon. The anchor was raised soon after for the journey through the Red Sea. Now the weather had turned really warm and we perspired day and night while going through this lap of the journey. We were, however, all day occupied with games like Bull's Eye, Cock Fighting, Auction Bridge and a number of other games including cricket on the deck. This cricket differed from the game of cricket on land in as much as the bat was about half the usual width and the deck was enclosed by a netting around to prevent the ball from going down the sea. The batsman did not run at all for their runs but the runs were scored depending on whether the ball had crossed the first, second, third or fourth line before being picked up by the fielders.

Aden, which is an extinct volcano, is about five miles long

and three miles wide, jutting into the sea and connected with the mainland by a narrow isthmus of flat ground about three-quarters of a mile wide. Barren and black, dreary and waterless, destitute of every natural gift but possessing the priceless advantage of a magnificent harbour, situated just outside the entrance to the Red Sea, nearly midway between Port Said and Bombay (1500 to 1600 miles each way), has a great strategic importance to the British who controlled it through the Government of India. It seemed that the rulers hardly gave anything to the place but got whatever they could of this possession, when I was told that the water storage tanks built on its outskirts were hewn by stupendous labour out of solid rock by the Persians and the British allowed them to deteriorate. Even the aqueduct about twenty miles long which had been built by the Arabs was now in ruins and was no longer functioning for carrying water from the interior to Aden. I could get no answer from anyone regarding this attitude of the British concerning Aden.

By the afternoon of the 25th October we entered the Suez Canal and the end of the Red Sea. This canal holds the field against all alternative routes between Europe and the East for inter-trade communications. Even in 1925 the work of widening and deepening the canal was still in progress and it may have taken us nearly fifteen hours to reach Port Said over a distance less than one hundred miles. After every three miles, the canal which had a normal width between 200 feet to 250 feet, became wider (800 feet to 900 feet) at the passing stations, where the passengers of one ship cheered heartily those of the other while crossing, and even if it was late at night when the crossing occurred, many passengers came to the decks for mutual greetings. This great international artery was controlled at the time by a company in which the British and French had large interests, but the Suez has its own history. It is now controlled by the Egyptian government but will it continue to do so or will the great powers that are capable of moulding the destinies of smaller nations, build an alternative route joining the Red Sea with the Mediterranean through the Gulf of Aqaba which was the scene of a great upheaval in the recent conflict between the United Arab forces and Israel? The Suez shall, however, always remain a posthumous credit to the French engineer, de Lesseps, whose statue we saw at Port Said on the morning of 26th October, 1925, with its finger pointing towards the canal at its junction with the Mediterranean. Here at Port Said I purchased picture postcards, which I posted to relations and friends. I was amused to see the tram cars in the streets of Port Said being pulled by camels. After three hours of stay in town we were back on the ship for the third lap of our sea voyage.

Although the next port of call was Marseille, we passed so close to Malta, which is a small island naval base situated about half way in the Mediterranean and about sixty miles south of Sicily. We could observe the various installations on the island as we crossed by it. We continued with the games for another four days so that before we got into Marseille, the winners were named and the prizes distributed. We landed at Marseille, handed over our luggage to our shippers, Messrs. Thos. Cook & Sons, and thereafter saying goodbye to our fellow travellers we went into town. We engaged a guide as both Autar and I did not know French but as we made some purchases, we could see that the guide had his commission from the shopkeeper over our purchases and that we could manage without him as far as shopping at big departmental stores was concerned. English, too, was understood by some salesmen. We dismissed him. I purchased an overcoat and a few other garments which I discovered were less costly than the prices in Anarkali, Lahore.

We left by the evening train to Paris, and then onward to

Calais from where we crossed the English Channel to Dover. From Dover we travelled by train to Victoria, London in the early evening of 7th November, 1925. We engaged a taxi to take us to 84 Sinclair Road, London. This place was used as a Sikh temple to which was attached a boarding house. It was the day of celebrations in connection with the birth anniversary of Guru Gobind Singh. Many Sikhs had therefore collected to listen to the recitations from Guru Granth Sahib.[20] We deposited our belongings at the entrance, paid off the taxi, and joined the gathering. After a while Autar was contacted by the manager to find out his needs, a meal and a room, and I was told to move to a hotel, as Sikhs only were accepted as paying guests in that institution. Autar (Mr. Sood), however, prevailed upon the manager to allow me to share his room for that night. We passed the night at 84 Sinclair Road.

I had been advised by Bakht to meet Mr. H.L. Kumar, who was a student at the City and Guild College in London, and was living somewhere on Wilkinson Street. I had not realised how great was the area of London, and how I could hope to find that address without knowing the name of the district in which Kumar was living. In the bitter cold weather I started out from Sinclair Road early in the morning, determined to find Wilkinson Street and Mr. Kumar. Through the courtesy of the London Police and as luck would help, I found this street in the shortest possible time, and a passerby pointed out to me a house in that street, in which a couple of Indian boys lived. There I met Mr. Kumar as also his friend, Gulati who shared his room.

I had an introductory letter from Bakht which I handed over to Mr. Kumar. Both of them received me with the utmost

---

20   The Sikh Holy Book.

courtesy and hospitality. They had two rooms between them, one of which they used as a drawing room and the other they used as a common bedroom. They cooked their own meals in the Indian style. They were cooking their breakfast when I met them and that morning they shared it with me, which I thoroughly enjoyed.

When I suggested to them that I could live in a hotel till I am fixed up in an English family as a paying guest, they dissuaded me from that course and escorted me to a house in Brixton, where one of their friends named Tandon was living. The landlady of the house had a bedroom to spare on the ground floor and she asked for thirty five shillings a week for board and lodging. They approved of this arrangement and I accepted the same. I returned to Sinclair Road, collected my luggage, and with Autar in my company, we were driven by a taxi to this house in Brixton. Autar left for Edinburgh the same evening – the 8th of November.

Travelling itself was an experience of some magnitude but having landed in London, the largest city in the British Empire in 1925, I looked forward for contact with newer facts and events. Even the first journey by the red bus was a new experience. London had both trams and buses in those days for movement of passengers along the roads. The bus conductors appeared to me to be quite clever in worming their way through the crowded vehicle, punching tickets, stopping the bus, or ringing it off. They gladly helped me on occasions about the best way to go here or there. I was quite sure at the time that I couldn't conduct a bus, even if I was paid hundreds of pounds a week. Later, I remember, during the General Strike of 1926 in England, a number of my class fellows offered their services to help their government in the emergency, and in fact, worked as conductors on the buses quite successfully.

Getting killed in a railway accident in England would leave

one's near ones five thousand pounds (or was it ten thousand pounds?), provided you took one of the London's morning papers that insured you. Later during my stay in London I learnt that in one of the serious railway accidents, several passengers died as a consequence. Those among the casualties, the largest were those who subscribed to the *Daily Express*, while none of the readers of *Daily Mail* had even received a minor injury. Both these dailies brought out advertisements in their own favour – one declaring that it had paid a million pounds or so against the insurance carried by its readers and the other proclaimed "Read *Daily Mail* and escape injuries even in a serious rail accident" – so on and so forth. Jokingly, what a grand event or a philanthropic act it would be to run a trip by train for those living in strained financial circumstances, having insured them all with newspapers, then wreck the train, killing most of them and leaving their dependents well-to-do.

While returning from Wilkinson Street to Sinclair Road I got into a London Tube at the Oval tube station. I was taken down underground by a lift and not by an escalator, which I had many occasions to use later during my stay. I was late in getting into the tube railway and was in panic, when I felt that I was going to be caught in the rubber grip of the automatic closing doors of the carriage.

Lahore had an automatic telephone system by which one could dial direct in 1925, and yet it was a surprise for me that London had, in most of the districts, still the old derelict system of asking the telephone exchange for connection. London had public telephones installed in small kiosks built on the footpath along main thoroughfares. Similarly, these kiosks with a name board 'Public Telephone' or 'Telephone Here' were provided in all important institutions and business undertakings. Not having used the telephone more than once before I landed in London, the thought of ringing up a friend from a public telephone set my heart beating. I wasn't sure if I would be successful. However, when I noticed that there was no one about the kiosk, I pulled its door open and when it was just half open, it was all lit up for everybody to see. I hunted through the dilapidated, moist telephone directory and found the requisite number with some difficulty. I took off the receiver and waited. Nothing. I rattled the receiver up and down and began to read the written instructions once again. Place two pennies – so one had to put his money in first – the telephone department did not trust very far. I could not find the money in my overcoat pockets. Instead of placing the receiver in its position I carefully allowed the receiver to hang at the full length of its cord, and after getting the two pennies out from an inner pocket and then placing them in, I hauled up the receiver and then someone was asking for the number, I uttered it. I had expected to hear the bell ringing on the other side much longer but it was soon through.

VISHAV BHAVAN

Part V: England

Experiences in England

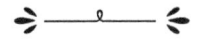

I settled happily in my room and later partook for my first meal with an English family. It was Sunday and all the family members and the boarders were at the dining table. The meal was sumptuous from my point of view. I was introduced to all present by Miss Loftus, who had received me earlier that morning. Conversation ensued when the luncheon had been served – everyone helped themselves for what he or she needed for food. I closely observed the mannerism of the English people at the dining table. An Indian boarder, Mr. Tandon, and I returned to my room after the meal and he poured out a lot of information to me which he had acquired during the four years which he had spent in London.

Dr. Gulati called at tea time and invited Tandon and I to Lyons – a well-known tea shop and restaurant. Later I learnt that Lyons and like them another establishment of the same kind called ABC, had branches in every part of London. We also went to a picture house together. I sent an account of my first impressions of London and its people to my wife and my uncle. I did not speak well although it was unreasonable for me to arrive at conclusions in the course of a day's stay in that big city. Then I had seen the slums of the city in the first glimpse as my train had passed on tracks overlooking their backyards. Looking at the clothes that were, in spite of washing, unclean due to fog and smoke, I formed the impression that people at large were extremely poor. The houses, also, appeared to me to be small and shaky. The nature, too, looked unkind, when I failed to see the sky as I knew it, studded with twinkling stars, but here it was hardly visible, and the few stars which I saw, looked to me, sick unto death.

In spite of a number of residents in the house I had a sense of loneliness. Except for Tandon, I had no companionship. Miss Loftus, the landlady, appeared to be more than sixty years of age. It was considered rude to ask a lady for her age. She was always dressed in black clothes, shoes, and stockings, which had a depressing effect on me. She was hardly intelligent and lacked the power of good conversation. I went to the shopping centre of Brixton almost every afternoon after college hours. It was a short walk from my residence.

My achievements in the first six months of my stay were far from satisfactory both at college and outside. I had made no friends either in the classroom or outside. I had my daily newspaper but I had a vacuum in the evenings. I did not have surplus money to buy entertainment. Life appeared to be passing without meaning or objective. I missed my parents and friends in whose company I had developed. "It is an ill wind that blows nobody any good." I had time to ponder over the struggle we were having against the English domination. Opposition or criticism of the British Government in India landed one in jail as the Government was paramount there and could not be changed by vote if the people of India wanted to do so. Democratic constitutional government in England was a new experience – a Conservative government of England could be replaced by a Labour Party government and vice versa if the people of England willed it so.

In the middle of June 1926, a 'General Strike' was declared in England by the English labour, but it did not have the support of the middle classes or the capitalists who carried on their activities in spite of the embarrassments. Even King's College did not close and students were expected to, and they did walk long distances from the London suburbs to attend their classes. That went on for a few days. I enjoyed the forced walks to and fro from the college. The people who walked the same distance every morning and evening got to know one another and began to wish one another 'Good morning' or 'Good evening'. Life, now, appeared full of interest as I used to have long conversations with the other co-walkers on all sorts of subjects. Many students volunteered to take up positions which the labour had struck from. The trains started running and the buses began to ply. The strike began to show signs of cracks and ultimately their labour helped to see the General Strike's failure.

In July 1926, when the college closed for summer vacation, Shri Kumar and I planned a holiday out of town – we went to Isle of White, a small island close to Southampton in the English Channel very close to the English coast in the south. We hired a car-van equipped with a kitchen and a bedroom. There was, not very far from our van, a small farm and a farmhouse from where we could buy milk, eggs, fowl, vegetables and we found the farmer and his family extremely friendly towards us. We stayed there for six weeks.

Mrs. and Mr. Carpenter, with their child about six years old, stayed in another car-van which was not far from ours. The child soon became attached to me and I also spent many hours with him during the day. When the Carpenters and ourselves, on one occasion, were together and posing riddles for solutions, my little friend butted in to enquire if any of us could tell him the difference between Tom and Mary. We all "gave in" and he told us laughingly that one was a boy and the other a girl. On another occasion he walked into our van at tea time and made us burst with laughter by asking if he could borrow a piece of cake.

The farmer's wife was an elderly lady. She asked both of us if we could give her the English equivalent of our surnames – Kumar and Nanda. We expressed our inability to do so, stating that there could be no English equivalents for surnames used in other countries. She ridiculed us at our lack of knowledge and was insistent that the *Encyclopedia Britannica* contained the entire knowledge of the whole world and that she would look into and herself give us the corresponding equivalents. The following day she informed Kumar that 'Albert' was his equivalent but she could not find one for Nanda. Maybe, she said, that the edition of the *Encyclopedia Britannica* she possessed was old and that the surname 'Nanda' may be of recent origin. We were naturally amused.

With the opening of the new term I became fully occupied at the university. My whole life was changing and my previous loneliness had disappeared with the companionship of Bakht Singh. Furthermore, I was spending a considerable amount of time in the college library. There were a number of Indian students in my class, namely, Ghose, Kapur, Gadhok and Bhuyan and we all had become friends. One English student, Mr. Fielder, by name, developed a great deal of nearness to me and we remained friends throughout my stay in England. Our friendship was strengthened further by my interest in his constant work and devotion to the cause of the poor in the East End of London. Later, I became a friend of all his relatives when I visited his village in the following vacations.

Bakht and I hired new lodgings in De Crespigny Park, Denmark Hill, London. The house was pleasantly situated on the corner of the two roads. Mr. Kemp, a bachelor and his sister, a spinster had rented this house. Miss Kemp kept the house. We were given a commodious bed sitting room fitted with a gas ring which we could use for cooking and which was quite simple and convenient to use. Miss Kemp soon developed a great admiration for me. It was my 'bowler' hat, as was normally worn by the business community in London, my spats, the walking stick and the gloves in my left hand – all together tended to convince her that I was a very sober person having adopted that attire at the age of twenty-three. She felt, in fact, that I was the only gentleman in England, if one relied on her opinion. There were a number of tenants in the house and we soon became familiar and often invited one another to spend our leisure time together when we were in the house.

Not far from our house there was Denmark Lawn Tennis Club, with twenty tennis courts and about four hundred members. Bakht and I applied for membership and were accepted as such. This solved partly our problem of occupying ourselves usefully in the evenings and over weekends. The club also offered new avenues of friendship. Mixed doubles at the courts was the means of meeting many English people of both sexes. Our own conservatism was slowly breaking down.

Early in summer in 1927, a room on the ground floor of the house in De Crespigny Park was let out by Miss Kemp to a new lodger who seemed different to most other English ladies. She was not really pretty but she seemed to elude me, and therefore I became desirous to be introduced to her. Very often, as I passed by her room, while leaving or entering the house, which was on most occasions open, its appearance and atmosphere was homely and artistically furnished. One evening when I was waiting for Bakht to come down with his tennis racket, I caught sight of her crossing the hall and going down to the basement. I followed her in the hope that Miss Kemp, who lived in the basement, would feel compelled to introduce us to each other. It exactly happened the way I had thought. On the following day I called on her for gossip. I learnt that she and her husband had mutually agreed to live apart.

I learnt from her that years ago, no English lady could think of herself as an individual capable of standing alone and her husband's wishes had to be her wishes. But the First World War (1914-18) forced many English women to compulsory physical separation during which period they had learnt to earn their own living and had by the process arrived at their own valuation. This new awakening had made many of them bold and they desired that their husbands should recognise their identities. I could easily see that my wife, who would not be able to earn, would remain docile and accept whatever position I would offer her. But, the change which had taken place in England, would also come about in India, whenever circumstances were identical.

This English lady, Mrs. Camebus had a car-van in Essex Downs, which Bakht and I visited and we met many of her friends, who also had their own vans. This car-van had been built by her husband which she now owned. Here we learnt a lot about English life in her and her friends' company. Listening to her wonderful experiences of life in the company of her husband, one wondered how two souls could ever think to live apart. I had read and heard about 'militant suffragette' for women in England and the success that the movement had achieved. I was not politically minded at the time to understand the implications of that movement but I felt that the English women may have achieved certain rights but they could not have done without paying heavily by losing their privileges in English society. It is unbelievable that anyone can get anything without paying a price first.

A strange experience which many may never believe is to have seen the rabbits dancing – dozens of rabbits rushing out of their holes about sunset, joining in couples with their front feet on each others' shoulders almost as Englishmen and women use their arms in ballroom dancing, and then they danced merrily for a short period, then scuttled and then rejoined. This I witnessed at Surrey and I could not believe my own eyes on the first occasion but this followed many evenings.

Once in the countryside I came across a gypsy woman. She seemed not even to possess a surname, if ever she had one, she had long since forgotten it. There was a great deal of similarity in 'outdoor living' to those of gypsies in our country about whom I had some knowledge. She eked out an existence by doing odd jobs for farmers, picking fruit and vegetables as their seasons came around, hoeing potatoes, and then in the autumn journeying many miles on foot working her passage. This was quite decent and honest and contrasted with dishonest means adopted by many of the gypsies seen by me in my village. This gypsy came to a number of homes for work living in Surrey. She assisted the women in their household like a help-maid, such as washing the clothes, bringing buckets of water, preparing beds and the like. She was illiterate but bowed to no man and always said, "I has me pride." She had, I believe, a thorough experience of rustic life in England. She had no house, as she felt and expressed that a house would just "hem her in," and she just "could not abide it." She was not seen there after some time and many people wondered where she had gone.

A Burmese friend of mine and I tramped together in the south of England. Both of us had rucksacks on our backs, one of them contained a small tent and its equipment and the other contained various other requisites for tramping. We were once seated in a field overlooking the sea. It was evening time and we had collected some dry wooden sticks and lighted a fire for boiling water for tea. A middle-aged Englishman approached, sat and gossipped with us. "Where do you sleep?" asked the visitor. We said that in any place we find a piece of land for pitching a small tent. He then wanted to know if the local folk allow us to use their land for the purpose. We told them that we have never applied our mind on that problem because we just wait until darkness falls and as daylight comes we creep away. He looked satisfied and rose to go away as darkness was approaching, walked some paces away and shouted back jocularly at the top of his voice, "Good night to you. I hope you sleep well. It is my land you are on." On another occasion when we had tramped all day long and found no resting place. Night was approaching when we came across an old lady with a rugged face and a body bent with much hard toil. She carried a heavy bundle which we insisted to carry for her. She agreed and together we trudged along wearily. At last we came to a small field in which there was a very small house. We enquired of the old lady if we could pitch our tent for the night in the field. She nodded without waiting for us to complete our question, as if the house belonged to her and so it was. We started to unpack our kit bit by bit in her presence. She ignored to look at them but when she saw a small tin container which had a small lock on it, her eyes lighted up. This box contained 'first aid requisites'. We could see that she was interested in it. However, she went away into the house and put no questions, but the following morning we presented to her this little tin and the contents without the lock. She felt greatly pleased, but when we offered her some money for the use of her protected land for the night, she returned the tin. We took her photograph and asked for the address. She said she lived in that house and beyond that she knew nothing, nor an address.

Once in the countryside we were taken over by a downpour and I was thoroughly drenched in a few minutes. I got into the nearest available enclosed land hoping to find shelter, which I did. The owners allowed me to get into the house and as the rains stopped and I still fumbled with my cold hands it occurred to me that I should pay them in cash for their hospitality. While I was still fumbling to find a shilling in my pocket, they felt amused and said that I looked so poor and for that reason they would not like to charge. I felt humiliated for my presumption.

I was once introduced to an Englishman of education and culture, who had once held a very good position in business but had totally abandoned his post and the life of town. With the capital he had in hand, he had purchased a small holding in the countryside, where he, being a bachelor, intended to live alone, eat only vegetarian food which he himself could grow and earn money by selling the honey products from the hives of bees which he reared. He seemed to have read every book he could find on the art and skill of bee-keeping. He tailored his own clothes, short trousers reaching about two inches above his knees, a flannel shirt of many colours and a green woollen coat which decidedly looked 'really home made'. He had a Scotch plaid shawl which he carried over his shoulders. He portioned out his meagre income that he could only afford new clothes once in two years, so that if one had met him when he had the new clothes on, he would look very fashionable, while if one met him about the close of the two years when would be getting ready for new garments, he would look a pauper. I was greatly interested in his project as I had in mind my own period of *'vanprastha'*[21] which I had hopes to enter. With all the experiences during my stay in England I had grown a liking for a trampers life.

People who have superficial acquaintance with both Western and Indian traditions will compare them in a way that does not penetrate below the surface. They either take a naive pride in finding in their past history the discoveries of the modern world, or obstinate in their insistence on things modern, make a point of disowning their background.

Whether it was at the insistence of the British Government or not Miss Katherine Mayo wrote a book titled, *Mother India*. In any case it was a deliberate attack on the Indian culture and her whole data was based on reports and visits to jails and hospitals. Many of my class fellows who had either read the book or the extract, found an occasion to draw my attention to it. Ours was a British colony and this gave my English contemporaries a complex of superiority and now with this slander in their possession, it gave them handle to talk lightly about our country. In my defence I quoted the English saying, "the whole world is a hunting ground where each seeks that which he hopes to find and invariably finds it." Miss Mayo had searched the gutters and found the stinking smell which she could have hoped for. If she had walked in a well-kept garden, she would have found beautiful and sweet smelling flowers. Would not they themselves encounter conditions in the sordid back streets of East End of

---

21 The third stage in life, when one hands over household responsibilities to the next generation.

London, which would equal, nay perhaps surpass the conditions portrayed in *Mother India*, and I often quoted Renan who said, "The Bible is a book which each dogma seeks, and each his dogma finds." Miss Katharine Mayo was a Christian woman and the author of *Mother India*, to which a rebuttal in *Uncle Sham* was produced by K.L. Gauba within a year or so but he wrote another book later, titled *Verdict on England*. Later, Lala Lajpat Rai wrote, *Unhappy India* which was more in defence of our own civilization rather than an attack on any foreign land or its people.

Among the few English friends that I had made there was an artist named Hjalmar. He did my portrait late in 1927. Among his paintings, he had one which stands out in my memory depicting the state of mind in which one of his friends was labouring in those days. The picture, which measured about three feet square, had in the centre, at the bottom, a dark, mucky pool with rushes growing all around its outer edge; but in the centre was growing a lotus flower, surrounded by its beautifully shaped green leaves. The flower itself was painted with pure gold. At the top of the picture, in the centre was a large golder star shedding its rays down on the lonely lotus. Around and beyond the water bullrushes beautiful and still, and beyond them also with their rich brown heads, was a mass of prickly thorny undergrowth or jungle land, and still beyond and above this was thick forest land and heavy cloud laden sky. He explained to me in detail. His friend was the lotus flower, lonely and desolate on whom the star of heaven shed its light. The lotus was incapable of getting out of that position as on the first effort she would get entangled in bullrushes and even if crossing them was possible, she would land herself into the jungle land with its prickly overgrowth and then beyond there is the forest land without a path and that she had no wings to fly to the star.

While I was quite familiar with carts drawn by bullocks in

my own country, I was keen to find out if similar carts could be seen in the rural areas of England. I expressed this desire to a friend of mine, who arranged for me a joy ride in a fascinating cart owned by a person who had built it for love. The cart was about two yards long and a yard and a half in width. In the front portion, measuring two feet into full width it had a box two feet high. This provided a driving seat for two, and had on its hard lid three cushion mattresses of the size of that seat. The cover was similar to the cover we have for the *tongas* in our country and this provided shelter against the weather. The cart was pulled by an old and worn out donkey who travelled slowly and deliberately. My friend managed to have it for our own holiday together in the countryside. We found, as it moved along the road leisurely, that only one of us would be able to sit and drive, while the other would have to pull along with the donkey. As the driving and pulling was equally tiring, we tossed a coin – "heads to pull, tails to drive and prod with the whip." Whatever we did, the donkey could not and would not set the pace. My friend either had a brain wave or he knew it before, that while he helped himself with a glass of light ale, he gave a glass of the same to the donkey which the animal seemed to like. The innkeeper brought some more for the donkey to the great amusement of his customers. When we started on our journey again we found the old fellow trotting along the road. Later we found the secret of that from the owner of the cart who was a dealer in chopped firewood which he delivered a considerable quantity to innkeepers, and the dealer being given a fair amount of ale by them, the owner always willingly shared the same with his donkey who was now a habitual drunkard.

Tramping in Europe

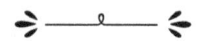

It was sometimes late in June or July 1928, that I purchased my ticket for the homeward journey by a French boat leaving Marseille late in August. I felt that I had time to see the continent of Europe before catching my boat. I decided to travel light so that I may be able to tramp, journey by the cheapest transport available, during my sojourn through the different European countries. I arranged for a rucksack which I could carry on my back and with the minimum requisite articles for such a venture. It included a water proofed ground sheet, one shawl, one light eiderdown, one small aluminium frying pan, a gladneck shirt, knickers, a necktie and a pair of socks, among other clothes.

When I left London. Many of my friends and some fellow students sent me off with their good will and good wishes. As the train moved out of Victoria Station, London, I changed into my dress of the tramp, and on grounds of comparative poverty I journeyed to Dieppe on the night boat for crossing the English Channel. It was a calm, warm night although the comfort was little and the boat crowded. I landed in Dieppe in the early hours of the morning and then travelled to Paris by train. Before leaving London I had arranged for accommodation in an inexpensive hotel in the Montmartre through the courtesy of a friend who knew Paris fairly well. I spent three days in Paris and then left for the French countryside towards the east near the Swiss border.

If my clothing and equipment were scarce, my diet was also frugal, which besides simple food included water, milk or tea for drinks. Occasionally, I cooked vegetables and eggs in the small frying pan but more often I hung the vegetables of every kind and shape on a thick stick of wood or a piece of wire over the fire built of wood in a quiet, secluded spot or meadow through which clean water flowed.

From France, crossing the Swiss border at Basel, I travelled to Neuchâtel through Berne to rest for a few days by the side of Lake Thun. From there to Interlaken and a few other places, and thence by train through the St. Gotthard tunnel and on the valley of Rhône and finally to Marseille.

In Switzerland I can recollect seeing the Jungfrau with its snow-covered peak at a time when the sun was sinking behind it. It was glorious and I sat with intense joy watching the crimson red of the sky as the sun went down. Then very slowly in the quiet hush of approaching darkness of night, with no other person around, I watched the rising of the moon – almost green and as clear as the deepest water of Lake Thun. This held me spellbound. I only remember one other sight on this track of mine from London to Marseille which was equally wonderful. This was at the Monte Carlo when I was standing at midnight leaning against the white marble parapet at the Casino and looking out to sea. The Mediterranean waters were not so deep a blue as seen in the bright sun, but a soft greyish blue colour. Small boats were tied in the shallows. Soft grey gulls flittered on the white horses, whilst above shone the pure white moon. Never had life seemed so pure, clean and beautiful before and that no heaven could offer a greater peace or more intense ecstasy.

Coming back to my journey through Switzerland, I have no intuition to describe the geography of that country, but some incidents of lasting interest. I decided to cross the Jungfrau on foot and hoped to arrive in Lauterbrunnen before dark. I started off very gaily early in the morning, but later in the afternoon I decided to leave the well-worn track down to the mountainside although the main track could obviously be the route chosen by most travellers and therefore the most safe, the other offered to be a real short steep which I could well see in the distance. I travelled along that route until dusk began to fall and I felt too tired to walk any further. I searched for and found a terraced spot of land with a patch of grass where I decided to rest for the night. No light or sight of residence was visible in the neighbourhood. Instead of managing in the darkness until daybreak I lighted a candle. In about half an hours' time I heard heavy footsteps approaching and the bark of a dog. Two powerful burly men each carrying a thick strong stick came nearer to the grassy plot. In very broken German I tried to explain that I was forced by circumstances to rest there for the night. One of the men, however, burst into anger and said that I was ruining the grass which they needed for their cattle. I suggested that I would willingly pay for the small damage that had or would be done by my trespass. They did not agree with the proposition and seemed quite hurt at the suggestion. Under their orders and with the dog barking all the time I packed my rucksack on my back and I took the trodden path wanting to walk down but the intruders intercepted and tried to drive me up as if I was a goat to be bullied by the sound of a dog behind me. I could not grasp their intention. However, I patiently plodded on with my wet clothing, as there had been a drizzle. Now it had started raining and I could see that it would prove disastrous to go uphill. I therefore decided to resist their orders and what helped me was that the lantern that they were carrying contained a candle which had reached the end of its life. They, somehow, asked me themselves, to walk down the valley.

I was once again alone, travelling down in pouring rain whilst they had turned back up the narrow path. At long last I came to a plank to cross a rushing stream and to my great joy I could discern that by crossing over it I should be on a highway. I continued to walk along the road in the continual rain, darkness and footsore to find some protection. I found scrubland under a large tree where I spread the rubber ground sheet using the rucksack as a pillow and covered myself with the almost wet shawl and eiderdown. I went to sleep and must have slept soundly when I was suddenly awakened by someone prodding in my side with a stout stick. As I woke I beheld two men and a dog and to my amazement in the intense darkness under the clouds a torch was flashed at me by one of the men, whom I on the first awakening had thought to be the men I had left behind on the mountain. To my relief, however, they told me that they were official tourist guides and they, having seen a heap covered with a shawl, one of them prodded it with a stick to discover its contents. They were amazed to find a human being. They offered me some drink from their flasks and assured me that all was well except that the place I had selected for rest was likely to receive a landslip from the adjoining mountainside. They asked me to join them for some rest in their homes but I decided to walk again on the broad highway under the moonlight as the clouds had cleared.

What a glorious tramp it was and how happy in spite of the inconvenient night before. The sunrise over the mountains was a wonderful sight to behold. On and steadily on I walked until I came to a thickly wooded area on the outskirts of a town. I was by this time physically tired and hungry. I had luckily been able to keep a box of matches almost dry and on this account I could call myself a confirmed tramp. Nothing daunted, I decided that I should take to the woods, drying clothes, sleeping kit etc. I lighted a fire, made some sort of meal out of the few scraps of food which were in the rucksack. I found a few dry twigs, stripped them of the damp outer bark and hunted for medium and large wood as it was possible to find until I had sufficient to have a really good fire which would last a couple of hours. All I could find in the way of food was one egg with its shell slightly cracked, one small loaf of bread soaking wet, one tin of condensed milk partly split, a small quantity of sugar and a very small amount of butter. I emptied everything in the frying pan, mixed them and fried the mixture. When cooked I found it wonderfully delicious, ate and enjoyed it.

Having dried my belongings I packed them back into the rucksack which again formed a pillow for my rest – a real rest for my aching head and limbs. I slept till midday and then went into town for luncheon. I was to leave this town of Lauterbrunnen the following morning and was now afraid of the coming night 'out of doors'. Although I thought it was wise to hunt for a hotel in which to stay, but on second thoughts, I thought it would be cowardly to surrender to fear and I also did not have sufficient money to continue to spend nights in hotels. I found a farm house where I was able to procure eggs, milk, bread and butter. I purchased them and was back to the wood I had come from and where I had stayed the previous night. I had an early breakfast the following morning and tramped to the railway station on my journey to Italy.

Late in the evening I arrived at the Italian village named Tanda – this place made me feel at home. I purchased a large green-skinned melon containing brilliant crimson fleshy pulp. I was even staggered at the amount of fruits and sweetmeats I was able to buy for what appeared to me a small price as compared to prices elsewhere in Europe. I felt coming nearer and nearer to my country. I loved simple village life more than the hustle and bustle of big cities. Here I found a small room in a very cheap little boarding house. The village had narrow streets with lines of washed clothes and lines upon lines of macaroni and spaghetti stretched from the windows of houses on either side of the alleys. Here the donkeys trotted along with their panniers on each side whilst the men and women carried their loads on their backs.

After a sojourn of a few days I travelled by coach over the hills past the many vineyards on the hillsides, through numerous villages and olive groves until I reached Menton having crossed the Alps. Here I was at Monte Carlo where I stayed for two days. I had travelled into the interior of Italy visiting towns and villages but there is nothing special which I like to jot down. I have already mentioned about the wonderful sight along the beach at the Casino in Monte Carlo. Casino and its life is too well known. Next I took my train to Marseille and on the following morning I sat in the band stand area and listened to the band for two hours and after a couple of days rest I boarded the Sphinx leaving the dock for Indo-China.

Farewell to England

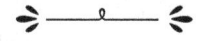

King Akbar, it is said, once asked Raja Birbal, one of his ministers, "Where is East and where is West?" Birbal replied, "If I walked in the direction of the rising sun which is east from the point on which I am standing, then the entire distance I travelled would be to the west. Sir, it is just not possible to demarcate East from West." Thus, travelling from Europe to India the entire journey east covered was going by to the west. The accepted axiom in England that "East is East and never the twain shall meet" was no longer apt in its essence, after I had lived among the English people for about three years. I returned from the country with a feeling that there was constant diffusion in progress between England and India when I contemplate objectively how we in our country have been influenced and conditioned by our contact with the English people and their language. In our day to day life, in thought and deed such as eating habits, dress, education, architecture, furniture, crockery, games, language, conversation particularly of the educated classes in India, are a mixture of the East and West – more of the Anglo-American than the indigenous. It was difficult for me to say farewell to England in these circumstances.

I learnt the habit of early morning tea called bed tea. On

and off I have tried to give up that habit but more often than not I have failed to drop it. I didn't adopt this from England but from the intelligentsia of my own country, who had it by their association with their English bosses. The afternoon tea and biscuits in place of roasted corn or gram is an accepted routine among the urban people and the same is creeping into the countryside. Even those who can afford milk have begun to shun it. In the days when I was a child, churned curd, butter, chapati and pickles formed an early meal. Its counterpart since the European influence is baked English bread called *'double roti'*, eggs in one form or another, tea, fruit and occasionally milk and porridge. Everything is now served in china ware, and the Indian thali and small cups are hardly ever used.

Although I have returned to *kurta* and discarded the shirt, but by and large the shirt of the European style has been adopted exclusively. My own *'churidar pyjama'* is more tight on the legs than the drain pipe trousers used by western countries, I am inclined to suggest that this eastern tight pyjama has intruded into European fashion.

Even during the British regime, the rulers adapted themselves to Hindu and Muslim architecture and even in building New Delhi, Sir Edward Lutyens blended the East and West in design, but since Independence our engineers and architects who have been trained in modern Architecture and Science have preferred to use European architecture slavishly. The Secretariat at Chandigarh, the Janpath hotel in New Delhi, the new Central Offices on Parliament Street, the Secretariat in Calcutta and Bombay all speak with one style – un-Indian. We have copied them regardless of whether they are useful in our weather or not.

I learned ballroom dancing in England, but gave it up after leaving the shores of that country but I found later in life after the English left India that ballroom dancing found its way among the urban upper middle classes.

We expressed our indignation against the English language when the Language Bill was moved in our Parliament in 1967, and debated on it in English, shouted slogans in English. I wonder if we could ever be able to discard its use, or is there a real need to do it.

It may be true that the British or European culture is alien to our land and as such has done much emotional and spiritual injury but those who believe in the laws of nature and its dynamism must accept that the blending of East and West is bound to take place with new forms of quick communications in thought and contacts.

The British rule ended in 1947, but they did not say goodbye to us. I could never have imagined that they would accept Indian men in turbans and women with *salwar* and *kurtas* as immigrants in their own country and I feel sure that the English, however conservative, are bound to be affected in the process in spite of the apparent non-intrusion of each other's culture and just co-existence. Fare well and no longer farewell.

Back to India

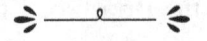

In the month of August 1928, I boarded S. S. Sphinx bound for Indo-China. I remember that I had only the clothes in which I stood upright, plus the garments and equipment which I was carrying in the rucksack on my back and by this time must have been regarded as a tramp. The remainder of my luggage I had not yet collected from Cooks. I was placed in a cabin which I shared with P.K. Atre. We also shared a table at meal time thus we became friends. He told me that he was a schoolmaster whose home was in Poona, to which he invited me on my journey homeward from Colombo. He was dedicated to a Society known as Seva Sadan, a group of men trained as teachers, who were giving to an educational society, time and energy to help raise the standard of living and education of the poor and the low castes. Mr. Atre was returning after a year in England which had given him the opportunity to teach in schools situated in poorer districts of London and other industrial towns. I met him in Poona and a number of times later in Bombay.

I was happy to sit and walk on the deck and wait for the sunset and often for the sunrise whether the sea was rough or smooth, cold or hot. When the Sphinx quayed at Port Said, I spent an hour or two on shore. Everything I saw was exciting, the town, the people, the goods for sale, the coffee houses and the shops, the small boats which hung around the large ships in the harbour, the young boys who dived into the sea to catch and place in their mounts the coins thrown by the passengers on the ships. The ship then moved on through the Gulf of Suez to the Red Sea and then to Jibuti, the French port opposite to Aden and in French Somaliland.

It was late evening and darkness was creeping in and the sun was slowly sinking when the Sphinx was piloted into the harbour for refuelling. Its engines were maintained and driven by coal. Mr. Atre and I along with several other companions stood enraptured by the beauty of the colours spreading over the sky, sea and land. Leaning over the deck rails I saw the coaling barges in partial darkness awaiting our arrival. As the boat drew nearer and nearer to the dull looking coal dumps I discerned, lying on top of the coal heap, in great heat, figures of men wearing only a loincloth. I felt that I was nearing home.

The following morning the Sphinx left for Colombo. The year was very troublesome in India as I could get from the news, although my journey from Jibuti to Colombo was very restful, and uneventful across the Indian Ocean. I was never tired of watching the flying fish, the porpoises, the gulls and many coloured birds and the beauty of the sun and the moon. As the bright golden sun sunk into the sea on one side of the ship, its glow was reflected for a short time on the moon rising on the other side of the ship. On some nights the heat made it impossible to sleep in the cabin and I, with many other passengers, slept on the deck.

Our country was in a state of great upheaval at the time and many of our leaders fighting for our freedom had been imprisoned by the British Government ruling India. Every newcomer could be a suspect. When I disembarked at Colombo

I was at once suspected probably because I had no luggage other than the rucksack as I had left the former with Messrs. Thos. Cook and Sons, the shipping agents for delivery at Bombay. I was therefore, again a tramp. I produced my passport and was asked several questions by a police officer who may have been an Anglo Indian or British. Nothing came out of this and I was allowed to get into the town where I roamed around for the remainder of the day and travelled by the night train to Talaimannar. From here I crossed by boat to the Indian Coast.

This last lap of my journey from Talaimannar (Ceylon) to Dhanushkodi (India) proved both interesting and embarrassing. The lower deck of the coastal boat was crowded with Ceylonese and South Indians – men, women and children, all of whom seemed to be peasants. Most of the ladies, young and old, had bracelets on their arms and ankles, and jewelled ornaments in their pierced ears and noses, and also around their necks. I was there in the crowd. A police officer came up to me and asked me to go to the top deck for queries. I followed him without showing any anger, I was given refreshments and questioned regarding my identity, purpose of my journey from Columbus to Lahore etc. All I felt was that I was a VIP needing the attention of the Government and the absurdity continued during my travel throughout my own homeland. I had already planned the places which I wished to visit in South India. As my financial resources were limited I had decided to travel in third class compartment and by night trains while visiting the countryside villages and towns by day. After getting down from the boat at Dhanushkodi I entered the train for Madura. But, alas, there was little hope of getting sleep because most of the passengers from the boat were travelling up country as I was. Still, being a suspect, the police came to my aid as no one was allowed to enter the small third class compartment in which I seated myself and there was police guard on duty outside the compartment. As the train moved, there were three policemen in uniform who shared the compartment with me. I spread my ground sheet on the floor for sleeping as it was more comfortable than the narrow seats in the railway carriage. In the early hours of the following morning the train steamed into a junction station from where the people could change for Rameshwaram. The policemen left my compartment and many passengers got in their place. However, no one occupied my seat although the compartment was occupied to more than its capacity.

The men were mostly clad in loincloth only except that a few then threw a small sheet of cloth over their shoulders. The small children were mostly naked except for some jewellery, the small boys wearing a small medallion on a cord tied round the middle of the body. Many women and children were squatting on the floor whilst the men occupied benched seats. As the day hours passed the compartment became hotter and hotter and I wondered whether I could possibly endure the night under those conditions. The following daybreak I reached Madura, where I was again met by a senior police officer. From questions put to me I could see that I was still under investigation regarding my political views and leanings. I spent two days seeing the Madura Temple and an ancient palace but all the time the CID was close at my heels.

The Temple, which was an admirable structure with four entrance gates called *Gopurams* and in their precincts several small traders sold small articles of apparel, jewellery, toys etc. besides the things required for offering *puja* to the deity. It reminded one of the story of Jesus of Nazareth who turned out the Jew traders away from the proximity of the Temple – the house of Prayer in Jerusalem. Jesus had said that people like that make the holy place a 'den of thieves'. The deities were not kept clean as I would have expected but looked soiled with the oil which the devotees used while offering their prayers. Things may have changed since with the advancement of scientific thought. I continued to go round seeing the idols, the buildings in their detail, the plaster statuary – stories which told the life happenings of Hindu gods. I can recollect the octagonal pillars which produced different tones from each face when struck.

I decided to search for a hotel in which to have some rest for one night as I failed to get shelter in the municipal rooms reserved for visitors. Luckily rest rooms were available at the railway station and I made use of the same. After Madura or Madurai, I visited Trichinopoly and then Madras. All along the journey the people were generally shorter in stature and darker in colour as distinct from the Indo-Aryan type of men living in Punjab and Kashmir. They also possessed broader noses depressed at the root and resembled to an extent with the coolie labour I had seen at Jibuti. A small minority of population with fair skin and more akin in size and build to the Aryan could be observed particularly in towns quite distinct from the mass of the people. Even at a glance one felt that there was no fusion between these two types. One also felt convinced that our population is a mixed multitude in different stages of material and moral growth, exhibiting an extraordinary variety of peoples, creeds and manners. While travelling in Europe the different races like the Italians, Germans, French and the English have by some process of blending produced a more or less uniform type of European. Here in our country I appeared as much a foreigner in the South just as a European would feel there. Similarly the languages of Southern India were as unintelligible to me as the French or the German medium of exchange of ideas between us, and that brought us closer.

Having witnessed the temples in the South I felt a sense of

pride about the singularity of our art. Our artists seemed to have complete freedom to weave an unending texture of innumerable interlacing plastic forms over the surfaces of the temples and rock-cut chapels. Their art is bound entirely with religious mythology and the splendour of the temple is a genuine offering to God, for as a race we give religion a place higher than the State or the Crown.

I was genuinely struck by the simplicity and the austere life of the people of the South, after having travelled in the same first class railway compartment with an Indian judge of the Madras High Court. He was bare footed and had a *dhoti* and *kurta* for his dress. He might be having a different dress for his official work but I couldn't dream that another person of his eminence under the British Administration in the North would dare to be so scanty in his dress. I stayed in Madras for a couple of days and to my utter surprise I could not find a modern restaurant in any of the market streets. I used the railway station restaurant for my meals. My next halt on my way to Bombay was Bangalore where I spent a week in sightseeing. I stayed with an Anglo Indian family as a paying guest. From the station I made a journey to and fro Kolar Gold Mines. The visit was worth the time. The management was very kind and hospitable.

From Bangalore I travelled to Poona, where I was received by my friend Principal Atre, with whom I stayed several days. Atre was a very popular Maharashtrian writer and known for his learned discourses. He ranked high among the educationists of the Land. Here I had the opportunity of seeing a famous Maharashtrian drama, *Ekkas Piala* (a glass of wine), in which the principal part was played by the late Bal Gandharv. I was introduced to him at the end of the play. I had occasions to meet Shri Atre in later years, when he had settled in Bombay as director and producer of films.

The whole of the South has been much more a citadel of Hindu orthodoxy and convention than the North. I had observed in Madura that its temples were closed to the lower castes. The untouchables could not even use the roads approaching the temples within one hundred feet or so of the *Gopurams* although Christians and Muslims could do so, even carry liquor or meat with impunity. The moment untouchables became converted to Christianity or the Muslim creed, the restriction vanished. No wonder that the country lacked integration and continues to do so, in spite of the later reformation of throwing open the gates of all temples to the so called untouchables when Gandhiji gave the name Harijans (God's own people). Even in Maharashtra the bane of untouchability existed although less intense.

Next I moved to Bombay, collected my kit from Messrs. Thos. Cook and Sons, and after spending a couple of days there I travelled to Ahmedabad. On my way during the night in the train I could see Gandhiji's face quite vividly. Next morning I was going to have his *darshan*.[22] I had seen him earlier in 1919, and now after nine years or so, he had on his face, which was considerably aged, the marks of an ascetic. Sabarmati Ashram, which he had made his abode, was a spiritual centre of the Gandhian movement. I felt quite keen to stay at the Ashram but both because life was too rigid there as I could feel at that time, and that I had some responsibilities towards those who looked forward to my return, I bade farewell to that sacred refuge.

I decided to stop in Delhi for a couple of days before proceeding to Lahore. I had some relations there but I met none of them and instead stayed with an Anglo Indian family as a paying guest. New Delhi looked like a dead capital as compared to the

---

22 Being in the presence and beholding a revered person.

capitals of other countries. The Central Secretariat had moved to Simla for the summer months. I have seen Delhi grow since Independence into a truly international city and now compares well with Bombay, which even during the British regime, had a varied and composite population, and in its diversity it presented unity in the life of Bombay.

My next halt was Lahore. It was a short one as I had made no effort to meet my old friends that were still left there. I purchased some fruit for my people in Jaranwala whom I was going to meet soon. This last lap of the journey was exceedingly tiring.

After three years' absence I was going to be back home. I sent no telegram to announce my arrival, knowing that my uncle had lost his only son two months ago at an age when his sensibilities would be keenest. I, too, having received the same blow when I was far away, felt embittered with fate. In order not to dwell on so painful a subject in a public place like the railway station I had decided to reach home quietly and avoid homecoming reception. It was well after sunset that my train arrived in Jaranwala Station and I made my way out without being observed and within fifteen minutes I knocked at the door of my uncle's house. Joy and courage were mingled in his reception as he folded me in his arms. I burst into sobs. There was no need to utter the child's name that trembled on my lips.

Random Thoughts

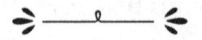

[Editor's Note: This section was written at the end, but noted to be inserted here. It offers his retrospectives late in life, examining the events and circumstances that caused him to be who he was.]

Conditions and circumstances are forever changing, and constantly creating political threats to our security. Old age and ill health could destroy my sense of security but it has not done it so far. Like most of us I have come across many factors which impaired my security – loss of a good job, loss of loved ones, loss of property, ill-will of superiors, loss of hard earned money, long illness of my wife, but none of these ever worried me. I don't believe that there is anything in this world which could have permanent stability. Even this earth itself, I have personally experienced, trembles during a quake. Solidly built structures fall to the ground. Mountains split and crumble. What kind of resilience did I have which provided me with confidence to meet every changing condition and every emergency. What kind of faith is this? Is it indifference, and if so, how have I developed it? Is it the result of the various influences to which my mind has been subjected?

When I was without a job in 1928-29 I lived in a condition of expectancy. It was an exciting state of mind to be in. "Anything might come up at any time," was wonderful, and such a state to come to a close, would have amounted to another loss. When I came to look back on that period of unemployment or of any gainful employment, it amuses me how like an adventurer I visited several offices and even a number of towns in search of work. I applied for the post of the Chief Engineer's job in Faridkot state and to my astonishment I was sent for the interview. I went there and stayed with a friend who was then occupying a high executive office under the *Rajah*. He showed me round, the kind of work I shall have to do resulting in loss of all association with my own profession and finally dissuaded me to join that service. He was of the opinion that even unemployment would be more useful as I would utilise my time in equipping myself with more learning.

Modern human society comprises the powerful 'haves' and the poor 'have-nots'. The former are the so-called defenders of our civilization while the latter remain devoid of all means of advancement – scientific, economic, and political. Although human progress depends on friendliness, neighbourliness, tolerance, sacrifice etc. but we observe continuous tussle between these two groups. The root cause of the strife and conflict lies in 'haves' amassing wealth and power through their privileged position by illegal means and ignoring the rights and claims of the poor. Experience has testified that those who are provided with basic needs of life have no need for creating unrest.

I believe that it was in the twenties of the present century that England introduced dole for the workless so that he and his family would not starve. People had to queue up at the Labour Exchange to draw the dole. I do not quite remember if it was at all successful, but looking at our own country with innumerable workless souls, I wonder if we would ever try this. Poor relief has been in vogue from the earliest recorded history and the stories of voluntary philanthropy in times of famine and disaster are well known. In 1947, when Hindus and Sikh evacuees entered India, both individuals and organisations used to serve free *dal-roti* and the same held true in camps. I have not only been a witness to this but accepted this charity twice in those days – once in Amritsar and a second time in Ambala.

Charity and alms giving has been treated as a mark of devotion in our country. Our temples and the approaches to them are lined with the infirm, the handicapped and the poverty stricken for getting alms from men and women who go to worship. Some of the temples even provide some kind of rudimentary shelter. Social service, unlike the organised doles from the State, has a religious background in this country and therefore has remained spasmodic in character, but the joint family, in which the members of the family grew up under one shelter, provided social security to them whether members earned or not. They would not lack food as long as the joint family had the capacity to provide and they shared the plight of hunger if the joint stock dwindled to nothing. Unemployment, sickness and the like were not quite frightening when the common pool of the family was adequate but the poor families faced hardships.

The joint family system with which I was well acquainted in my childhood and I have recorded facts about its functioning under the control of my grandfather, introduced some rigidity in rules of conduct for otherwise a community of people living close together could not function. Enlarging upon this simile the Nation, which ought to function as a joint family in a democratic set up, would normally impose certain duties to be observed by its members strictly for them to pull together – the living expenses of well off members should be reduced with regard to the economic conditions of the whole family so as to provide food, clothes and shelter as also education and medical aid. The

State must work out such a scheme – Five Year Plans must aim at meeting the 'five needs' of every individual in this country.

The community development programme, in which I had a hand, is a movement on a large scale similar to the joint family system with which I was quite familiar. But having worked for a few years in Government administration I always felt that the rust that clogs it would not allow the new programme to flourish. If however, some of them would do well and catch the fire, then conflagration would set even the cold and wet, ablaze. My friend, S.K. Dey was at it, while he was by and large, able to cross administrative hurdles, he was up against political aspirants who ultimately pushed him out from the Ministry of Community Projects. Our country is large, inhabited by multifarious societies whose ways of life are determined by traditions of the area and who promote parochial political interests – a factor which, to my mind, came to play for the exit of Shri S.K. Dey.

Having been in-charge of Nilokheri and Fulia rehabilitation centres which were visited by men of eminence from India and abroad, I had come to believe that literacy drive among the children was the correct approach for the rejuvenation of our country. Once the upsurge for development was created among the children they moved their parents to work and raged a war against their misery. Bengalis had known the 1943 famine when thousands of people died of starvation without resistance, but at Fulia they felt like men and women of a living race and entitled to a livelihood in the country they belonged to. At Nilokheri, the people were desirous to have training in new trades if those could give them increased income, yet at Fulia they, at least in the early days of our campaign felt satisfied with evacuee's relief and dole. Gradually they adopted the same attitude towards their rehabilitation, as their counterparts at Nilokheri. They would accept no degradation in asking for free relief of any kind.

We have a democracy in which the National Congress because of its past association with the freedom movement is still dominant. It lost considerable ground in the 1967 elections and the opposition parties have jointly in some states dislocated the Congress party from power and from the economic and social advantage that they had as ministers. National integration has recently received a big jolt and I observe that we are divided on the basis of language. When I look back towards our past history as to how we lost our freedom whether to Mughals or the British, we did so not because we were poor or militarily weak but because we were divided. When I read the threat of further partition of the country and its Balkanization, I shudder but being an optimist I have faith in my countrymen to turn towards integration.

From Free Country to Enslaved Land

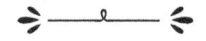

The joy of meeting gave a poignant new life to the sorrow from which we were suffering. I straightened myself up after the embrace with my uncle to look at my parents, my aunt, my wife and cousins, who had assembled at Jaranwala. In fact, they all knew my homecoming was in September 1928, except the date. In our meeting after such a long absence all the grown ups tasted the peculiar flavour of human life with mingled joy and grief. Gradually the conversation became general and restored to calm. It was quite late when we retired to bed. I spend a week at Jaranwala before proceeding to visit my in-laws at Chopala and then spend some time at Kakrali.

On my way to Chopala, accompanied by my wife, I passed through Jalalpur Jattan – the hometown of my mother. I have never made any mention of my mother's sister in my narrative so far, for I never visited them even once. My mother's parents and brothers had died even before I was born and she was left with an elder married sister Lakshmi Devi, who had no children. She had come down to Jalalpur with her husband to make her home there to inherit all that my (maternal) grandfather left behind. Some misunderstanding had developed between her and my mother in the division of their father's property and as a consequence they had snapped sisterly relationship for good. Without exposing my plans to anyone I decided to meet her enroute. The result was extraordinary. Both her husband and she were overjoyed when we went to their house. Their emotions touched a great height and within an hour they arranged to distribute sweets among their neighbours to announce my homecoming. A lasting relationship was revived between the two sisters.

Next I proceeded to Chopala, two days there, and then we went to Kakrali, where we were in the most familiar atmosphere. We were entertained wherever we went or stayed. At last, we returned to Jaranwala, as it was convenient for me to make journeys between there and Lahore where I had to go in search of employment. Within three months of my homecoming from England my wife conceived. It was good news for everybody in the family.

By this time I had grasped the political situation in the country. The Indian National Congress had grown in size, while the Muslim League had taken a positive shape, whether with or without Government support, for counteracting the influence of the Congress over the Muslim masses. The British Government had sent to India a commission under the chairmanship of Lord Simon to report to the British Parliament the type of reforms that should be introduced in the Indian Administration for satisfying the Indian aspirations for Dominion status. Both the Congress and the Muslim League had decided to boycott the Simon Commission although on different grounds. However, it was the Indian National Congress which was organising black flag demonstrations and *hartals* (strikes) wherever the Commission went on its mission. Further, during my absence from India revolutionary activities had been organised by some daring youth who hoped to bring about a violent revolution in the country to drive out the Alien Government. Many Congressmen who leaned towards socialism were silently supporting the revolutionaries. The Marxists had helped to organise the working classes in militant trade unions. Jawaharlal Nehru's popularisation of Soviet achievements after a visit to Russia and Subhash Chandar's ascendency among the youth had developed leftist tendencies within the Congress ranks. A huge procession demonstrating Indian boycott of the Simon Commission headed towards the Lahore Railway Station when it arrived there on 30th October 1928. There was a sea of black flags and shouts of "Simon Commission, Go Back" and *"Inqalab Zindabad"* (Long Live Revolution), outside the station. Lala Lajpat Rai, the Congress leader of Punjab, who was leading the procession received injuries on his head when the police lathi charged the processionists. He bore those baton's like a true *Satyagrahi* and the only words that he uttered before he lost his senses and which were engraved later under the statue created in his memory after his death were, "Every lathi hurled at me indicated the last nail in the coffin of the British Government." That statue now stands at Scandal Point in Simla. He died on November 17. A revolutionary organisation known as Hindustan Socialist Republican Association had been formed for violent freedom struggle by a small number of young men in Delhi. Bhagat Singh and some of his comrades of the HSRA, in order to avenge the death of Lalaji, shot Mr. Saunders, the Deputy Superintendent of Police, who was responsible for the lathi charge on 30th October, exactly one month after Lalaji's death. A red leaflet was circulated in Lahore by the revolutionaries stating that Saunders was an insult to the Nation and had therefore been shot dead while he left his office and rode slowly on his motorcycle.

The above is a brief account of the conditions in the country when I returned from England in order to join the engineering profession in my country. If the recruitment to the Indian Service of Engineers had not been stopped in 1928, I may have been admitted into the Service directly in London for being posted somewhere in India. Simultaneously with the government policy in London, it had cut down its expenditure on development works in India with the result that new recruitment to Indian Service of Engineers was now limited to a few replacements, for which All India competitive examinations were held in January. I tried at the competition in January 1927, but without success. In fact, my mind was greatly perplexed whether it was at all wise to join Government service in the face of prevailing political unrest and then with the doors to entry into Government Engineering Services almost blocked and with no opening for the profession it looked much easier and comforting to join the political ranks. On the other hand my people were very keen that I must find lucrative employment to be able to look after myself after the financial crisis over which my uncle had not till then crossed. I accepted an unpaid job in the Punjab Public Works Department (Buildings and Roads) to work as an apprentice personal assistant to a Superintending Engineer in Lahore. As this did not involve any commitment of loyalty to the Government from my side I associated myself with Gandhiji's edicts such as spinning and the *Swadeshi* cult. Naturally this did not find much favour with my Superintending Engineer, but all the same he showed no indignation and was always willing to help me with my professional work. I gained experience under him. In 1930 I was selected by the Jammu and Kashmir state as an Assistant Engineer at Rs. 300 per month as my salary. I joined at Jammu and was placed in charge of His Highness's palaces.

The Simon Commission fought shy of conceding even the demand of the liberals, namely the Dominion status, the Congress under the leadership of young Nehru (Jawaharlalji) declared its goal as complete Independence on 26th January 1930, at the Congress session held in Lahore on the banks of the river Ravi. Lord Irwin who was the then Viceroy of India, brought forward a new move as a substitute to the Simon Commission recommendations which had already proved futile and thrown as unacceptable to any section of the Indian community. While accepting the issue of India's constitutional progress as the attainment of Dominion status, he with the consent of the British Parliament, announced a Round Table Conference of all Indian political parties to be held in London to discuss the Simon Commission's report. In December 1929, Pandit Jawaharlal Nehru declared a campaign of civil disobedience under the guidance of Gandhiji although it remained in abeyance for some time, till Gandhiji launched it on 6th April 1930, with his historic march to Dandi against the Salt Laws. There was spontaneous response from Nationalist India and there were witnessed outbursts of Nationalist excitement on a huge scale all over the country. When the National movement proved too strong against the Government's repressive measures the Round Table Conference which met in London had to be adjourned to a future date with a view to bring Congress into the conference. The Gandhi-Irwin agreement came into being on 4th March 1931, when the Congress decided to discontinue civil disobedience movement and the Government declared a general amnesty for all political prisoners. The Congress chose Gandhiji as its sole representative to participate in the Second Round Table Conference in London.

Leaving further account of the political situation for another place I return to family life. My mother was getting extremely anxious, as my wife's gestation period passed month after month, about the birth of her first grandchild. In spite of my contempt for popular superstitions, my mother had a great deal of respect for them and my wife was at the time under her care. Horrible tales were told, e.g., if expectant mothers did any work during lunar or solar eclipse, the child would bear some peculiar markings on the body. Similarly during the last month of her gestation a woman must be very careful about her desires and ambitions as her child on birth would show their effects both on the body as on the mind. On this premise a number of photographs and paintings of pious Indian leaders hung from the walls of the room occupied by my wife. I used to have jokes with my aunt regarding these superstitions and the whim of the 'evil eye'. Once I said that it was lucky for a particular woman to keep her desires within modest limits during that specific period of gestation, since if she had allowed herself to hanker after a motor car, a house, all sorts of furniture etc. etc. there would not have been skin enough on the body of the child to record all these ambitions on the body at birth. She, however, laughed away at my jokes. In spite of the fact that they all hoped for a male child and all precautions having been taken, my wife gave birth to a daughter – a lovely one (with no markings). My mother hailed the birth of her granddaughter who she saw was the forerunner of her brothers to follow. We gave the child the name Sarla, and she was born at Jaranwala on 29th September, 1929.

My wife did not desire to cramp my career, and never insisted to live with me in Lahore while I was out of employment. She was strong enough to bear the separation and stay with my parents or with my uncle although having had a long separation earlier she would have preferred to be close to me. In fact what would have been our love worth if we did not adjust according to the circumstances facing us. My mother too, who had placed high hopes on me, never looked perturbed about the bad luck I was having while in search of Government service. My mother had, in fact, the strength of a stoic, which she had, according to her, developed while too young at an age when life was opening with all its charms. She had lost her father and brother before her marriage and had no patronage from her close relations. After her marriage she lost the affection of her only sister, but in spite of these sorrows she had a bitter pride about her, and would not give vent to her feelings of despondency for my sake. It all worked well. My wife and my daughter were well looked after. My uncle provided me, my bare minimum monthly needs for another year. However, I was very keen to 'do things' and get my house in order. I recognized that the most important things in life were making for myself a successful career to provide a sure shelter for my family. The rest then appeared subordinate. I was finding it difficult to live away from my child. Today parents may thank God when they do not have children but my feeling was that a child is such a rarity and such a joy that one must live for them and work for them. They make life worth living.

In the life of the Nation struggling for freedom there was a call to every man to take part in the struggle without fear, but the uncertainty of our livelihood in case of my imprisonment kept me out of battle. I satisfied myself by reading papers every morning in order to be able to place my views on the affairs of the Nation and to encourage those who proposed to sacrifice everything for the Nation. I had already reduced my ambitions even in my profession, limiting life and setting bounds to my destiny. I was prepared to accept an official career with a fixed salary and a pension even under the British Indian Government, although I even failed to secure that, even though I had spent three years in a British university – the London University. The great hopes with which I went abroad were now shattered.

Every life demands effort, no one is exempt from failure. In fact, obstacles often bring and merit courage. Having been selected as an Assistant Engineer by the Kashmir state government, I felt quite happy with my lot, to work for myself and for those who were dependent on me. My wife – my companion who was extremely fond of her child, was keen to found her house and be the housekeeper, which she looked upon as an occupation.

As a spinster she had not relished independence. Even her freedom to move about in the village of her parents was restricted with strict limitations. She had been brought up in economic dependence. All the training helped her not to ask for or to snatch the liberty which marriage had offered her. She always looked fresh and her whole joy was her daughter and her husband. She never talked to me about any of her day time problems or about any economic troubles. Besides, she was not weighed down with the trivials of the household as my mother helped her to a very great extent. Even later in life when she knew that my earnings had gone up, her demands remained limited to the conveniences she wanted to provide for her three children. When her health made her bed ridden she never looked morose and faced her troubles boldly for recovery.

When I was working in Jammu and Kashmir state as an Assistant Engineer and was posted at Jammu city, the movement for the eradication of untouchability had gained considerable momentum under Gandhiji's leadership. I found in this an opportunity to go to the localities of the so-called untouchables, Gandhiji named them Harijans, to render them some service. During autumn when malaria took the form of an epidemic I visited their quarters to distribute quinine. I could never make myself agree to clean their houses or streets. In fact, the Christian missionaries, who not only looked after their children's education, went to the extent of cleaning their little children free of filth to which the children seemed quite accustomed. While they inspired me with selfless service, yet I failed to reconcile myself to tasks which looked to me unbecoming for my status in life.

Time went on and I was gradually turning towards fellow feeling for the discarded by society but it was not until 1948 that I was able to shed considerably my arrogance towards them. Traditions die very hard and even today I am only capable of exhibiting a kindlier approach to the *jamadars* who work for us as sweepers. My father beats me at this as he feels one-ness of the *Atma* (soul) in himself with theirs. Unless we can follow that principle, untouchability will continue as a body sore or as a fatal cancer of Hinduism.

London As I Saw It

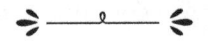

Having spent almost three years in London, a period quite enough to know the city I lived in (1925-28), it would be unfair to leave it out of the account. From the point of view of dimensions London was vast, immense with miles and miles of streets, with tramways, and buses carrying huge masses of people one way or the other. It had a railway system both over and under ground, the trains rushing along these arterial routes either way. It was along these communications that I could see the Londoners, besides those whom I met every day at the King's College or in the humble digs where I stayed. The General Strike provided a great opportunity for me to walk with Londoners.

London's population was as much, if not more class ridden as I had known in Lahore. Here I lived among the serfs, and there being no intermingling between the 'idle rich' or the upper classes, and the lower middle classes, I had no opportunity to know them. It was even quite difficult to know the inside of the English family with whom I lodged and boarded day in and day out. Their home life remained a dead secret. I was invariably introduced to the relatives of the family when they visited them. I was a stranger and always remained so as long as I lived with an English family. They behaved like shopkeepers towards their customers. It was always quaker oats or corn flakes as the first course for breakfast. After wishing "Good morning," because of London's undependable weather, was followed by a remark about the weather – "good" or "rotten."

At college, too, the Indian students mixed among themselves as the English class fellows remained within their own group. There was no visible antipathy but there was a display of indifference between the two groups of students. In fact, there did not appear to be any affinity even amongst the natives of London. I accepted it as English character. I had, however, one friend who belonged to a rural area, had a religious background and who spent some weekends in the East End of London, where the poor lived in London's slums. His name was Hugh Fielder. He was also brilliant in his studies. He often invited me to his home in the village and I spent some holidays with his parents. I learnt more about the class barriers through his association than I could have ever done otherwise. He was frank and had no reserves of a normal Englishman. Through him I was able to see the plight of the poor, ill fed and ill clad and badly housed. The poor could almost be compared with the untouchables in our own country.

London was the Capital of the British Empire which ruled the waves. It was said in those days that the sun never set on the British Empire, but it did not belong to the common people. The Empire was the preserve of the very upper classes who had set up a Parliament of their own with a constitutional monarch as the nominal head. The London businessmen, small or big, followed their King – King George V in the style of their dress with a bowler hat, gloves in left hand, and spats on their shoes. The college students generally followed the Prince of Wales in adopting felt hat as the head dress, worn slightly tilted to the left. The ladies drew their inspiration from the dresses that the Duchess of Kent used or borrowed from Paris.

The Parliament had two principal parties in the House of Commons, the Conservatives and Labour. The Liberals were there only in name. The Conservatives formed His Majesty's Government at the time and the Labour, His Majesty's Opposition. Together they formed the 'Ruling Clique' which was the government of the clique, by the clique and for the clique. Each party however was equally desirous of gaining political power more for selfish ends than for promoting the ends of democracy. Unfortunately because of our educated community's close association with the British, we adopted the same Parliamentary system after Independence and were consequently infected with the virus from London.

With the technological growth, the Christian religion was losing its past hold on the English people. The old, the infirm and the children observed the Sabbath generally, the rest spent the Sunday in pleasure hunt. Whether it was the Hyde Park Serpentine or the Clapham Common, the open parks drew large crowds on Sundays in summer months, but in winter the same crowds filled the cinema halls.

Whenever the King, seated in a gilded coach pulled by eight white horses, was driven from Buckingham Palace to the Parliament House the people thronged along the entire route and took slavish delight in seeing the monarch. They were thus made mentally slave to the clique, while we were kept politically enslaved in India.

The Englishman in India was a specimen quite different from the natives in England. He possessed a conceit which he showed outwardly. There may have been exceptions but by and large those in the Civil and Military Services of the then Government of India behaved as the ruling class which made them repugnant in my sight.

VISHAV BHAVAN

Part VI: Civil Engineer and Businessman

The Maharaja's Service

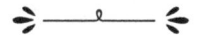

Jammu and Kashmir was a princely state in 1930 under the reign of Maharaja Hari Singh. Its population had a Muslim majority. Once the abode of Hindu seers, it became an outpost province of the Mughal Empire with their conquest of Northern India. Later it was seized by the Afghans on the dissolution of the Mughal empire and when Maharaja Ranjit SIngh was building up his Sikh kingdom, he turned the Afghans out of Kashmir and granted it as a fief to Gulab Singh, one of his generals. The British on the conclusion of the first Sikh War left the grantee in the possession of his fief (a payment of two crore rupees to the British was agreed to by the fief) and admitted him into alliance with them. Maharaja Hari Singh was a descendant of the Sikh general. After the first War of Independence (1857), which India lost and during which the then Maharaja of Kashmir remained loyal to the British and with the transfer of India to the British Crown, a policy of 'union and cooperation' was initiated between the paramount power and the Maharaja. A *Sanad* (royal warrant) was granted giving assurance that the British Government desired perpetuation of the Maharaja's Government and its suzerainty over the area held by him. The state was, therefore, governed as it pleased His Highness, but the British Resident, an agent of the British Indian Government had to be kept informed of the affairs of the state. The Resident could be authoritative in giving advice on administrative matters when the situation, mainly political or that of law and order, was uncomfortable. The civil administration in the state was almost similar to that in British India although the scales of salaries paid to civil servants did not compare favourably with the salaries in Punjab.

I was posted as an Assistant Engineer to look after the building and roads either in construction or their maintenance and attached to His Highness's palaces and the Central Secretariat. There was considerable scope for utilisation of the technical knowledge which I possessed, and for learning and showing originality in design as the Maharaja himself took keen interest and made his own demands and suggestions in all new building construction in the palaces. The post also offered a fairly close contact with the head of the state and the cabinet. I was placed in Jammu, the winter capital of the state. The Central Secretariat was still functioning from Srinagar. Therefore I had a very light demand on my time from the ministers or His Highness's personal staff. His Highness was away to Europe for a holiday accompanied by Her Highness. The grandmother, an aunt (wife of the Maharaja's predecessor) and the mother of His Highness occupied the Inner Palace which were heavily guarded by army personnel, and an ex-Army general was in overall charge of these Palaces where these grand ladies lived with their women retinue called *'golies'*. No men lived inside, nor was anyone allowed to enter without military escort in plain clothes, while both the visitor on duty and the escort had to be in *burqas* as long as they remained inside these Palaces. The *burqas* were simple sheets of cloth which covered one's body from head to ankles with holes in it opposite the eyes. I, too, had to observe these rules therefore I avoided to offer any assistance or advice on normal constructional defects, but whenever the pressure was put on me by the Controller of Palaces (ex-Army general) for my personal attention I made occasional visits. Just because of the imposition of this kind of taboo, the *golies*, invariably manufactured emergent situations which necessitated on the spot study followed by some kind of work by male labour and skill. It is, however, beyond the scope of this narrative to give a detailed account of my experiences and knowledge of some of the mysteries of these Inner Palaces of Jammu and Kashmir.

Within a week of my joining the State service we set up our new home. My cousin sisters from Jaranwala came to stay with us. It also provided an opportunity for the two girls to receive their education at a girl's school in town. They were also company for my wife while I was away on duty. She often appeared quite reserved in those days and readily took to the new set up joyfully. She had tasted long separation without flinching and now she made me see that this round of life would depend on her companionship. Besides, I observed that she was not only interested in her own welfare as her ideal but strove unselfishly to make herself the link between my parents and her children. She was extremely fond of Sarla and so was I.

It was probably very early in 1931 that the heir apparent was born in Nice (France). The news was called to the Prime Minister, who ordered a holiday and a programme of rejoicings all over the state. Dr Karan Singh, the Union Minister for Tourism in the second Indira Gandhi cabinet, an ex-Governor of the Kashmir state, is that child, son of Maharaja Hari Singh, the last ruler of the state. His reign could not be smooth as the Indian political upsurge influenced the people of his state in demanding popular government with him as the constitutional head. It was the Muslim majority in the state, who was backward and became vocal in this demand. Earlier the movement was purely communal but later it allied itself with the Indian National Congress in British India.

At this occasion it seems necessary to write briefly about Islam. The Mohammedan religion took its birth in Western Asia, where it was embraced by the nomad races, to whom it provided the stimulus, the ardour and the bond of unity for a mission to win the lands and the goods of the non believers by the sword. There was a kind of brotherhood among the believers who had religious zeal. The plunder of India was a magnet that never ceased to attract successive hordes from the northwestern gates. As one set took possession of some territory, it tried to defend its possessions and this made subjugation of India by the invaders a gradual and protracted affair. The religion of the Prophet found a great attraction for the low caste depressed and despised among the Hindus but the latter having an elaborate theology offered a great deal of resistance to conversion. But it must be admitted that Islam assigned to the lowliest convert the full privileges of a believer. It has always appeared troubling to me that though there are more Mohammedans in India (Bharat and Pakistan) than in any other country, Indian Muslims have at no time exerted an influence corresponding to their numbers either in India or upon the Islamic world at large. The Mughal Empire was largely secular and when it became an ardent theocratic State in the time of Aurungzeb it began to disintegrate and in fact wrecked. When the British established themselves in India, the Muslims no longer remained men of war, and they, whether invaders or converts, remained inferior to the Hindus in learning and peaceful pursuits and this prevented them from occupying their share of administrative posts both in British as well as Indian India. When the British found a new awakening among the Hindus for self-government and later for full freedom they exploited the educated Muslims in towns to demand their share in the administration, admission to educational institutions and the rulers also sowed the poison of 'Divide and Rule', the effects of which were witnessed in communal riots and the establishment of 'Two Nation Theory' of Mr. Jinnah and consequent division of the country.

Here in Kashmir the Muslims were ruled and they had no ill will against the ruler, who was very secular in his outlook, but the fire of communalism was fanned from outside the state. About the close of 1930, riots broke out in the state. I recollect that Hindus of Jammu who had a preponderance in population over the Mohammedans, attacked Muslims, looted their shops and when the police started arrests they disposed off their booty by throwing the same away into open spaces, lawns attached to large houses – hundreds of new shoes were dumped overnight into my lawn. Although stable conditions were soon brought about in Jammu but the Muslims were astir all over the state. In Kashmir they burnt bridges and Government buildings. The British Government in India intervened and on the advice of the Resident, the ministerial appointments were given to senior British Indian officials.

It was prominently visible that those who excited the communal passions did not themselves jump into the communal fire. Even later in life I observed and can testify from my past experiences that those who are provided with basic needs of life, by and large, hate communal tendencies. The atrocities committed on the innocent and the poor in the name of religion can bring tears in the eyes of even gods. Sheikh Abdullah, the veteran Kashmir leader who incited the Muslims in the early days of his campaign, courted imprisonment but with the passage of time became the first prime minister of his state in 1947. How many unconcerned poor people received flogging or bullets in the name of law and order, and their families suffered hardships of life for the benefit which they neither understood nor received. I was then a part of the administration that ruled the state in the name of His Highness.

Like most of my colleagues, although I remained strictly honest in my profession and performance, I was gradually taking to a life of ease and club-going and becoming a man of society, but all was suddenly brought to a halt when in early 1934 after the birth of my third child, my wife fell ill with tuberculosis of the spine, which needed nursing, care, and a life full of hope to bring her back to recovery. I accepted the challenge wilfully, and ever since a new and closer understanding developed between my wife and I, who loved our children and for their sake she offered cooperative response to the long treatment, and I spent almost every spare minute by her side, talking and reading to her. This continued effort, good medical attention, and the Kashmir climate helped her to be back on her legs by the middle of 1936.

I was not a native of the Kashmir state and in accordance with the policy of His Highness's Government my services were retrenched in 1936 to make room for sons of the soil. While in service of the Jammu and Kashmir state I managed to live comfortably but had no surplus or a bank balance. Two sons were born to me in 1932 and the other in 1934 for which I was grateful to God's blessings. Unemployment now stared me in my face as I knew that there was recession all over the country and the openings for employment were few and far between. I decided to leave my family in my village while I went out to Karachi in search of work. I did not expect smooth sailing.

I felt that there were going to be hardships and a great deal of effort would be needed in the adventure. In fact we were living in a world in which there were hazards and in which every advance had to be won. There were opportunities for struggle and victory and those made life more interesting.

Sarla was already in her seventh year and she had not been enrolled in any school till then. She had, however, had her education at home and her street knowledge came from my father and it included reading, writing and arithmetic. I too helped her. She wrote and spelt her Urdu pretty well for her age. A Kashmiri *pandit* tutor was also employed to see that she maintained, if not excelled to standards laid down in the school curriculum. My parents and wife felt that my daughter was too young and delicate to go to a mixed school, where, it was reported, the boys often belaboured girls of their age. I never tried to find out about the correctness or otherwise of the report but I thought that there wasn't a school in Srinagar at a reasonable distance from our house where she could be sent. The tutor came to teach Sarla at the appointed hour every day. My mother conducted them both into her own room and installed them at a little side table and saw that no one disturbed them. Few days passed off well. The tutor never spoke a word to her except when he read over from her book or the copy book. Gradually she began to feel a peculiar disdain for him and only after she had been reprimanded for her behaviour did she agree to sit at the small table for her tuition. Perhaps, if he had shown the least symptom of kindness the spell of horror would have been broken but, during the two months or so that Sarla had lessons from him, he did his work as a routine and never displayed the smallest interest in the child. We had to drop him. Vinod was just beginning to learn his alphabet when we had planned to leave Srinagar for the plains and Kailash was only two years old.

Soon after my wife fell ill seriously in 1934, my mother's sister lost her husband and after the funeral ceremonies were over, my mother persuaded her to stay with us in Kashmir. I had been stricken with grief to have learnt about the death of my mother's brother-in-law but I was about three hundred miles away from the place where he died and could not be by his side when he was ailing seriously, in view of the condition my wife was at the time. I had known of his illness and his demise from the communications that my aunt sent me by post. Although it opened the wounds of grief afresh and made our tears flow once more when my aunt told me herself the details of his suffering and his end. She told me that his closing words were that he had full faith in me to take care of my aunt. I promised to do it and she is with us till today although her health is gradually giving way.

Bakht Singh had returned to India as a Christian missionary. He visited Srinagar and stayed with us. He was a changed person. The sort of ardour, which impels youth today to cinemas and to journals like Filmfare exhibiting accounts of upcoming pictures, of actors and actresses, had taken the form in Bakht Singh's case of romantic elevation to social service and to an intense interest in the state of his own soul. He was almost obsessed by the ideals of saintliness and was convinced of the supreme importance of not eating too much. I sat by his side whenever he sat for his daily prayers but he never appeared satisfied in living with us, and in a couple of days he moved into a houseboat, where he felt free to propagate his mission.

My wife's illness brought greater responsibility on my shoulders to spend a great deal of time with my children, although my parents showered all their love and care towards their upbringing. I was keen to provide the requisite emotional security of the parent-child relationship so that they do not develop unconscious tension, frustration or neglect. As our home was completely free from any kinds of quarrels or conflicts, the children were not under unwholesome influences.

Feelings and Incidents

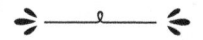

There are some memories never-to-be-forgotten in one's life of events which bring him face to face with situations of extreme anxiety or of great joy. Such incidents are of transitory nature, but their impressions are of permanent nature, and they produce feelings which come to one's mind again and again. I was once, riding alone on horseback through a forest of overgrown bushes. It was after dusk, and the sky was already dark. My horse was moving slowly along the beaten track which was visible because of its contrast with the surroundings. Suddenly the horse stopped. Around him I could only see the silhouettes of a few stunted shrubs. Neither pats nor spurs had any effect; the animal refused to move and his body trembled. Was there some living thing in the shadow beside him? In the dead silence of the dark and deserted place some invisible presence made itself felt. With this mysterious peril I was overtaken by extreme fear but I did not lose strength and energy. With a violent effort I forced my horse forward until it galloped away into the darkness beyond the forest area. I never knew whether the animal had shuddered at some imaginary fear or if we really had passed within reach of death.

    I purchased my first car – a Baby Austin or Austin 7 sometime in the middle of August 1931, and sought the assistance of a part time driver to learn driving. Within a few days of strenuous training I felt confident that I could go about without the trainer by my side. One evening towards the close of the month, I left my office at about four in the afternoon for inspection of works in the town. It must have taken me quite an hour or so to finish when I decided to drive out of town for a distance of thirty or forty miles from Srinagar and then to get back before dusk. On my return journey after I had covered about seven miles or so, and the sun was setting, I began to accelerate my drive as I found myself master of the road. For several minutes I neither crossed a truck or a car, nor could see any vehicle following me. All of a sudden the fast moving little car bumped over some depression in the road. I put my foot on the brake instantly, the car overturned and I was under it. My right arm was fractured and the left badly cut and bleeding profusely. I lay alone helpless, injured and bruised. Within a couple of minutes I heard the noise of an approaching truck or bus, and as soon as it came within yards, I yelled for help. The vehicle stopped and all the passengers came out either to see my plight or help me out of the mess. They lifted the little car bodily and turned it over away from my body and then lifted and placed me on the floor of the bus in a kind of gangway between the seats occupied by the passengers. The bus was going towards Anantnag and it was also the nearest station where I could get medical assistance. I received first aid immediately and was then kept in that suburban hospital for the night. The following morning I was moved to the State Hospital, Srinagar, where a large crowd had gathered whom I thanked from the stretcher while I was taken out from the ambulance car.

Once an article appeared in an Urdu weekly of Jammu regarding the rampant corruption in a local sub-division of the

Public Works Department of the state and the simultaneous suggestion by the editor that I should be posted in place of the officer who, it alleged, was corrupt. Both he and I were not only colleagues but were working under a common boss, who himself was known for his integrity, and felt puzzled into thinking that I was responsible for the appearance of that article. It was untrue. I was shocked by the conclusions drawn by my boss, whose respect for truth was insufficient in spite of the fact that he was himself scrupulously honest. The State Government had taken serious note of that article and acted promptly in meeting the popular demand. My boss however, being thoroughly annoyed with the whole episode and failing to resist the commands of his superiors, transferred that officer from the specific project to take my place and I was asked to work as staff officer in the Divisional Office – so to say as personal assistant to the Divisional Engineer to supervise the project. I worked as directed and in due course of time my boss felt that he had done me wrong, when I was given full charge of the project.

Having spent three winters in London I had seen fairly heavy snowfalls but I had never experienced motor driving while the snow fell. Here, in Kashmir, it was part of my assignment to see that the roads were kept clear of the thick snow for vehicular traffic and I had to go about the road in my own little car for inspection. Once, when I was returning from Tangmarg to Srinagar, the snow was falling fast and I had journeyed about a mile from Tangmarg when it became difficult to distinguish the road from the berms, of course the trees along the edges of the road demarcated its width. One of the men engaged on road maintenance raised his hand and requested me to stop and not to attempt to go further. He advised me to return to Tangmarg as the valley ahead towards Srinagar was in the thick of heavy snowfall. I did not take his advice as I thought that going back uphill may land me in greater difficulties. The snow continued as I drove along, so that even in the middle of the road it was between four and six inches deep. Although the top of the engine was well insulated by a thick quilt made to size, yet I feared trouble from the engine. Personally I was warmly clad with a thick tweed long coat. The evening, rather dusk, was drawing in as I plugged slowly onwards. In a journey of about four miles I had not met a single living soul. I was carrying no food or drink because, had travelling been normal, I should have been home in Srinagar by that time. In order to allow a car to pass which was going to cross mine bound for Baramulla, I turned the car through thick snow, the off-side front wheel, owing to a skid, sunk into a ditch which was frozen, leaving the car with me inside tipped to starboard. The other car passed along the trail left by me on the road and did not stop. I switched off the engine and looked as if I must spend the night. The nearest village was about a mile ahead. I decided to get out of the car and move to habitation but during the time that I spent on making up my mind the windows and doors were almost frozen stiff and it took me quite a time to even open a window, the tools being all in the boot at the rear of the car. I did not have sufficient strength to force open the door so I had to labour to remove sufficient snow to be able to squeeze my body out of the partially open door. I removed my shoes and stockings which were already soaked through, and leaving them inside the car I started to walk in my bare feet. At last I got near the village and called for help. I asked a couple of men to walk beside me up to the car with shovels so that I could get the car out of the rut. On reaching back to the point where I had left my car, they shovelled the snow aside and lifted it bodily and put it on the road. It took all my reserve of courage to start again on the snow clad and snow bound road to Srinagar where I knew my people would be anxiously awaiting my return. The journey was slow and arduous and it was past midnight when I reached home.

In my professional work I was once engaged in widening a road. In the process I had to pull down a retaining wall built in rubble which was all pointed with lime mortar. When dismantling was actually taken up, I observed that the wall was built without mortar and the engineer-in-charge, who had it built, camouflaged it by external painting. I remember to have remarked that both the contractor-builder and the engineer-in-charge must have conspired to build the wall below specifications and shared the savings between themselves. I felt quite certain about their guilt from what I had seen. Later, by a simple deviation in the project I had in hand, the estimated cost of work proved inadequate to complete the work. There were two courses open to me, one to send a revised estimate and secure its sanction while holding up progress of work and the other to build the long retaining wall below specifications and camouflage the external appearance in the same way as I had seen the one I had dismantled and thereby complete the job well in time and earn the 'shabash' of my superiors. I adopted the latter course successfully but felt miserable about my attitude towards a colleague who may have been involved in similar circumstances while building the wall which I dismantled. If I had given a reverse twist to my judgement by following my attention to his grace in preference to blaming him without reason, I would have been saved from the morose I suffered as a consequence.

I once read a story called *Open Country*. It tells of a university youngman named Percival, who was engaged to marry a young woman whose name was, let us say, Sylvia. He, tired of his books and attempts at learning, left the university, bought a trek-cart and wandered from place to place alone, asking, not knowledge, but peace of mind. His lady, who was intensely religious and orthodox, tied by habit and upbringing to the ways and customs of her set, was concerned with his departure from her accepted way of life. The book is exceedingly interesting and mostly consists of letters which passed between them. In one of his letters he writes, "I must take my own course. I think that every man must work out his own salvation." Her reply was, "What do you consider to be your way of salvation?" I am writing this entirely from memory but this is the essence of what passed between them and that in his reply he said that a man should hunt as a stag and run like the hare and that he should use all his faculties to the uttermost limits and his muscles to the breaking point – his emotions to the swooning point and then he should sleep like the dead. I believe that the name of the author was Maurice Hewlett, who wrote two sequels to it, *Halfway House* and *Rest Harrow* and in this latter book he ended with a happy marriage between the two. I was almost twenty-four and a university student in London, and did feel like Percival, to be in possession of an inexhaustible strength and could afford to squander it. My religious training regarding life's transience, and the incessant flight of time was out of the picture. I had read an Urdu couplet, *Ghafil tujhe gharhial yeh deta hai munadi, Gurdoon ne ghari umar ki ik aur ghata di,* (While you pay no attention, the hands of the clock move another round and you are another hour closer to the end). But what significance can this have for a young man who knows nothing of value of days, leave aside the value of hours or minutes.

 I must mention a highly educative lecture which I heard at the Brixton Town Hall in London when I was there for my studies. It concerned the subject of venereal diseases and the lecturer emphasised that syphilis, gonorrhoea centres of medical inspection had been opened by the London County Council and curative medicine was given free of cost. I was horrified by the statistics revealed by the learned lecturer as the prevalence of those diseases had been observed in the city. I understood the necessity of self control from a new aspect.

An incident occurred in the classroom at King's College, London, which I remember vividly. The professor of mathematics was writing on the black board with his back to the class and I threw a piece of chalk which hit his bald head. He turned around and enquired, "Who?" While I was about to rise and acknowledge my guilt the whole class rose up in their seats to protect me from punishment. I was a stranger and the kindness of my class fellows has remained a pleasant memory.

In India I had no training in any craft, therefore I lagged in smithy and carpentry practicals. I was once ridiculed when the foreman in charge of carpentry laid some wood shavings on my head and then drew the attention of the class that I was being crowned as the 'king carpenter' for my inefficiency in the craft.

Bakht, my dear friend, who is now a Christian missionary, was a Sikh gentleman before going to London for his studies. He and I stayed together. Bakht felt, one day, very strongly that he should discard his long hair and beard which was out of place in the country of our sojourn. Thus he had a clean-shave one day when he returned from college and it was soon followed by a hair cut. He used his turban for quite a time to conceal his hair cut for some time more, and then started using a felt hat.

When I was at Quetta, I had Jack – an Alsatian in the house. He was very faithful and equally intelligent. He could frighten any stranger by his frantic barking and it was hardly possible for anyone to get past the entrance to the house unless Jack was directed to keep quiet. Once during the period of the second World War the night warden of the area in which we lived, was on his round to see that no one violated the rules of the 'black out'. I heard Jack barking beyond our main gate, and came out to find out who it was. The dog stopped barking and stood patiently by my side while I talked to the warden. The dog trotted off towards the verandah when he was told to "Go back." On another occasion when I was laid in bed for a few days after a minor operation in my bedroom, the dog would insist to lie underneath my bed and it became his nightly routine as long as I was not fully recovered.

My daughter had a small cat as her playmate. Jack must have observed the affinity between the two and on that basis he adopted the cat as his little sister and the two together sat side by side at meal time. It was a great experience to watch Jack and the kitten sipping their milk from a common bowl. When our family had tabooed meat diet for a period of a few years, Jack, too, relished his changed diet of vegetables and chapatis.

When communal disturbances broke out in Quetta a year before the country's Partition, I found him restless and he continued in that condition and lying awake day and night, till things became normal. When we started packing for leaving Quetta he looked very unhappy, and while we were loading our luggage in a truck, he disappeared on his own. This last act, we failed to understand, as we had every intention to maintain his association both during the journey and keep him as long as he lived. We failed to find him, but a week later he was reported dead via a postal communication.

It was sometime in April 1947, when as a result of communal tension I witnessed one of the wildest eruptions of mob fury and hysteria in Lahore. After seeing how the area inside Shah Almi Gate which was the hub of the Hindu population and their shopping centre – not so fashionable but known for fair prices, the Muslim mob had burnt a sizable portion of the ancient city in a few hours, wrecked and burnt many houses and shops, I decided to leave the city for a more congenial town for the safety of my people. It was a city gone mad, that is how I felt. I booked seats by a railway train leaving Lahore for Dehradun on 17th May, 1947. When the evacuation of minorities was settled between the two parts of the Indian subcontinent, then I left for Amritsar and the horrible scenes I saw on my way from Ambala to Amritsar have remained in my memory, and ever since I am convinced that people – the people of this subcontinent whether Muslims, Hindus or Sikhs, who can kill each other in the name of religion – are capable of greater fury and bloodshed when they are aroused against the 'haves' as being responsible for their lack of basic needs.

I remember an occasion in 1947, when I was working as the Secretary of the Refugee Association in Dehradun, when I took some gifts for families of displaced persons. One family that I visited consisted of a widow and her four children whose ages ranged from five to eleven years. The mother was seriously ill. When I offered some sweets to the youngest child, he refused to eat it – "Give these sweets to mataji who is sick." When the mother heard this she wept and the little boy comforted her by saying, "Mataji, don't cry, soon I will grow up and study and earn a lot of money with which to buy all the things and then we will live well."

The New Setup

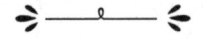

After leaving my job in Kashmir I wasn't sure of another employment in the near future. Civil engineering, at the time, offered no promise. It occurred to me that I should start as a consulting architect in Karachi, as its Corporation allowed only qualified engineers and architects to submit plans for constructing buildings in its area of jurisdiction. I had neither friends nor relations there, on whom I could count for contacts and I could see the difficulties ahead. Anyway I found no hurdle in enlisting myself as an Architect Class I for the Karachi Corporation.

A firm of engineers styled as Messrs. Herman and Mohatta, I was told, were on the lookout for a civil engineer. I went over to their office and met Mr. Herman, to whom I gave a resume of my scholastic qualifications and of practical experience in the profession. I impressed him. He then introduced me to Mr. Mohatta, the director of finance, who explained to me the type of work for which the firm stood in need of the services of a qualified engineer. He was satisfied with my credentials and offered to employ me on eighty rupees a month. When I flatly refused the offer, he raised it to one hundred and fifty rupees per *mensem*. I made a counter offer to him suggesting that I would not mind working for them without a salary for one month, and at the end of that period terms of service may be negotiated on a rational basis. This was accepted with the proviso that I would start work immediately. I agreed and faced the situation in the right spirit. Within a week the director fixed my salary at three hundred rupees, which I accepted provisionally for the first month and that my terms of service would be finally negotiated after the expiry of that period. The firm, however, within the month allowed me the use of the company's car for official work and added a house allowance of fifty rupees per month. Thus I dropped the idea of starting practice in my profession.

The firm had taken up building contracts for the Army and their supervision and management was entrusted to me. Alongside, I was asked to prepare a lump sum quotation for building an *abattoir* (slaughter house) in Lahore for the Army in India. Within the first six weeks I secured a number of works in Lahore as well as in Peshawar.

My aunt Lakshmi Devi, who had informally adopted my elder son Vinod Chandar, had been left a widow after my uncle's death in 1934. She lived in Jalalpur Jattan and with the strictest regard to economy had managed to live on my uncle's slender means. My aunt who was older than my mother had a much stronger build and used to roughing. My mother was afraid of her stingy ways and was not quite confident if she would be able to adjust herself in our house if we decided to accommodate her as one of our own family. I was able to convince my mother that my aunt's coming over to live with us for the rest of her life was quite welcome. We had her with us, and she proved herself to be an asset. With the shattered health that my wife had in 1935-36, both she and my mother looked after my children. Respect for old age does not come naturally to children, it is the result of education, which they received from me in abundance. They loved my parents and my aunt. When I went to Karachi for the first time, my wife went to our native place for a short while till I settled again somewhere.

All mothers have their children but my wife was a real companion to them even at their tender age. It was always a treat to see how after her recovery from that long illness, she found the greatest pleasure in associating herself with the childish activities of her three children. I had brought them down to Karachi, where I had set up a new home for them. I desired to settle down for the sake of my children, who, I felt, should be brought up in congenial and stable surroundings. She was immensely home-proud, she seldom went out, and we were members of no clubs, and rarely called on anyone in Karachi. We knew only a few families and did not care to extend our acquaintanceship. By this process our three children who were aged approximately seven, five and three hardly sought relaxation away from us. We had no servants in the house and she never seemed to mind that, in spite of the fact that only six months earlier she, on account of her invalidity, received attention and service in abundance from my parents, as also from attendants.

By March 1937, I had shifted from Karachi to Lahore in order to supervise closely the construction of the *abattoir* and organise its execution so that the job could be completed within the contract period of six months. I acquired on a rental a very big bungalow with expansive lawns in the Lahore cantonment for my residential purposes. Two or three rooms had English type baths fitted in. All this was for seventy rupees a month, which the firm paid. I was also given an increment of Rs. 150/= per month and was provided with a car and driver on the firm's account. Two peons were attached to me within a week of this new acquisition. My parents and my aunt Lakshmi Devi joined us. Although my financial circumstances had now improved considerably, my wife remained simple and unassuming. She gave the front seat to the elders in the house and received their immense love in return. She had particular reverence for my people, rustic or urban.

[Photo captioned "1937, KARACHI"] [Photo captioned "1940"]

The construction work had an excellent take off, as within the first two months the entire steel frame for the four-storied building was in position and some of the ancillary buildings were nearing completion. Just then in some quarter of the city the Hindus started expressing indignation against the construction of this slaughter house, which was intended to produce large quantities of tinned beef for the Army in India. It did not take many days before protests turned into a full-fledged agitation not only in Lahore, but in the whole of Punjab and Sindh. Pressure was brought upon the proprietors in Karachi and a number of leaders approached me to close down construction and when we expressed our inability to agree with them we were threatened with serious consequences. The directors did not like to put up any resistance against the public opinion, but I persuaded them to leave the whole matter in my hands, as any voluntary action by the firm to close or slacken the job would result in serious financial losses. I saw that the Government suspended the works in view of serious civil commotion and the directors were immensely pleased with my performance. I was still not sure if the work would be resumed, therefore, while retaining a partial office establishment as also my parents and aunt in Lahore, my family and I left for Srinagar to have a holiday till such time that the Government took final decision to give up the project altogether and bow before the public agitation. We had six weeks or so in Kashmir before it became necessary for me to return to my office for preparation of bills and claims arising out of the foreclosure. After completing all that was necessary for final settlement, I returned to Karachi along with my mother, aunt and my family.

I prepared and tendered for the construction of earthquake resisting buildings both commercial and residential for the Quetta reconstruction. It may be mentioned here that Quetta had a very severe earthquake in 1935, when the whole town was razed to the ground. The town was again being rebuilt. I succeeded to secure a few contracts from the Military Engineering Services of the then Government of India and later from the North Western Railway for my firm, who posted me there. My family and I reached Quetta sometime in March 1938 to settle down there till the completion of those contracts. But we were beginning to realise that the education of our children had already had a setback and it was time that I chose a station to make a permanent home. The weather of Quetta gave us a good reception as it resembled Srinagar.

The firm gave me an increment of one hundred and fifty rupees per month in my salary in addition to several facilities like a free furnished house, free conveyance, a personal servant, a driver for the car and a personal assistant. Thus my wife had any amount of free time as she had not to attend to trivials of the household, which were looked after by my aunt who found the greatest joy in doing that, and the servants were there for all other jobs which were difficult or unbecoming for the old lady. Thus my wife has no day time troubles about which she could complain and yet she was always home stuck. Her children loved her and she loved them and she had, or for that matter, I had never employed an *aya* (nanny) for entrusting my children to their care.

As soon as the schools opened after the winter vacations, the children were admitted to the schools. The co-education of children was taboo, therefore Sarla had to go to a girls school and the boys to a different school. Every morning they were taken and brought back in the afternoon in my car. The schools did not provide any school bus and there were no public conveyances either, and we lived in the cantonment area quite a couple of miles away from the educational institutions.

For almost a year I carried on with my assignment, but I realised that my technical knowledge and experience, valuable no doubt, had a limited earning capacity. I could see that my own employers, who had vast financial resources and business acumen, had hired me and a number of my colleagues with engineering qualifications at a high marginal profit. On the other hand I, in spite of six years service in the Kashmir state, and already about three years in the service of the firm, was still without a bank balance. All this was not a happy picture and I still possessed the urge for growth, and a desire to have an income from which I should be able to save for bad weather in life. I was never so ambitious to desire the moon to come down and to keep me company.

I decided to leave the firm and even face the hardships and difficulties that I knew to be inherent in any new adventure without adequate financial resources. I could, therefore, not start out with any cut and dried picture of what I should finally aim at. I hoped that through my own technical work as a consulting engineer on earthquake resisting structures new avenues of earning will come to the fore. There was hardly any competition in the field but people's capacity to pay good consultation fees was exceedingly poor. It did not, therefore, bring in a return which could give me confidence. As luck would have it Messrs. Siemens Schusest - a leading German firm manufacturing electrical goods and well known for their quality products, offered me an exclusive agency for pushing their sales in Baluchistan. I accepted the offer and within a couple of weeks they equipped me with bulbs, electrical metres, hot plates, irons, switchgear and electrical accessories. They also included Telefunken radios. All materials supplied on two months credit during which period most of them were sold off, and in fact more than fifty percent were disposed of in less than one month. The commission was handsome and the sale was good even at the start.

While I was struggling with my new venture in Quetta, my mother who was reported unwell, was at Jaranwala. My mind was not at rest. I left my business in the hands of a trusted lieutenant so that I could give my whole time to my mother's care. She was a great courageous soul, that I had known all my life, but her courage had grown with her illness. When I asked her how she felt, her answer was "Alright," although she knew too well that she was hastening towards her end. No medicine seemed to work, and gradually over the days she began to sink. She wanted to know about employment and it was my uncle who conveyed to her how well I was doing after leaving the firm. She could accept that version and retorted by saying *"maa beemar, beta bekaar*", i.e., mother unwell and the son without any gainful employment – was not a happy situation for the family. A week before her fatal condition she expressed a desire that *mundan* (initiation) ceremony of her two grandsons be performed before she collapsed. We could, however, see that such a course would bring us into ridicule, as it was a time when she needed the greatest attention. Then the time came when her breath became fainter and fainter with each passing hour. Overwhelmed with anxiety I walked out of the room where she lay and paced and prayed for strength to bear the trial to which I was being put to. She died. The whole family including my uncle and his family were all present. She had the traditional funeral. Many friends and relations joined the mournings and she was cremated with age-old customs.

My mother was an inspiration. Her death was a great setback in my life at that time. My father bore her loss quite well. We all returned to Quetta and with faith that we all possessed we drew the requisite strength to do our duties. The business was going well but when the Second World War broke out in September 1939, Siemens were simultaneously declared an enemy concern and as a consequence my business in electrical goods and radios came to a close almost suddenly. It meant a new hurdle but this proved a tonic. On the one hand I started negotiations with Messrs. General Electric Co. and on the other I enlisted myself as a building contractor in the government departments. In both directions I met with success. Now, Messrs. Nanda & Co., the name under which I commenced distributorship for GEC, and secured a building contract. The difficulties that had arisen were solved and they left me richer in experience which helped me transcend in the two lines of business which I had then adopted.

Both my wife and I were watchful of our children in their childhood to see that they do not go unchecked on heedless trails. I did not encourage them to be 'clever' nor would I accept falsehoods or small acts of dishonesty which could form firm habits over the years. After the death of my mother and my father's indifference towards family affairs I had taken upon myself the position of the head of the family. I concerned myself mainly with the inherent integrity of all members. Even little twistings of truths, 'minor' thefts of small things, and intended wrong impressions irritated me. I had it plainly known to everyone that by freedom from corrosive sham and blurred values which accompany deceit, honesty will find firm roots in the whole family. It did work.

The Second World War was raging in full fury. Germans were proving to be invincible. Many countries had already fallen against their might. The alteration that took place in the two decades since the end of the First World War in the psychology of the German peoples was so vast and powerful that it influenced their minds. It was a change so profoundly and dynamically affecting the entire German nation in its attitude to other nations of the world that it influenced the history of civilization of mankind. And when the Japanese entered the theatre of war on the side of Germans against the Allies they showed that within the space of less than two generations they, who were regarded as unfit for association with western nations, attained an efficiency in war and superiority over the known leading nations. They had, by collectively submitting themselves to a new kind of social inheritance, achieved extraordinary excellence in warfare. I have no desire to write even a brief history of the Second World War but it did help India in bringing near her cherished goal of Independence. It was the exploding of an atom bomb over Hiroshima in Japan that brought about Japanese surrender and psychologically it brought degeneration also among the Germans.

The New Setup

Both the victors and the vanquished in World War II suffered losses and privations. The rapid fire machine guns, the long range cannons and the 'blockbuster' bombs of the war made the lives of both the combating forces and the civilians quite miserable. We were far from the theatre of war but when the Germans were approaching Stalingrad and they were pushing ahead, we in Quetta began to feel unsafe and it was being openly said that if Germans score victory over Stalingrad in Russia, Quetta would be within bombing range of the enemy. I remember to have made a reasonable study of the conditions through which Great Britain passed in the early years of war and particularly during the Battle of Britain in September 1940. For a month and a half the Londoners hardly slept and it seemed Hitler had decided to destroy the city and to kill all its hundred million inhabitants. He did not succeed but more than twenty thousand Londoners were killed and many seriously wounded. The city was battered nightly for one hundred days and nights with incendiary bombs with great crashes and fires so that in a month's time every street in London, it was reported, had its fires. People lived in constant terror, and yet the large majority remained calm outwardly and did not exhibit the kind of panic the people of Calcutta exhibited after the first aerial visitation over the city by the Japanese. As an engineer, when I studied the nature of their air raid shelters I came across an account that people slept on pavements of London's tube stations, men, women and children. People of all nationalities residing in London kept themselves from fear by playing cards, giving concerts and arranging games for children and many comedians moved about on those platforms where people gathered. From the press reports I observed that the effect of the blast was a great deal similar to that of an earthquake with which people of Quetta were quite familiar. Gas pipes were cracked and water pipes burst with the incendiary bombs and it was all chaos, but gradually those who were unhurt felt sure that the falling bombs were not for them and it is probably this humour that saved their sanity.

[When in 1965 the war broke out between Pakistan and India even the sound of an aeroplane passing overhead disturbed my people in Chandigarh. The shriek of the warning hooter which implied "Take Cover" and the wail which indicated "All Clear" was a constant nuisance every night but here too we gradually got used to the inconvenience and the black out which my people had some experience during 1944 at Quetta. Luckily the war lasted only a few days and Chandigarh had no aerial attacks.]

While the war continued away from Quetta and in fact we were nowhere nearer the theatre of combat after the Germans suffered crushing defeat at Stalingrad, my business flourished. Some English officers who were working as reservists in India, told us that their families in England were suffering from all kinds of shortages as England was blockaded, but we had rationing in petrol and sugar and even that could hardly be called serious. Contractors who were working for the Army were given coupons far in excess of their needs as it was expected that they would make requisite petrol available for those who issued the coupons. Same was true about sugar rationing. We earned and we spent lavishly. With every successful large contract I added an extra car to my fleet – at one time I had four of them in my possession, but for most of the years I was able to afford three.

With financial prosperity local people of all communities and shades of opinion began to dispose of my liberty. The Railwaymen's Federation of Quetta selected me as their president for three years. The Khaksars gave me a march past and made me the local president. *Bazem-i-Iqbal*, Quetta, an organisation comprising the Urdu poets of Baluchistan made me to head the society, regardless of the fact whether I could compose and poetry myself. The Arya Samaj made me a member of the Managing Committee of the local D.A.V. School. The lovers of Hindi held a Hindi *Sammelan* (Conference) and I presided over the meeting. There was hardly a function for which I did not merit all the honour but I could contribute money, not that all organisations looked to me for financial help. For societies that needed it badly, some wanted my association because they felt that I could secure certain privileges for them from the government, as I had gradually built up good contacts with the local officials. One of my colleagues in business told me that some of the older well established people were jealous of me. That I told him was human nature but it is better to be envied than pitied.

I began to expand my business. I opened three branches in the course of time – at Karachi, Lahore and one at Katro (Sindh). At the last station I had a branch manager whom I trusted and gave him the general power of attorney but he absconded with fairly large deficits, but I bore the temporary storm aroused by his flight. He did not return to Quetta for over three years and when he did he apologised and I accepted it.

I also became a member of *Anjuman-i-Watan* of which Khan Abdul Samad Khan was the leader and he was known as 'Baluchistan Gandhi', and through him made friends with many Muslim *Maliks*. My business, too, brought me in closer contact with many local *jagirdars* (landlords), who were also running identical businesses, namely army contracts. The Khan of Kalat, who ruled over the state of Kalat – part of Baluchistan invited me both as a guest and as a consultant to his capital and gave me VIP treatment. On the strength of these associations, organisations looked to me for benevolent patronage, which to my mind in that setting, was the exclusive privilege of aristocracy to perform.

Unlike the exacting conditions of life in my village even in a prosperous family like ours, the family and the daily routine for the members were much easier at Quetta. By the time I was eight years old, my childish pranks, mischief and laughter had largely disappeared in spite of the fact that I was the darling of the family. But as it was the general custom that responsibility for handling all kinds of odd jobs were given to the children, I too had to fall in line with the practice to some extent. This process developed in me the air of a little grown-up – in my childhood. I became anxious that my children must deviate from that path and should be allowed to have the maximum amount of carefree growth during their childhood.

The children grew up as children. Sarla even when she was preparing for her matriculation examination was not taking any interest in our household work. When she was not at school, she spent her time with her girl friends, provided however we did not go for a picnic, or to see a picture. At times we arranged a campfire in our own premises. We used to sit around and spend the evening in merry making. Both the boys participated equally in those meetings or in the rendezvous. We were also fond of social meets and often invited friends to teas or dinners and vice versa. Life was full of lustre.

During the World War that was still raging the Congress started the 'Quit India' movement. Although the Government adopted all kinds of repressive measures to crush the movement, yet they had obviously realised that India was determined to throw off the British yoke. They sent out a Mission headed by Sir Stafford Cripps to negotiate with the Indian political leaders for setting up in India a representative National Government. Although the Mission was not successful, yet it paved the way for further progress. We began to reckon how the likely changes would effect the political setup in Quetta.

The New Setup

Father & Scouts   Mother & daughter

The family in Quetta.
Front: daughter Sarla. Sitting: wife Ram Pyari, father
Mathra Das, cousin sister Shanti.
Standing: son Vinod, brother-in-law Pyare Lal Bhasin, self, and son Kailash.

Mud Houses and Brick Walls

The Eminent Businessman in Quetta, seated center right.

1946 - 48

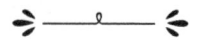

Mr. Attlee, the British Prime Minister, through the Cabinet Mission Plan in 1946, announced that "My colleagues are going to India with the intention of using their utmost endeavour to help her attain her freedom as steadily and fully as possible. What form of government to replace the present regime is for India to decide, but our desire is to help her set up forthwith the machinery for making that decision. ..." Charged with the work the Cabinet Mission and the Viceroy negotiated with the leaders of political parties but the differences between two major parties, namely the Congress and the Muslim League were great and an agreement under the circumstances did not seem possible. The Mission, however, all the same, formulated their proposals. I need not go into the pros and cons of their proposals as it has nothing to do with my own biography but the Congress having accepted them decided to form the Council of Ministers with the Viceroy as the Constitutional Head whether or not the Muslim League agreed to participate. Mr. Jinnah fixed the 16th August, 1946,[23] as a day of 'Direct Action' by the Muslims and one of his main followers declared, "... If Britain puts us under Hindu *Raj*, let us

---

23 This is one year ahead of Independence.

tell Britain that the destruction and havoc that the Muslims will do in this country will put into shade what Chengiz Khan did." It did not turn out to be a mere threat. Many towns in the country where the Muslims had majority and including Calcutta where a Muslim League government was in power had an orgy of arson, loot and rape the like of which India had not witnessed before. The flames of communal vendetta reached the far corners of India, and in Quetta the Mohammedans attacked Hindus, who did not retaliate at all. I was a victim and my elder son found shelter with people unknown to us for a whole night and I must record here that he was helped and protected throughout that dreadful night by a Mohammedan friend. One of my nephews was also hurt by a flying brickbat and I had a number of injuries, and if the street in which the Muslim mob attacked us was not completely dark where we were not visible while we took shelter behind a fly proof wire gauze door, we would have seen our end. Neither I nor my nephew shrieked as the brickbats fell on the door leaf. Within minutes of the Muslim's attack on the Hindu *mohallas* (neighbourhoods), the police was on the job and the streets were cleared of the miscreants, at least where we were hiding about a half mile from our house. No transport was available, hence both of us walked back home while bleeding on the way. My aunt fell a-sobbing when she saw me and all others looked terrified and worried about the missing child (my son) who was delivered to us in a car in the early hours of the following morning.

We had a fairly large number of relatives living with us at the time. They had come to Quetta on a holiday, and after what they had witnessed, the charm of Quetta was gone and they were keen to get back. Many Hindus having decided to return to safer places, the trains leaving Quetta were always crowded and it was a problem to find berths, leave aside reservations. I decided to send them back within a week but while they were there, the nights hung very heavy on all of us. From time to time every night there came the uproarious shouting of "*Allah-o-Akbar*" and sometimes in the distance the rattle of musketry. These things kept everyone awake in the night except those children who did not understand the events. My two next door neighbours were Mohammedans whom we suspected for an unfriendly act, but they too had their own fears. As soon as I was able to clear the guests from Quetta, we moved to the cantonment area where we felt safety of life. We now began to plan our future under the changed conditions.

Quetta was, incidentally, having elections – the first of its kind in Baluchistan for a representative advisory council to the Agent of the Governor General. I was fighting as a nominee of the *Anjuman-i-Watan* – a sister organisation of the Indian National Congress in Baluchistan. It was in fact in connection with one of the election meetings that my son and I had gone out and were later caught or attacked by the Muslim mob. In spite of what had happened, I still wanted to fight the elections while my family members were averse to the proposition. I was defeated by a few votes and to my utter astonishment I learnt that my wife, in thanksgiving to the Almighty for my defeat, distributed alms to the poor.

There was bitterness and trouble throughout the country and the Viceroy Lord Wavell was still trying to persuade the Muslim League to join the Government and finally he succeeded when the Muslim League decided on 15th Oct 1946 to join. This brought some relief to those who were feeling insecure. I felt that it was the time to move to Lahore. I withdrew my two sons from the D.A.V. School, Quetta so that they could join some school in Lahore. My daughter Sarla was already studying in Hans Raj (D.A.V.) College for Women in Lahore. By the beginning of

November 1946, we were able to rent a house – an annexe of Rai Bahadur Sohan Lal's house opposite the University grounds.

I did not close the establishment at Quetta but began to take interest for starting professional work in Punjab and in a couple of months suitable premises were fixed up in the old Anarkali near The Mall, Lahore. The Congress and League being as apart as they were before the latter joined the Government, the communal passions kept on mounting and the administration had become lax. The English officers were no longer interested as they were marking time for their final departure. The situation was growing from bad to worse with unchecked rioting in many parts of the country and with a paralyzed Central Government, the new Viceroy Lord Mountbatten, who replaced Lord Wavell when the latter resigned, suggested Partition of the country which meant partitioning Bengal and Punjab. While the Congress seemed amenable, although Gandhiji opposed it all the time, the League, being intent upon wresting as much land from United India as possible, encouraged violence and bloodshed. Leaving politics aside we found life very unsafe for us in Lahore. We never went out in the evenings, nor would we stir from our digs while street fighting was reported to us in any part of the city. In the premises, part of which we were occupying, there were many tenants all of whom began to fraternise with each other and whenever we sensed any trouble in the vicinity, we gathered in one place, usually the most secure and ready to face any eventuality. The tidings were received and talked over with the liveliest manifestations of terror and pity although the aged like my aunt kept saying "*Ram Ram*", or moving their lips in silent prayer. From time to time some good friend of ours would come in and tell us how and where the trouble was progressing. Things were in a terrible state, several parts of Lahore were in flames. Early in May 1947, we decided to leave Lahore for

Dehradun with as little as possible, but we found it difficult to find transport which could take us to the Railway Station. We had our seats reserved and our friend offered us the use of his station wagon up to the station. We took the train in time and arrived in Dehradun the next morning, where we were welcomed by a friend of the family. Within a week or so, we moved to Mussoorie in a large rented house.

The Partition having been accepted officially on 3rd June, 1947, and a White Paper issued on the day, it became clear to us that we have paid a very heavy price for our freedom. But having paid it, or our leaders having agreed to pay it, the people would reconcile and settle down to constructive work for improving their lot. That is how I began to feel, and looked forward to an opportunity when I could return to Quetta and live amicably with my Muslim friends in the new country of Pakistan. I had no fears. My own office informed me that conditions there had improved and the two communities have adopted a healthy attitude of 'forgive and forget'. The business was normal and that I could be back with my family in my own home, and that Quetta would remain quite free from disturbances after the Partition of the country had been announced. I accepted the advice, to the extent that I alone went to Quetta by plane, and found a warm welcome from everyone I met. Although it was really peaceful there, we read and heard woeful tales of carnage in many places in India. Many people were of the view that Hindus of Pakistan were quite safe as millions of Muslims were hostages in India and for fear of retaliatory measures by the Hindus in India, the Muslims will show the requisite tolerance towards the Hindu minority. Lesser people took the other view that whenever the majority community in one country treated the minority country with hostility, the majority community in the other country would retaliate and a vicious cycle of extermination of minorities would set in. It was also announced that India would be finally divided into two states on 14th August 1947, the day on which Lord Mountbatten inaugurated the Dominion of Pakistan. In the first week of August '47, I was told by my Muslim friends that my life would not be safe and that I should make arrangements to fly out to or get to India before 7th August. I accepted their advice and was back in Mussoorie on the 10th August 1947, and the Indian Dominion was born on the 15th.

The Congress government under the leadership of Pandit Jawaharlal Nehru at the Centre and all the Chief Ministers of several states heading Congress ministries owed their existence to the halo of the freedom movement. Their training was mainly nonviolent civil resistance against a foreign power and its bureaucracy. They had little experience of administration and with the common enemy removed, the unity of the movement days lost its meaning. The Muslim civilian officers had opted for Pakistan and Hindu counterparts for India. The Army had been divided on a communal basis. Communal troubles began within a couple of days – murder, death, cruelty on both sides particularly in divided Punjab and Bengal. The evacuation of minorities was considered the only feasible solution.

VISHAV BHAVAN

Part VII: Partition and Resettlement

Nilokheri

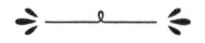

Once the question of mass evacuation of Hindus from West Pakistan had been settled, East Punjab and the areas bordering it were suddenly faced with a multitude of humanity who had suddenly lost every material possession, and within a short space of time human beings were moving about like disturbed ants. I had left Lahore earlier with my family some time in May 1947, and moved to Mussoorie, 'the Queen of the Hills'. My uncle and his family and all my in-laws were among the people who were to be evacuated under the protection of the Indian Army. The Government of India set up a transit camp at Amritsar and an Army Administration which worked day and night for the movement of Hindus from inside Pakistan. I left my abode and my family in the hills and in order to secure the evacuation of my relatives to Amritsar at an early date, I went down to Amritsar. Whatever I witnessed on my way in the train and the carnage in Amritsar in dealing with Muslim evacuees, and the reciprocity of the vice versa of the train loads of dead bodies of Hindus moved to Amritsar by the Indian Railways, is the sad story of the inhumanity that prevailed at the time. I have no desire to describe the awful scenes that I saw or heard. It is enough to say here that they were heart-rending.

Somehow, with or without my effort, my relatives reached the transit camp around the middle of September, from where they moved to places where they could get welcome shelter, but the place that came under the impact of migration was Kurukshetra, a place which was and always will be on the lips of every student of history. It was here that Free India had to welcome without warning a million helpless souls. Immediate relief was provided to wipe their tears, but they had to be put to work to render them self reliant citizens. With this in view the State set up an experimental vocational training centre where some of the displaced persons could be trained in certain vocations under the guidance of Shri S.K. Dey, a volunteer social worker. This centre was moved to the jungle land of Nilokheri – a tiny village near Kurukshetra. He advertised for a Civil Engineer, who could build both man and township and was prepared to share the hardships of life with the refugees and face the inclemencies of weather and the risks involved in marshy jungle land while clearing it. I met Shri Dey in Delhi. He drove me to Nilokheri and on the way he unfolded his dream about the future India as also his own past life, which helped me make up my mind to join him in that noble task.

In passing I would add a few lines about Shri S.K. Dey who impressed me immensely and I must confess that I learnt many new lessons about life and human society during my stay at Nilokheri almost entirely through my association with him. He hailed from East Bengal, completed his electrical engineering – a Master's degree from an American university in 1939, when nations of the world were in the throes of the worst economic crisis. Even America, where employment is known to be always around the corner for the asking, had millions out of jobs. Shri S.K. Dey found a job – the digging of the foundations for a large building under erection, in order to earn enough for the yearnings of his 'aching stomach'. He told me that his hands and feet were soon in blisters but he earned nine dollars and was ordered to get out as he was not fit for the job according to his foreman. So this Master of Science had to take to the open road. In the intervening years between that event and my meeting and staying with him at Nilokheri he had found comfortable, lucrative employment with Messrs. Victor X-ray Corporation of America and had at the time of the Partition of India left his princely palace in Lahore to the mud hut he was occupying in the jungleland of Nilokheri. He designed the scheme of Nilokheri with an eye to the eventual balanced economy of the whole country. The once legendary villages of India, neglected through generations and bled white by our British masters were to be given a special treatment on the lines envisaged in this experimental scheme which Shri Dey called The *Mazdoor Manzil* (The Worker's Destiny). This township was therefore, to be basic in concept and execution, for the elements of social structure promised by our leaders – namely a socialistic pattern of society. Besides, this experiment aimed at transforming relief into rejuvenation of the refugees. The author of the scheme believed that this would be the forerunner of the total war against poverty, ignorance and disease, which must be waged and that he would be able "to integrate the best features of communism in Russia, capitalism in America, and the spiritual heritage of our own country, with malice towards none and welcome to all."

My task, in planning and building Nilokheri of Shri Dey's conception, was by no means easy. The construction of the township to house a thousand families was not an end in itself but the displaced people in my charge had to be rehabilitated - their livelihood was to be kept in view all the time. Among the refugees there was a complete lack of bricklayers, carpenters, blacksmiths and other skilled workers required for construction.

They had, therefore, to be trained and the requisite supervising staff had to be trained not only in engineering practices but in developing new social values. It became necessary for me to eliminate the middleman – the contractor, altogether so that the displaced persons could draw the maximum benefits of their employment during the construction period, and become self-reliant. I would admit that a contractor's resources could have been helpful if construction was the main objective. Workers on the project formed themselves into small cooperative groups of their own choice, who received payment for their work on the basis of results of their effort, which they gradually improved both in quantity and quality. The training of workers and supervisors was carried on simultaneously both at the central polytechnic and in the field on the works, and the trainers also earned or received stipends during the period of learning.

It was an experiment in construction amidst adverse conditions of all sorts. Food shortage, materials shortage and requisite labour shortage and above all the watchword of the Government to spend within the distress budget, which meant economy in all directions including specifications, finishing or furnishing, and yet to produce everything structurally sound. Thus it was a lesson in adventurous planning, and of bringing into existence a small town against all odds natural or man made, for the sake of the people and their prestige.

If I were to write all that actually happened and everything that concerned the establishment and growth of the township, it would fill many a page. As for the technical side, the planning and building, with which I was engaged, there were two distinct processes. The former was purely dreaming a dream while the latter was fundamentally living a dream. Between the two, the difference was of sky and earth. I could not afford to remain in the sky but remain all the time on the ground being faced by blatant facts of shortages of all kinds and the fear of being pushed aside by political pundits who were not prepared to spend anything beyond the accepted per capita subsidy for refugees in general.

We struggled in this marshy land to develop a modern basic town which was expected to have its circle of influence in the surrounding villages, whose economy was to be linked with it. It was assessed that it would affect an area of about 80 to 100 square miles. Many dignitaries both Indian and foreign visited the place, but it was only when Mr. Chester Bowles, the US Ambassador in India paid a visit and examined its underlying approach to the development of rural India that the Government of India with the cooperation of the USA worked out a workable scheme for community development. India was divided approximately into five thousand blocks and each block was to be placed under a Block Development Officer for intensive work by combining subsidies by the two governments with cooperative effort of the people inhabiting the block. Nilokheri, thus, gave birth to the Ministry of Community Projects and Cooperation of which Shri S.K. Dey became the first Union Minister.

When this scheme was taking shape I had been posted in Bengal to build Fulia township for the displaced persons uprooted from East Pakistan. It was intended to be similar in concept to Nilokheri but the financial provisions were further curtailed by the Government of India. I built the town complete with all services in about fifteen months and I was then transferred to the West Bengal government to prepare detailed schemes for eight development blocks in that area.

Whether it was Nilokheri or Fulia, any towns for that matter, Delhi could build them through the agency of the Central Public Works Department, while the small scale industries, the consumer shops and other undertakings could have been set up without investment from the Government if traditional classes like contractors and shopkeepers were employed or given licence. The Government had, however, chosen an arduous route as under Shri Dey's leadership they had hoped that the two experimental towns held out promise in the direction 'India-to-be', and a hope in casting men for the purpose. Is it an irony of circumstances or the villainy of the administration, or the impractibility of the whole scheme that the experiments failed to produce the socialist island that it was to be?

From a builder's point of view I am satisfied as Nilokheri has today a population of ten thousand or so and has already paid back a very substantial part of the government investment and the town is humming with activities. The Haryana government has set up its provincial police training centre, an engineering training school, a Government Press etc. I have visited the township a number of times after it was handed over to the government, there still exists a camaraderie between the people inhabiting it, and the Hindus and Sikhs live without any communal rivalry. Some of the cooperatives are functioning successfully. Fulia too stands out as a planned township in West Bengal.

Experiments in rural development were being carried out at Etawah (U.P.) simultaneously. There, it was Albert Myer an American architect who was the planner builder and another enthusiastic American, Mr. Home, who worked in the field among the villagers. They laid special emphasis on agriculture and followed the pattern of the Extension Service of their own country. Mr. Myer visited Nilokheri on invitation and we had occasion to discuss both the schemes both in resemblance and contrast. Nilokheri was visualised as an Agro-Industrial township as described earlier. Another American planner of great international repute by the name of Dr. Trone was sent over to Nilokheri by Nehru ji. He was accompanied by his personal secretary, her name I have forgotten. She looked after the comforts of old Dr. Trone, took down dictation from him and was herself quite intelligent and well read to be able to discourse on all matters relating to rural development. She must have been about twenty to twenty-five years his junior. They stayed three-four days at Nilokheri and accepted my hospitality. Later I learnt that he was working out a blueprint for Independent India's economy – a sort of five or ten year plan. He did it, I know for certain but it was not allowed to appear in the Press – probably it was revolutionary in character or the concept was not in keeping with India's tradition. I remember during our mutual exchange of ideas, he would not accept Gandhiji's constructive programme for rebuilding the life of the countryside, nor was he wedded to aided self-help projects. He wanted the rural people to profit from science and technology through a crash programme organised by the State. He was against setting up of projects to produce heavy equipment, or manufacture aeroplanes and motor cars, which he thought could follow after the Indian Nation's inertia in scientific and engineering development had been completely broken by directing their energy into the production of articles and small machines needed for higher production of basic needs. He would not discourage the cooperative way of development but he would not adopt it if it stood in the way of progress. He did not seem to possess much faith in democracy but in social justice combined with a totalitarian regime.

Shri Dey had visualised Nilokheri as a demonstration model for emulation at all other refugee centres and eventually by India at large. It was this vision which made my task difficult. Many of my colleagues had ideas about rehabilitation and even outsiders made suggestions from time to time. All these prophets made the confusion, as it existed in the country about rehabilitating the displaced persons, worse confounded. A Union Minister wanted to give each displaced family a milch cow, so that each family could, besides adequate milk supply for itself, be able to earn a livelihood from the sale of surplus milk. He could only change his mind about the project, when he was made to understand the impracticality of his scheme. Some blindly hoped for miracles, something in the nature of Alladin's lamp to produce quick results and on a self-help basis. I was told that houses could be built at 0.60 *paisa* a square foot when the general construction cost for a home with modest specification was between Rs. 6/= and 7/= per sq ft. Rehabilitation based on *moonj* and *durries* (grass fibres and jute) or on silk worms to be reared on mulberries yet to be planted was as much a self-deception as the conception of a house built on self help labour hired at no cost, when the refugees did not have a surplus to live on for their immediate existence. It could only be planned on the basis of full time work for the refugees based on normal payment. Only then could it be copied elsewhere.

We took cognizance of the individualistic outlook of the people and provided enterprises for impetus, and to do this introduced a blitz programme of adult education designed to produce the enlightened conscience en-masse.

Pandit Nehru, the Prime Minister of India, accompanied by Lady Mountbatten, the wife of the Governor General of India, visited Nilokheri on February 21, 1949. Pandit ji made a demand that Nilokheri shall be repeated throughout the country. Shri Dey told me that he had conveyed his reaction to the Ministry of Rehabilitation and his helplessness in the matter, as he felt that there were easier ways of committing suicide and bringing about the ruin of that nascent centre than undertaking its repetition at that stage. His arguments proved of little avail and it was ordered that we should set up training centres for supervisors, social workers and administrative officers. This was done but, as often happens in government schemes, when the original zest loses its urge, those trained could not be absorbed and that they had to look for a job elsewhere if they did not maintain liaison with their previous employers.

In any case, Fulia – a township for refugees from East Bengal was built under the Nilokheri Administration.

Nilokheri Township

Welcoming Lady Mountbatten to Nilokheri. Pandit Nehru, Indira Gandhi and Lady Mountbatten. I am looking on, at the extreme left.

Mud Houses and Brick Walls

Adult education. Studying by the light of a hurricane lamp.

Work is Worship – Swami Vivekanand

The Community Projects

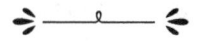

➤ ──○── ❈

For nearly four years I had lived a rustic life either at Nilokheri or Fulia under trying summers, monsoons and the biting chill of winter along with the people who were co-partners in building these townships. It was work all the time and hardly any respite, but under the guidance of Shri S.K. Dey I had become one with the communities in the making at the two places. When he asked me to shift to Calcutta in the Writer's Building[24] I felt very reluctant to do so. I resisted for a time because I was convinced that the two experiments, which to my reckoning, were still in an embryonic state, might collapse when the concentrated effort in building the community was removed. Dey was keen to enter into a wider horizon for developing the community of India. I accepted his advice and instead of building townships, the proposal to plan for building the hinterland – the villages of India with a nucleus at the Block level for Extension Services. For three to four months (Dec 1951 - Mar 1952), most of the time I was rushing about in a Jeep from village to village in several parts of West Bengal and with the cooperation of Bengali officers of the Ministry of Agriculture, it was possible to produce blueprints for

---

24 The secretariat in Calcutta, now Kolkata, is housed in Writer's Building.

eight development blocks. It is difficult for me to forget the dust that covered me from head to foot every day, the *kacha* (dirt) paths that my Jeep moved and the bodily aches that I suffered from. What made me accept that life, the external influence of Dey's dynamic personality, or an inner urge, it is difficult to analyse. My wife was certainly unhappy, particularly whenever she witnessed my body and clothes covered with lateritic soil, which I used the name 'saffron soil'. She became very nervous about my health and had herself a nervous breakdown. She was removed to the Presidency Hospital in Calcutta and after a fortnight's treatment she was declared incurable from her physical ailments – mentally she was alright. I could see no other course except to remove her from Calcutta and she was keen to return to Nilokheri where my father and aunt were living. I resigned from my job and acted as she desired. Having telegraphically conveyed the serious illness of my wife to my dear friend Dr. Bhagat Ram Khanna, who had been our family doctor for long, he met us at Delhi Railway Station. He assured me that she will get well with due nursing and treatment. He followed us to Nilokheri, examined her thoroughly and gave us the prescription. In a fortnight she recovered from her serious illness. The love of the community with whom she had shared the hardships of open air life at Nilokheri gave her the requisite courage to get well.

Early in April I received a call from Delhi to join the Planning Commision. I accepted the work as Officer on Special Duty and was attached to the housing division. For days, my lot was to go to 'L' Block, sit there at a table without work, to which I was not used. No specific assignment was given to me. I raised a protest but to no avail. I received a few circulars for perusal and my colleagues were sweet to me but there was no guidance as to how I should usefully employ myself. The First Five Year Plan, which began in 1951, was on the anvil. Large sums were earmarked for the large river valley projects, but the social welfare projects came in only on the periphery. It was felt that rural housing being a colossal problem should not be touched and the emphasis be laid on industrial housing. This appeared to be an opportunity on which I might engage myself earnestly. I set up a study circle consisting of prominent engineers and architects who could jointly study the problem and produce a report on which I should base my recommendations to the Planning Commission. Besides, I was instructed to prepare a paper on 'housing' jointly with Dr. Gupta who was in charge of the Housing Division at the time. Both these papers were in final shape by the end of August 1952, after which I was transferred to the Ministry of Irrigation and Power to work as Member Secretary of the newly constituted Damodar Valley Enquiry Committee. The venue of my work now shifted to Calcutta, although my office remained in Delhi attached to the Ministry, and my family had shifted to Civil Lines, Old Delhi, in hutment accommodation provided by the Government.

My work both in connection with the rehabilitation of refugees at Nilokheri and Fulia, and the planning of development blocks for the West Bengal government gave me satisfaction and tended to offer joy regardless of the fact that it was physically very tiring. But, the consequent physical fatigue led to good appetite and sound sleep and the contact with the refugees and the poor peasants in the Bengal villages produced the requisite incentive to work hard. Not even on a single occasion did it cause me any nervous tension.

The programme of rural housing, to which I was indirectly attached in the Planning Commission, was closely linked with agricultural production which when it goes up, creates surplus purchasing power. The Agro-Industries, too, when promoted will produce identical results. If that augmented purchasing power is not utilised in improving rural housing, there is a grave danger that it will find an easy outlet towards the middleman in towns. This is an activity related to national reconstruction dependent largely on the technical agencies and it is my view that engineering personnel can be inspired to give their best by a democratic government provided the elected representatives can, themselves, become real servants of the people.

In passing I should like to state that the community projects programme, and later the rural works programme as its adjunct, were very widely accepted by the people of Punjab. I noted that the Nilokheri experiment had its greatest influence in the state whose people showed pluck and courage even though displaced from their original moorings, than the people of Fulia, evacuated in similar circumstances from East Bengal. People's complement in rural development of Punjab, it has been my observation, was more than the share which the State or Central Government contributed. For the social revolution which was taking place in the country since Partition, the displaced people of Punjab, Northwest Frontier, Sindh and Baluchistan contributed a very prominent part.

Multifarious Experiences of Interest

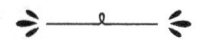

While building the township of Nilokheri I came across several *'balmiks'* – strong and enduring houses built by white ants. I had seen similar ones before, but here I had the chance of a closer study of the structure and the master builder. Although she is a wee little creature she is able to build a structure larger in proportion to their size as is the greatest skyscraper in America built by man. Her home contains a throne room where the Queen ant lives, then there are granaries, nurseries for the young, apartments for workers and for soldiers etc., and besides there there are multifarious halls and corridors which communicate with the apartments. Nilokheri had large eight feet high clay mounds of these wonderful structures. It was surprising how many of the colonies, who had enjoyed a peaceful life for ages in the *'dhak'* forest which I was clearing for building sites, began to disappear from the area. The various Queen ants must have realised that their armies, officers and generals would not be able to fight to victory against the human beings, and yet some of them did stay behind to attack the wooden door frames and timber battens in the structures that I had put up. The insect community has an elaborate system of government and well planned under the Queen that is also the mother of the community. She has a totalitarian regime, a crowd of slaves, a hard and unjust employer of forced labour with no strikes. She is thoughtful when under the altered circumstances and an encroachment on her monopoly by a powerful enemy in possession of lethal weapons she concludes to shift to places of safety.

In the performance of my official duties and social work I have been lucky enough to do a good list of touring in the country, and have nearly visited all parts of India except Assam. I have stayed in some places for weeks and even months while on a holiday. Thus I have had glimpses of my own country, the account of which one can read in countless books written by historians and travellers. I have no intuition to deal with India's past or its geography but it would be interesting to relate some of my personal experiences.

During my first visit to Cuttack I had hoped to stay with my class fellow Shri Mahindar Nath Bhuyan who was an *Oriya* posted as Superintending Engineer (Building and Roads) in Cuttack. He had his own house. He preferred that I should live in a hotel. I accepted his advice. Later, the same day I came across another friend of mine Mr. Desai who had worked as an Assistant Engineer under me at Quetta. On his invitation I went over to stay with him as his guest. Nath Bhuyan, as I used to call him in England at King's College London, asked me to tea with him at his residence. It was served in the courtyard and none of the members of his family joined us. I was very inquisitive why his wife would not meet me. I was told that she observes purdah.

The next three days I spent visiting Orissa. Compared to Punjab, Orissa appeared to me to be quite backward in physical development. Poverty stalked everywhere. Even the roads connecting the capital with its surroundings were either not metalled or stone for metalling some of them, was just being collected along the berms. The rivers were still unbridged and the work of building bridges, along one of the National Highways connecting Madras and Calcutta along the east coast and passing through Cuttack, was in hand. A very large population of the state dwelled in *sal* forests and looked quite primitive.

It is in sculpture that Orissa presents excellent work. I had the occasion to see the Jagan Nath Temple at Puri, Raja-Rani Temple at Bhubaneshwar and Sun Temple at Konark. They are superb both in architecture and stone work The innumerable figures and figurines on and around the temple walls are things of everlasting beauty. The excellence of chisel work is comparable to the best I have seen anywhere in the world.

I do not know why the temple stone masonry has been plastered on the outside. I was told that the many representations in chiselled stones were too obscene but I did not accept this explanation as a few full size figures and figurines showing sexual perversions are still left uncovered.

Near the sacred city of Puri there lives an artist – Rama Maharana who expertises in temple murals and in traditional, auspicious designs for Oriya homes and also paints on canvas made of handloom sari fabrics. He uses locally made vegetable dyes.

Orissa's handicrafts particularly in silver filigree, horn products, Sambalpur saris, art pieces attract foreigners and our own countrymen alike and are popular in large cities.

When I was posted in Calcutta under the West Bengal government who did not provide me with any State owned accommodation, I found it exceedingly difficult to find a suitable house. It was beyond my means to live in a hotel or to hire accommodation in any posh locality or to pay *'pagri'*, which often meant a payment of several thousand rupees as black money for securing a house at a reasonable monthly rent. Through the courtesy of a known friend I was able to have a flat in a bungalow built in an area where persons in a lower income group were residing. I was fairly familiar with the housing conditions in rural areas but did not possess any intimacy with the appalling state of housing in poor quarters of cities. Here, not only was there a lack of living space in the hutments, but there was almost total absence of even essential sanitary facilities to provide for the health and comfort of the occupants. Houses, many without plinths, windows and adequate ventilation, usually consisting of a single room, the only opening being a doorway often too low to enter without stooping. In dwellings such as these, human beings lived and died. It was very hard to shut one's eyes to these realities and yet I did not know if I could do anything except for writing a note for the Planning Commission, to which I was later posted in dealing with this very problem.

The upheavals on account of the Partition of India in 1947, contributed no small measure to disturb the housing balance in the city of Calcutta. There was a large influx of refugees not only wanting shelter, wherever they could find it, but building ramshackles on unbuilt areas. The way they had occupied railway platforms as permanent residences for themselves had rendered travel by rail highly embarrassing.

My first visit to Calcutta was late in 1947. While passing through it on my way to Cuttack, where my friend late Mahindar Nath Bhuyan lived. I rested for almost six hours in the waiting room of the Howrah Railway Station after the arrival of the Calcutta Mail by which I had travelled. When I changed over to the Puri Express in the late afternoon I realised that I had been pick-pocketed. The pocket's bottom seam had been clean-cut by a razor blade by the pick-pocket who got away with Rs. 265/=, the entire cash I had. I borrowed Rs. 10/= from a fellow traveller to meet with the immediate needs of the journey and at Cuttack Railway Station I happened to meet an acquaintance who gave me Rs. 100/= against a cheque. This eased the embarrassment.

It was some time in 1957 that I was posted again in Calcutta as a Special Officer, Damodar Valley Corporation. I was lucky enough to secure a flat as a caretaker lessee. This was fairly well furnished and the entire neighbourhood consisted of upper middle class Bengali families. After I had been settled there for over a month I learnt one afternoon that a Bengali family living in the street had received the dreadful news of the death of a young army officer who belonged to them. He was the only support the family had and his mother and sister were in mourning. In their solitude the two crushed women received the innumerable testimony of sympathy which came to them from many relations and friends, from the state, from the brother officers in the army, known and unknown. They leaned on each other so as to be able to bear their sorrow, and found no consolation but in prayer and in their mutual affection. Visits from some close relatives were, however, of some comfort to them as they understood what to say to those who had suffered the great loss.

The world of society decided not to stay back at this occasion as the deceased died a heroic death. Some leading aristocratic families decided to organise a public gathering for a condolence meeting in a big way. I believe that it is the aristocratic way of expressing sympathy by monopolising the dead hero. I do not know if they had made any collections for helping the two women financially. I felt deeply interested to know how these unaffected people offered to console them. I managed to get the assistance of a Bengali neighbour for knowing the details of the ceremonies to be held and the conversation that took place between the visiting ladies and affected women. He translated for me what was said in Bengali. The visiting ladies told the two women that they wanted to pay homage to this beloved memory to share the latter's grief. The elite of Calcutta, to which the officer belonged both because of his family and his splendid worth, desired to honour these merits adequately, and reward his death by expressing regrets for the national loss. They proposed to invite the Mayor of Calcutta Corporation, high officials of the state and local senior army officers and the meeting, they said, would be worthy of the illustrious dead, in the type and grandeur of gathering. The mother and sister of the deceased had listened to the aristocratic lady visitors without interrupting but declined to have any outward demonstrations. Wealth had visited poverty with a desire to extend its patronage to it. This is how it was understood by them and therefore they refused to accept the offer. They believed that God does not measure His blessings by the magnitude of the ceremonies, and were satisfied with the simple cremation ceremony devoid of ostentation and parade which they had already performed without any one of them participating in the funeral gathering.

Of all the Hindu festivals, Dussehra followed by Diwali could be considered a national festival. They are celebrated all over the country. In the North, Diwali marks the coronation of Rama and his triumphant return from Lanka. I observed in one of my tours to the South as also from the Tamil Nadu press that southern India objected to this narrative and would rather prefer that it should be reckoned as a festival for celebrating the commencement of sunny winter at the end of the monsoon. There is also a legend connected with the adventures of Lord Krishna. It is said that rain poured for weeks and the part of the country in which Krishna lived was flooded. He saved the whole cow herd under a huge umbrella until the rain stopped. That being the *Kartik Amavasya* day, the same is celebrated year after year, particularly in the United Provinces (or U.P., today referred to as Uttar Pradesh).

Lakshmi, the goddess of wealth is also worshipped on this night and this is practised in a much larger part of the country. Money, cash and even some ornaments are left unlocked in a dish in front of the goddess for the whole night in every home with the hope that the goddess would bless them with financial prosperity in the year following the festival. The business community reckons Diwali to Diwali as their financial year.

It also surrounds the mythical story of Lord Shiva, and Parvati, his consort, having played the dice on this night. The occasion has thus become synonymous with gambling. However, when I was in Bengal I found that the local population celebrate this festival as Durga Puja and the mythological story runs thus – The whole world was being ruled by the demon king Mahishasura, and godmen and even the Gods were tormented. Lord Shiva sent his own consort Durga into the world to prevail on the cruel demon king and if persuasion failed, she should incarnate as Kali, the goddess of violence and force to kill the demons. She had, perforce, to start her 'Dance of Destruction' for annihilating the whole human race. The gods trembled and Shiva had to leave his heavenly abode to come down and pacify her. He laid himself prostrate on the ground in close proximity to her and inadvertently, she touched his body. She then stopped the murder of the human race and repented for what she had already done. I believe the legend is metaphorical and its significance and parallel is modern caricature. In Bengal, beautiful models of Durga are prepared in lakhs in various sizes and *puja* performed, after which those models of goddesses are carried over shoulders, carts and trucks, by crowds singing her glory, to the holy river Ganges where they are submerged in water.

Diwali is a festival of lights and the morning following it is *'bhai-dooj'* – a very old custom maintained for the promotion of link and affection between brothers and married sisters, the latter, having developed new relationships after marriage, have the occasion to strengthen their parental relationship.

My visit to Kashmir in 1955, brought back pleasant memories of the time when I was about thirty, of Srinagar, and of the mountains and valleys in which I had then spent five years or so. I travelled by plane from Pathankot to Srinagar and before I landed at the airfield which I had built in 1934, I saw from afar a sheet of pearl and gold, which was Dal Lake, its sleeping waters bathed in sunshine. This aerodrome is located on high table land situated about eleven miles outside the city and is surrounded by valleys around it. I can recall how this project, the airfield and the connecting road from it to the city, was built in almost five weeks to receive His Highness the Maharaja of Kashmir in his first landing from his own plane. The countryside around the airfield is exquisite. From the airfield I was taken to the city by an old friend of mine and all along that road I was breathing my native air – being so familiar to me. My eyes dwelt admiringly on the still delicate green of the trees and fields, the individual glory of the month of May, and I felt a happiness and that joy of life which begins with the dawn. The scarps of the neighbouring mountains to the valley lose their jagged shape in the morning light and those who have visited Kashmir in spring would be familiar with the grace and charm displayed by nature by its clear sky smiling all over the valley – the heaven on earth. I stayed with my friend Bir Sen Anand in Sonwar Bagh and on my way I passed though the arch of *chinar* trees bordering the road, and stopped to see these familiar sights which had been part of my life. I was once more among the outlines of the valleys and mountains, that mixture of precision and softness, which gives Kashmir its unique character.

When I was working as an Assistant Engineer in Srinagar one of my functions was to control the embankments along the river Jhelum, of the flood channel, as also general control of the waterways, and observation of the behaviour of the river. The river starts rising when the snows melt and if there are heavy rains in March when the level of the river is already much above normal, then there is danger of flood. The city of Srinagar is in panic. People with nothing to do, squat on the bunds, watching the rise of the water, inch by inch. We had gauges along the river from Sangam to Baramulla but those from Sangam to Srinagar are of great value when there is likelihood of flood. Although year after year the river reached the 'danger level' during the incumbency of my charge, it was always lucky that the water receded without any damage to the banks.

My wife and I visited Varanasi in the middle of 1963, on our way back from Patna. We arrived after sunset. After settling ourselves at the office of the Bharat Sewak Samaj, we went to Vishwanath Temple. Gandhiji had pleaded to throw open the temple to untouchables and he was met with hostile demonstration. This was the impression that I carried in my devotion to the institution, but my wife who has *bhakti* (devotion) in every age-old custom and institution, in spite of her close association with the Arya Samaj, was keen to offer her prayers. She felt rather disappointed at the whole affair. We returned to our lodging and decided to go to the Ganges the following morning and then later see all the other places of interest.

My wife, having all the fervour and spirit of surrender to God, was up at dawn, and I accompanied her to see the rituals performed along the *ghats* on the banks of the Holy river and listen to the chanting of mantras by the *brahmins* and *sadhus*. I could see hundreds of devotees offering prayers and having a dip in the Ganges and my wife in spite of her indisposition, could not be stopped from having her bath in the stream as she was performing certain rituals on payment of small money. I stood on the back and looked after her clothes.

After breakfast we went around the city, Sarnath and the two temples of Buddha, and we must have visited dozens of temples, which our guides were keen to show us. The two new temples – Vishwanath built in the premises of the Hindu University and the other built by Shri Fotedar – Tulsi temple or Ramayana temple, are excellent pieces of a mixture of old and new architecture.

[Editor's Note: This section is left incomplete, with several pages left blank].

The 'Underground Movement' in the War

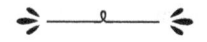

In the early spring of 1943 an RAF Pilot was making his way over Holland to Düsseldorf and Berlin (both German towns). Whilst still over Holland the crew was ordered to bail out. One of them, who did not know where he came down, but found himself in a messy ditch when he gained normality. His parachute was still near his body. His watch had stopped. He was exceedingly hungry and consumed all the food which he had. According to the RAF rules he burned his parachute and papers indicative of his rank and calling. In such circumstances he could have surrendered himself in uniform and with evidence of his rank to the Germans as a prisoner of war but he tried alternatively, as directed, to obtain help from friends of Britain known as the 'Underground Movement'. (Combating nations set up such movements in enemy countries).

Feebly he crawled along, not knowing where, until he came to a river and swam across and thought that the side on which he landed was German territory. He therefore, swam back assuming that to be Dutch territory. He waited on the river banks until darkness made it possible for him to seek a resting place for the night. He tramped for several hours in the darkness until fatigue overcame him when he spotted a small village and in sheer despair and starvation he knocked at the back door of a cottage. It was opened by an old lady. He explained to her his position and dilemma, she was sympathetic and gave him a hot bowl of soup. She then drew the curtains so that not one streak of light was visible on the outside, put out the light and added fresh fuel to the already burning fire. He was then dressed as a woman and every particle of his kit was destroyed by burning it in small bits slowly in the open grate, causing as little flame as possible. As morning light came, the old lady left the house, unable to explain her movements to him because he could not speak her language nor could she speak his, but they managed to understand each other. After a short time she returned and made him understand that he should sleep in her bedroom all day. At dusk, two plain clothed policemen called and presented him with a policeman's uniform and a bicycle.

The two visitors told him that at dawn that a company of six policemen, of which he would be one, would patrol the road near the village and return to the station. The RAF officer was to be the last man at the rear and a code of direction would be given if the Germans became suspicious in which case he was to escape from the road to the nearby thicket where he would get further help. He was not allowed to carry any written directions which would be evidence against the 'Underground', but must always commit them to memory. All this worked successfully and he reached the station where he was offered a cell. He was given old, shabby but clean clothing for use in the cell, and the policeman's uniform for outside use. He was now pledged to the care of the Underground and also threatened that he would be shot dead, if he surrendered himself to become a prisoner of war.

The 'Underground Movement' in the War

After six weeks or so he was informed that he must move on. He was taken to a forest under cover of darkness and had been shown a map directing him to cross the canal which divided Holland from Belgium. He was to memorise the whole route and appear all the time to be a Belgian 'idiot', unable to work and both dumb and deaf. This was infused upon him as he was unable to speak French and it would have been disastrous to reveal that he was an Englishman. He was also given a passport with a photograph which represented him as an idiot.

He was asked to cross the bridge over the canal which was manned by German soldiers, at the time of changing of the guard, not to walk openly on the bridge but to crawl across the open supports under the bridge. He accepted the challenge and was told to walk straight on after crossing the canal to the town of Liege, where at a certain place, he would meet a woman attired in black and wearing a bright red rose in the lapel of her coat. She would conduct him to her home.

With great courage he managed to carry out his instructor's directions. He met the woman with the rose. She instructed him to follow at a distance behind her. They then arrived at a small cottage in a back street of a poort district of the town. He was escorted to a small bedroom. After a few hours a young girl entered the room and explained in English that she could be trusted. She made it clear to him that the woman in black was her mother who had joined the Underground movement and that she would do everything in her power to reinstate the British airman. Her father was out all day and returned for his evening meal at ten in the evening and then a night's rest. She explained that her mother worked secretly even from her father and that he would be called to breakfast only after the old man had left for his work. He was also not to be seen by the neighbours as they would in fact report the so-called visitor to the Germans.

All went well for weeks, but one day when all three real occupants of the house were away, he was disturbed by a series of loud noises in the adjoining houses. He dared to look from one of the windows and to his horror there were German soldiers pounding on the front door of every house as they came along the street and even breaking windows to gain entrance. He felt sure that these soldiers with bayonets would discover him. He decided quickly to retire to the darkest corner of the kitchen and surrounded himself with litter and any coverings that he could quickly lay his hands on. He waited scarcely daring to breathe, when he heard the breaking in of the front door and the heavy footsteps of men ascending the stairs. Finding no one, a soldier flashed a torch light into the cellar, then flashed it across and then banged the doors and then apparently departed to carry the operation in the next door house. He waited patiently until the whole street was cleared and then made up his mind to depart, imagining that it was him they were seeking.

As soon as he walked out in the direction by which he had entered the house, he met the lady. She hurriedly grabbed his arm and turned him in another direction. They walked together through many side streets for hours until they came to open country. Not a word was spoken between them until they were met by a highly cultured man who dismissed the lady with a smile and then had a long conversation with him. He explained to him that the Germans had declared that they would enter every house with or without the permission of the owners to obtained forced labour and that irrespective of the status, health, age, all were to work or to starve and that is why the Germans had entered the house where he was hiding The lady having known the orders, hurried to the solicitor of the branch of the Underground for his escape.

It was this solicitor who had met him. He showed him the

drawings which he must read until he could manage to memorise the route by which he would find a farm house while still journeying in the direction of Paris. He thanked him and took leave of him with a new passport and some ration cards by which he could buy food on the way. He walked seven or eight miles and found the farmhouse as and where it had been described to him. He was still posing as an idiot and grew to look like one everyday. Here, he was given a hay-loft in which to sleep and hide.

By day, he was given a deep pit to dig, and planks were at hand, so that in an unexpected emergency he could be hidden there. The labourers looked upon him as a newcomer and considered that the boss was daft to employ such a fool of a labourer. He was given food along with the family who could speak English fairly well, so that in privacy they could and did converse. Here he began to learn French but only when he was alone with the family, otherwise he was still the deaf and dumb idiot with long hair, unkempt moustache, untidy outworn clothes of cheap Belgian cloth, and heavy boots which only labourers would wear.

Here for a time he found peace and some degree of happiness among the farmer's family. As time passed, the solicitor fellow arrived at the farm house to instruct him in the use of a tiny radio instrument which could be fitted into the ear to receive messages regarding the landing of the American troops at Dunkirk. These messages were received in a code known to the Underground receivers and those instruments were made and issued by the Movement.

The RAF officer had known the code and the news that the Americans had landed at Dunkirk gave him a new life and hope. In a few weeks time the Americans were driving the Germans back and the owner of the farm had received a notice from German officers that the sick and wounded would be brought in lorry loads to the farm, to be cared for, until other vehicles would come from Berlin to fetch them. One day when the farm family and he were having a meal some of the German officers rushed into the kitchen to insist that they would take possession of the house in order to place beds for the wounded men already on their way from Dunkirk. Reluctantly the family went into the ground surrounding the house and hinted to him to remain seated with his food and return to the role of the daft idiot.

The soldiers now had come to the window and began to joke at the idiot, who was spilling his soup and staining the front of his shirt. They jibed and jeered at him, and he answered not a word but continued making a mess of his food on his plate whilst this was continuing, the farmer returned bringing with him a woman. She was pushing a perambulator in which there was a screaming child. She spoke to him in French in vain trying to convince the idiot that he was the father of the child and that he must push the child's perambulator home. The farmer pushed him forward and placed the handle bar into his hands and hissed at him to "Go." He now understood what was happening and slowly began to move along with the new lady trustee – a nagging wife screaming her anger at his unwillingness to "push the pram" and the child being scolded by the angry mother drew the attention of the passers-by away from the stupid husband. They travelled nearly three miles along the road by which the wounded German soldiers were travelling.

The idiot with his presumed wife and child reached 'home' safely and he was again welcomed by a new friendly family. The lady changed her dress into a colourful costume and became gay and they had a hearty laugh. After several weeks news came to him that Dunkirk was in American hands and that Germans had been severely beaten back from there. The Germans yelled as they passed the road and the villages alongside that they would return to collect their wounded comrades.

In another few weeks time the farm where he was now staying received an SOS to ask for help and to bring any weapons they could find with which to strike the German soldiers who had started attacking each house in desperation. He along with his host drove to the village battlefield armed with sundry agricultural implements such as forks, spades, shovels and with hatred in their heart. When they reached the village they saw that most of the cottages had been set on fire. He saw many terrible sights. A woman who was rushing out from a burning cottage with a child still feeding at the breast was shot dead by a soldier and the child which he snatched from her was dashed against an iron gate. At one time he witnessed a train carrying Jewish men and women and children – all refugees, and moving slowly being shot by dozens of German soldiers through the windows and, when the end carriage came in sight the train was put to fire by fire bombs. So bitter was his hatred for the Germans that he would no longer linger in idleness and comparative comfort, and at all costs even that of death he could make his way back to England in order to fight again.

The news of the massacre must have reached the American Army as after the Germans had left, an American corps followed within a few days. He placed himself in such a position along the road that the American driver had no alternative but to halt or run him over. The driver stopped and the RAF officer disclosed his identity. The driver asked for evidence and he could produce the stump of a cigarette with an English marking on it. The officer inside the lorry accepted the evidence and took him into the carriage, which was going in the direction of Berlin. He requested to be dropped so that he could be picked up by an American or English lorry going towards Paris or Dunkirk.

It was later arranged to transfer him to another vehicle in the direction he wanted to go. At the American Headquarters in Paris, he was flown to London.

This story was related to me by his near relative and I considered it worth recording here.

I Build My New Home

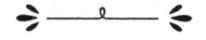

The new city of Chandigarh came into being as a project almost five years after the Partition of India. By then the uprooted people from West Pakistan, both urban and rural, had found some sort of refuge in different parts of the country; most of the urban population having settled in Indian towns like Delhi, Calcutta, Bombay, Jaipur, Lucknow and many others. In fact, they spread throughout the length and breadth of the country according to their associations, talent and resources. When the Government decided to construct an ultra-modern city in the foothills of the Himalayas near Kalka and about 150 miles northwest of Delhi, it could not attract those who had already settled elsewhere.

I had not yet built a new home for my family after having lost the one we had in areas now called West Pakistan. I chose Chandigarh and acquired a thousand square yards plot for building a residential home on it. Linguism coupled with communalism were raising their ugly heads in the Punjab at the time and I wasn't keen to settle in this part of the country although I admired the surroundings of Chandigarh and its climate. When however, the Prime Minister made an unequivocal declaration that this model city would remain bilingual for all times to come, I made my investment. Later under the Regional Formula, Kharar *tehsil* of the Ambala District was divided into three parts – the Punjabi area, the Hindi area, and the bilingual area of the Capital project. In fact, after the Regional Formula, it looked as if the problem of linguism was finally solved, but in 1965 it took a grave turn. The Government of India agreed to bifurcate the already truncated Punjab into Haryana and Punjab and appointed a commission to report on the demarcation of boundaries between the two states. I am not concerned here with the history of the events leading to or subsequent to the bifurcation, and it would suffice to say that the Parliament constituted Chandigarh as a Union Territory, by an Act. This town as a Union Territory came into shape on 1st November 1966, but stands as a bone of contention between the two states, Haryana and Punjab. Each state claims that it should be included in its territory. While the dispute continues, both the states have Chandigarh as the capital city. No one can predict with confidence whether it will go to Punjab or Haryana or remain a Union Territory.

I had settled down here because it is near Delhi and close to the hills and it provides well all the amenities that are needed in modern living – education, medical aid, etc. Public transport is inadequate and the rates charged by rickshaw pullers are high. Taxis and scooters are not easily available and they have no metres and fleece the customers. I have faith that these hardships will disappear before long. The citizens have to play their role in respect of their rights and obligations to make a really beautiful city.

Soon after I built my house in 1953, my daughter Sarla gave birth to her third child in this house. Both of my sons Vinod and Kailash completed their scholastic careers after we had settled in our new home, and they got married by which my two daughters-in-law Shashi and Shukla were added to my family fold. We have quite a commodious house to accommodate the whole family.

Vinod and Shashi were settled in Bombay for some time while Kailash stayed with the joint family but later they changed places as the latter found employment in Bombay and Vinod joined the Panjab University as a Reader in Mathematics.

Chandigarh is coming up as a cosmopolitan city. Many Indians from Africa, Middle East and Southeast Asian countries have built their homes here. Whenever I have had an occasion to talk to them they feel very morose about the political instability of the people of Punjab and Haryana. Having lived abroad and away from the triangular public life of the pre-partitioned Punjab, free from friction and communal wrangles they have a catholic attitude. There is a large section of the people belonging to both communities, namely Hindus and Sikhs and inhabiting this town who are above communal considerations in social sphere but it was observed during the 1967 elections that their catholicity did not penetrate deep while casting their votes.

Political events and cross currents keep on surging even after the state of Punjab has been cut up into Punjab and Haryana and parts of it have been merged with Himachal Pradesh. Those currents influence the life of the city and arrest its growth. While the chariot of time raised this insignificant place to a glamorous city, the political instability whether it will form part of Punjab or Haryana does not give its people a place of pride in the country.

So far Chandigarh does not suffer from overcrowding and hardly any problems of slum clearance. The average lower income group, namely the labour is housed in labour colonies, which are in no way ideal but considering the mobility of those living in these colonies, planning for them seems to have offered difficulties. Those who adopt the town as their home buy plots for building at reasonable cost. The Administration has built houses for the industrial labour and also some cheap houses for the lower income group of the Government services.

The cost of living has gone up everywhere in the country but it is my belief that the cost of basic requirements are relatively higher in Chandigarh than in any other town within a hundred miles of its neighbourhood.

[Editor's Note: Incomplete. Three pages are left blank. The home he built in Chandigarh was named Vishav Bhavan, and much more about life at Vishav Bhavan in the nineteen sixties and nineteen seventies has already been said in the Preface.]

Retirement from Business

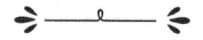

It is true that to meet my own basic needs of life, and of those who were largely dependent on my effort, mundane occupation was necessary, and that it required both energy and common sense directed towards that aim. Whatever spiritual outlook I had it did not distract me from working for procurement of the essential requirements for comfortable existence. Events like illness, accidents or business setbacks did not at any stage produce any imbalance and consequently never made any fuss about ill health or financial losses. Considering that most people have to work, rather struggle very hard, for their existence, and only a small minority of them are well off, and even those who are conscious about their worldly riches or power are a few in number, I reckon myself amount the lucky ones, who had slipped through my *'grihastha'*[25] quite comfortably and without any extraordinary effort. I began to have thoughts about retirement from business, but not one of inactivity.

I had, though dormant, a predetermined passion for social service but I was motivated to secure for myself a kind of

---

25 The second stage in life, leading a married life, with the duties of maintaining a home, raising a family, and educating one's children.

influence over the community I served. By 1960, all my children had finished their education, were married and had settled down in their own avocations. Kailash, the youngest, was practising as an Income Tax Consultant, but struggling and did not feel satisfied with his station. I was trying to persuade him to stay at this post and work in Chandigarh. I offered to build up an industry there so that he could improve his earnings but he was adamant to try his luck in a bigger place. He worked for nearly one year in Delhi in his profession and concluded by joining a business concern as a trainee for a business executive's post. During this period, I planned and built the requisite buildings for a factory to manufacture pre-stressed concrete products. After he joined the business firm in Delhi and I could see no easy return for him to be in his own business, which primarily I was hoping to set up for him, my course of action, namely retirement from mundane occupations became clear. I let out the buildings I had built and moved to Delhi for joining a social service organisation of an All India character. I had earlier contact with the Bharat Sewak Samaj which I joined.

I did not look forward for a colourless and dull life or shirk from taking up responsibilities and meeting obstacles. It meant freeing myself from earning money for myself and my family, otherwise it amounted to hard work, and an uphill journey without the rubber tyre conveyance. It meant a kind of leadership in society by which I could take on myself a very large share of work of organising public cooperation for the benefit of a developing nation. I desired to work hard, almost as hard as I could humanly bear, and plunge myself exclusively in that kind of work which would benefit the community even at the expense and neglect of those who were near and dear to me.

I have not been successful in the fulfilment of the new ideal I placed before myself. The requisite emotion was not fully developed otherwise even after recovery from a heart attack in 1964, which did not leave me infirm bodily, I would not have altered my direction. My devotion was not of that calibre which would have created a capacity for sacrifice in the service of that ideal. I could not rise above self interest in not risking my own life, and did not move independent of my reasoning faculty.

When Kailash was struggling at Chandigarh, my wife wanted that I should resign from Damodar Valley Commision and be by the side of my son. She had too great a faith in my capacity to do miracles. I, on the other hand, felt that my son held a particular picture of himself in his own mind, and eventually the environment underwent changes to fit in with his picture. He has probably moved to his goal in spite of himself. I tried, it seems to me, to side-track him. I am glad that I failed. What may have appeared to him fantastic when he joined Messrs. Bajaj Electricals Ltd. Bombay, has now become a matter of fact. I did not bind him to my views which could even be dogmatic if my assessment of his capabilities was inadequate. In fact, his decision to work without my assistance came very handy in my relinquishing to do any business. From Bajaj he joined Messrs. Bharat Carbon and Ribbon Ltd in New Delhi as the Secretary of the concern.

VISHAV BHAVAN

Part VIII: Social Service

Bharat Sewak Samaj

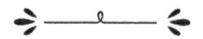

Shri Gulzari Lal Nanda was the Union Minister of Irrigation and Power as well as the deputy chairman of the Planning Commission. He was also the Chairman of the Bharat Sevak Samaj and the founder of the organisation. I was working in the Planning Commission of the Government of India when the Bharat Sevak Sangh (later Bharat Sevak Samaj) was founded. Nandaji held that there is great deal of necessary good and useful work for which no provision may be possible for years to come in the Five Year Plans but the means to carry out those programmes are available in the shape of unused time, energy and other resources accompanied by the desire for serving the community, and in order to bring about the union of the resources and programmes an All India organisation was necessary. This assumption of Nandaji had an immense appeal and when towards the close of 1958, I gave up my professional work for mercenary gains, I offered myself and my experience to the Bharat Sevak Samaj for setting up the B.S.S. Construction Service.

I had just resigned from the Damodar Valley Corporation, which was engaged in taming the Damodar River known as the river of sorrows. During the monsoon this river created havoc in the shape of floods in Bengal and those large volumes of water were gradually carried down to the sea without yielding the benefits which those could bring to the people if the water could be conserved by building dams and then used as and where its need is felt. The conservation and adequate utilisation of vast resources of the Nation's time and energy, which was otherwise being wasted, involved social engineering and an organisation which could serve as a dam, was the Bharat Sevak Samaj (B.S.S.). A constitution was drawn up for the B.S.S Construction Service and I was appointed as its first General Manager. The task was colossal and the government administration whether Public Works Department (P.W.D.), Military Engineering Service (M.E.S.), Irrigation, Railways, were not favourably inclined towards this project. Pandit Jawaharlal, the founder President of the B.S.S. and the Prime Minister of India desired its success. Many co-workers within the Central B.S.S did not like the idea that a social welfare organisation should take up activities in which large finances were to be handled and could be at stake. I made a good start and carried on my work for about nine months after which I was persuaded by Nandaji to join Damodar Valley Corporation as Special Officer.

I returned to Bharat Sevak Samaj in the middle of 1962 and was asked by the Chairman to study the *Report on the Welfare of Weaker Sections of the Village Community* and then meet him. The study group which had made the report was headed by Shri Jay Prakash Narayan, the Sarvodaya leader. "The task of finding work for members of the community who have to live from hand to mouth so that their children must go hungry tomorrow if they do not work today, must receive the first and highest priority and not be left to the general processes of economic growth to solve in due time." The Rural Works Programme was a step in that direction adopted by the Planning Commission, but it had almost failed in execution over the first two years of the Third

Five Year Plan. I was asked to put up a scheme by which Bharat Sevak Samaj could bring the programme to fruition. I expected a number of projects in operation by the State and then drew up my own blueprint, which although adopted by the Planning Commission, had to be dropped soon after sanction on account of the emergency created by the Chinese military offensive on 20th October 1962. The Bharat Sevak Samaj created a '7-Point Programme for National Defence' within a couple of days of the Chinese attack and I was named to take up its overall charge. With this new programme the B.S.S emerged from secure obscurity to unsecure eminence as while it was engaged in a work of first priority for the Nation, it was face to face with the curious yet sceptical country.

The war did not last long and the programme had to be abandoned for peace time projects. I was made the Joint General Secretary of the B.S.S., but with virtually all the duties of the General Secretary. During the emergency the Samaj had raised a large band of volunteers called the Bharat Sevak Dal (Service Corps). They had been trained and disciplined, and I had witnessed a number of rallies which convinced me that workers of sterling qualities were available in the organisation but unless the lowest paid menial earned enough for an optimum existence and produced some surplus for the organisation, he could not attach himself to the B.S.S., for long.

After the passing away of Gandhi ji, the public life of the country had suffered from lack of inspiration, which through various causes, by no means of historical importance but only ephemeral, was being smothered in a wave of materialism. There was a difference between material progress which was desirable and materialistic outlook on life which was undesirable. Both are not synonymous and the whole of our own past history has shown that material progress is absolutely compatible with a non-materialistic view of life. The Indian mind, history proves, has always been inspired by men and women of integrity and renunciation, not by persons holding high positions living a life of luxury and personal bodyguards to protect them. I felt certain that there was still a large number of sincere men and women in the country, who can be centres of inspiration and produce a cadre of missionaries. In order to attract such persons to the fold of Bharat Sevak Samaj a charter of setting up the Bharat Sevak Mission was adopted by the Central Board. It was also a movement for self improvement of the organisation for bringing at the helm, tried and trained workers.

Earlier in July 1962, when I was examining the possibilities of the Samaj taking up the Government's Rural Works Programme for implementation, the Samaj resolved in the meeting of its General Council held in Bombay that "the Samaj will henceforth lay greater emphasis on the fulfilment of the objective of creating conditions in society in general such that every human being gets, as his birthright, the needs of life to an optimum standard, good for his growth." Nandaji, the Chairman of the Samaj stated that "a human being was sacred, and the moment a person was made free from fear of lack of needs, he was capable of doing work many times more than he does carrying the burden of fear. Hunger could be no incentive to work. If the people can be provided with basic needs of life they could move mountains."

With the above noble objectives for fulfilment, my task, though exhilarating, was by no means easy. I also knew that many of my colleagues had accepted these highly idealistic programmes without faith. I had, therefore, set myself to the task of finding men who were honest about the resolutions. Bharat Sevak Mission, with a network of Bharat Sevak Ashrams, not *ashrams* of the traditional type which meant peaceful abodes, where the disciples lived under the guidance of a Guru for practising self control aimed at individual salvation, these Ashrams would be instruments of social salvation – residential institutions for learning the art of life, self-reliance and cooperative living. I asked all branches of the Samaj to submit plans for setting up Ashrams of the kind in their areas. The response was far from encouraging and those working at the headquarters considered the resolution to be preposterous. They had no faith and given time and laxity the resolutions became dead letters.

When an organisation gets funds from the State even though for specific Government projects, the Government has the right to direct their use and will not naturally leave the recipient free to use them as they would like. The State, in fact, is like the parent who would give the child a five rupee note to spend on toys and then direct the child to a particular shop. The child may buy something with which he will be finally disappointed. The B.S.S. was the child of the Government's own creation. It was given funds and schemes to which they had to be directed. The accounts had to be rendered to the parent and they were being done year after year and yet the parent in one of its fits got very angry with the child, reprimanded, scolded and stopped these favours and then the growth of the child. I had apprehended this when I took over as General Secretary of the organisation. I was keen on programmes aiming at self sufficiency in men and money, and the Samaj to dig itself into rural India.

Man is endowed with the natural gift of an analytical mind and with proper training is able to develop it further to great heights. He is, therefore, not satisfied even when his immediate physical needs are met, but struggles further to secure peace of mind and eternal bliss. He thinks far ahead of the likely results of his efforts in respect of their applicability to himself and his family. Few even go beyond that boundary and seriously apply their mind to the happiness of the community in which they live and of the whole mankind. Those who care for personal ends only, are in preponderance. But those few, who have the missionary zeal, maybe for their own peace of mind, given a field to serve their fellow human beings without any fear of conservative communal sanctions, political harassment and the like, would be moved to greatest sacrifice for the love of the people, particularly for the weaker sections of the community. I wished the Bharat Sevak Samaj to turn in that direction, although it would have meant my own surrender for the sake of my own emancipation. During the struggle for Freedom from the foreign yoke there were large numbers of people on a steep climb and they reached the summit against many odds, but the pace became considerably slower and I saw that many climbers had given up the effort. The Bharat Sevak Samaj had come into being with the blessings of all parties mainly to arouse public cooperation for Government plans but when one saw the Government failing to fulfil its pledges to the people, I felt strongly that the B.S.S. should even challenge the State if it did not work for the amelioration of the masses. This approach, or for that matter, setting up the Bharat Sevak Mission was not willingly accepted by those who held the various offices of the organisation. For myself I had a severe heart attack early in February 1964, and although I survived, I was left much weaker to attend to those bold plans. I retired in favour of an action worker Shri Ramchandra. Late, in the year 1967, Nandaji after his exit from the Union Ministry in 1966 and his re-election from Haryana, organised the Nav Jeevan Sangh with objectives similar to those outlined in the above paragraph.

Bharat Sevak Samaj held a convention in the 3rd week of 1963, in Bangalore. Many workers of the Bharat Sevak Samaj and its ancillary organisation the Bharat Yuvak Samaj had an interchange of thought and experience regarding the various activities on which they were engaged and examined several new issues brought up for discussion by me as Joint Secretary of the organisation. I was greatly perplexed over the marked decline of the national character and the convention desired to evolve a programme for the Samaj for rooting out corruption and other anti-social habits which were on the increase. Another serious problem was redress of people's grievances, in which the workers suggested that the branches should keep a live touch with the oppressed. The Chairman Shri Gulzari Lal Nanda desired to give this programme a priority and soon after his return to New Delhi, he became very keen to have a new organisation, in close collaboration with the B.S.S., for dealing with public grievances. Together we drafted a constitution for the Sanyukt Sadachar Samiti (S.S.S.) and had it registered under the Charitable Societies Act. Nandaji became the common link between the two organisations. It was only in 1965 when I felt fit enough after several months' rest in my home at Chandigarh, that I took up the reins of the S.S.S. as its Vice President, while the President's office remained unfilled after Nandaji had resigned from the office. My experiences of work in the S.S.S. are stated elsewhere.

My mind was also set on the cooperative movement of the country. I had seen that the B.S.S. by entering in the field of construction contracts had helped the Government in having lower bids from private contractors and in getting better quality of work. Prices of materials like sand and bricks had been brought down in the market as B.S.S. was able to smash rings established by private traders in those lines. I was keen that the B.S.S. should enter the consumer service and forge sanctions against anti-social elements in the trade. The Samaj set up in Delhi, price intelligence, assisting in setting up consumer cooperatives and fair price shops. It held, in collaboration with the S.S.S., an exhibition against adulteration in food articles.

I was a very poor speaker and equally so as a writer in

English. I could not write Hindi correctly nor could I grasp Sanskritised Hindi speech. My language was Urdu, which was no longer an asset in the conduct of my duties in the Bharat Sevak Samaj. For a while I shirked from speaking to gatherings but gradually I began to gain confidence. I was very reluctant to write an article for the *Bharat Sevak*, either in English or in Hindi, and I felt very humble when I refused to contribute to the two monthly journals published by the organisation. But I made up my mind to get over that shyness and I succeeded. I accepted the editorship of both the monthlies and personally wrote both the editorial as well as an article in each of them every month on current subjects. Every audience terrified me to the extent that I felt nervous and shaky. Gradually I was able to convince myself that it hardly mattered whether I spoke well or badly, the organisation was not going to suffer. In fact, it proved that this conviction alone gave me fluency in speaking and diminished by nervousness and the consequent strain.

My contact with the Bharat Sevak Samaj provided me with an opportunity to meet some *bhoodan* and *gramdan* workers.[26] While I understood the significance of the *gramdan* movement, which apparently had immense possibilities in revolutionising our village life through the forces of community action, self sacrifice, and mutual aid, yet it cannot make much headway without creating a strong public opinion in its favour, and would not be possible to succeed in its objectives unless there is a national agreement among the people as a whole. Nilokheri and Fulia which were islands of ideology could not be sustained as in building those townships they were not closely linked with the national framework.

---

26 *The Bhoodan-Gramdan* movement was started by Vinoba Bhave, a follower of Gandhiji. *Bhoodan* refers to land-donation for land reform, and *gramdan* where the entire land in a village is donated for community ownership.

Bharat Sewak Samaj

THE FIVE NEEDS OF LIFE MOVEMENT

CHAKRADHARI AGARWAL

STUDENTS of Social Science and Economics have often been asking: "What is the social and economic goal of the Samaj? what does it aim at"?

The answer is provided in a way in the Consitution of the Samaj in which it is declared that one of the objects of the Samaj is to promote the social well-being of the community and to mitigate the privations and hadships of its less-favoured sections.

Perhaps this required a clearer definition and hence the Bhilwara convention of the Samaj held in 1959 declared, "Gandhi gave to us the ideal of Sarvodaya. This will be for all the workers of the Samaj a source of light and guidance. This will inspire all our activities".

What does this mean to the people, the masses? Shri Gulzarilal Nanda, Chairman of the Bharat Sevak Samaj, while inaugurating the Five Needs of Life Co-operative Bank in Bombay, gave a lucid answer to it. It must mean freedom from fear. A stable peaceful society is to be created so that people grow peacefully in our country. Everything which is done in India must be based on the deeper spiritual culture of the country. The moment fear is taken away from a person, the moment he is assured of his Five Needs of Life, namely Nutrition, Shelter, Clothing, Health and Education, there is the liberation of his locked-up energy. There will then be a new type of humanity consisting of people who are free from that fear or insecurity. This is Sarvodaya".

The Bharat Sevak Samaj accepted this revolutionary programme of spreading the Five Needs of Life Movement, as an answer to the questions which are often posed before us. This momentous decision was taken with great enthusiasm at the meeting of the General Council held in Bombay under the Chairmanship of our leader, Nandaji.

This movement came into being in 1959 as a result of the spiritual guidance received by Dr. D. K. Mehta, the Servant of the Society of Servants of God. This movement aims at creating conditions in society in general such that all the human beings get as their birth-right the Basic Needs of Life which, in the present day world, are five: Nutrition, Shelter, Clothing, Health and Education. This movement does not aim at providing the minimum needs of life as is generally concieved, but the optimum requirements for the healthy growth of a human being.

In these needs of life, nutrition means scientifically balanced food, and not merely any kind of food, to satisfy hunger or taste; lodging means not merely a roof or shelter to live under, but a place conducive to human health and growth; clothing means utility clothes and not necessarily the clothes needed for the satisfaction of individual desires; education means not merely the present-day education in schools, colleges and universities, but also the education necessary for character-building and physical, mental and spiritual culture of human personality; and health means not only cure of disease but also maintenance of health and culture of human body.

Shri Nandaji said that this movement had its origin in another revolutionary concept, a new philosophy, the philosophy of God-Guided economics. In this world of science and "enlightenment" people feel an embarrassment in associating themselves with anything connected with the soul of God, yet the inner urge is there. The tensions of modern life find expression in the human life of individuals in the forms of all kinds of discord, quarrel and other manifestations which make life unhappy".

Proceeding, he said "we cannot provide our teeming millions with wherewithals of the Needs of Life. We have said in the Plan that socialistic objective means that there will be nobody in the country who has not got certain minimum standards of satisfaction of those needs. But this Movement aims not only at providing the minimum, but the level of optimum. I used to ask-how can you assure the

31

needs of life without extracting work first. I thought we could not afford to make people sit and eat. But gradually I have realised that this movement is much bigger than anything we have thought of. This movement considers the human being as something sacred, as something given by God. I am now fully convinced that the moment you have made a person free from fear, he is capable of doing work many more times than he does; carrying the burden of fear. Fear is one thing which exhausts energy and paralyses people. This movement will take away this fear. There will then be a responsible humanity the members of which will work more and produce more."

The Five Needs of Life Movement stems from the faith that there should be no link between work and wages. The question has often been asked, " If there is no link between work and wages, what is the incentive to work ?" The argument is often advanced that if workers are provided with the needs and necessities of life, none of them would work. In reply, one might as well ask, " What is the incentive for wives and mothers to work in homes ? They are not paid any remuneration in terms of money. Yet, they work longer hours than most of the paid workers do in offices today. What is their incentive ? " Their incentive is love, their incentive is the fact that it is inherent in human nature to work. Probably, the greatest punishment that can be given to an average human being is to satisfy all his needs of life and prevent him from doing any work.

It has been observed that the present trend of linking wages and incentives with productivity often defeats the very purpose for which linking is being done. Besides spiritual reasons, we must understand that the mind of the Indian worker is different from that of the Western Sector. To an Indian worker, money is necessary as long as it satisfies his needs and necessities and those of his family. Beyond that, he does not have much value for life. The result is that in industries where wages are linked with work, the worker works until he gets sufficient for his needs of life. After that, he leaves the machines idle because he no more cares for the money. Thus, the nation's productivity ultimately suffers in the case of those industries where the worker is able to earn more than he needs.

The question still remains : If needs of life are given free, what is the incentive for work? The answer, in the words of a saint, is : " Gultivate the Soul". Make the worker realise that work is worship. Make him understand that work is ennobling, that work should be performed not for gratification of one's needs but for the good of humanity, for the nation's productivity, and see how the workers respond. Let us give them their Needs of Life and cultivate within them the principles of Love and Truth and then see how the Indian worker responds to this call.

So two important principles are :

(i) Making Five Needs of Life free for all human beings, and (ii) inculcating in human beings the principle that work is worship, that work is to be done for the good of the nation and humanity.

So in the words of Shri Nandaji, the experiments being conducted in the country to give a practical powerful support to the movement are not experiments in the ordinary sense because its values are true values, its foundations are strong foundations. These are experiments for others to look up to and to get encouragement from."

The goal thus defined, Bharat Sevak Samaj now poses the question before social scientists, " Will they not join in the mighty practical implementation of this revolutionary concept of human relationship ? "

The Samaj has taken a decision and it intends to mobilise all its resources for giving shape to it.

गांधी जी के नेतृत्व में हमें आज़ादी मिली। जिस अंग्रेज़ी साम्राज्य ने दो विश्व महायुद्धों में शक्तिशाली जर्मनी को हराया उसी हमने अहिंसा के मार्ग पर चलकर स्वतंत्रता प्राप्त कर ली। यह भले ही विचित्र हो किन्तु यह गौरव प्रद है क्योंकि अहिंसा धारण करने के लिये संयम और आत्म-शुद्धि चाहिये। यह हम में प्रयाप्ति मात्रा में गुण थे। आखिरकार १५ अगस्त १९४७ को हम स्वतंत्र हुये। आज १७ वर्ष हो गये। इन १७ वर्षों में हमने बड़ी २ तीन ५ साला योजनायें बनाई। बड़े २ बांध बनाये। बड़ी २ प्रयोगशालाएं बनाई। बड़े २ पावर हाउस और कारखाने बनाये और लोकतन्त्रीय शासन कायम किया। स्वशासन के लिये विधान सभायें और लोक सभायें इत्यादि कायम कीं। मंत्रीगण नियुक्त किये। उनकी शान बढ़ाने के लिए उनको कोठियां दीं। सुन्दरी मोटरी और दूसरे ऐश्वर्यों से सम्पन्न किया। उनमें से अक्सर को संयमी जीवन से हटा कर आलसी बनाया। उनके नये नेता बनें जिनके पास त्याग का कोई सर्टीफिकेट नहीं है। उन्हें कोई परीक्षा नहीं देनी पड़ी। जितना कोई दलबन्दी कर सकने का साहस रखता और भारत आमेन आर्से दिला सकता उतना ही वे वज़ीर बनने का अधिकार रखता। सब जिलों में जिला परिषद बने तो उनमें भी यही पार्टीबाज़ी करने का मौक़ा मिला। वे हाकिम भी बने और नेता भी। जहां कोई अच्छा कर्मचारी था जिले के भाग्य जाग उठे और जहां स्वार्थी था वहां भ्रष्टाचार का दौर चला। सरकार अधिक से अधिक काम अपने हाथ में लेने लगी। इससे राजनीतिज्ञों को हाथ रंगने का अवसर मिला और हाकिमों को तरकीबयां मिलीं। नामे से और भरती हो गये। इस तरह बड़े २ राजकीय कामों पर न तजरबाकार अफसर लग गये। मंत्रीगण बड़ी सरकारी मशीन को चलाने की उलझन में लग गये और जनता से दूर होते गये। नये काम नये तजरबात, नये स्टाफ नतीजा हम देख रहे हैं। भ्रष्टाचार और मर्ज़ू बढ़ता गया ज्यों-ज्यों दवा की। शहरी उलझनों से फुर्सत ही न मिली। देहात में कोई प्रगति न हुई और उनकी आवाज़ के बिना लोकतन्त्र कहां। गांव वालों को परिचित करने की आवश्यकता है और यह पंचायातों द्वारा हो सकता है। पंचायातें कायम हो गईं किन्तु वे अशिक्षित हैं। उनमें से शिक्षित लोग नगरों की ओर भाग आये। गांव वालों को सभी सुविधायें मिलनी चाहिये ताकि वे वहां के लोग अपने क्षेत्र में काम करें और उन्नति करें। हमारी हमारी चौथी योजना इन्हीं लाइनों पर आधारित होनी चाहिये। यदि हमें ज़िन्दा रहना है तो अपनी जड़ों को सुदृढ़ बनाना होगा। हमारी विचार धारा बदलने की बड़ी ज़रूरत है। कौन बदलेगा? रचनात्मक कामों

- २ -

में कौन जुटेगा ? सयासी चालों से कौन परे रहेगा - भारत सेवक समाज और यह सब कुछ तब ही हो सकता है जब हमारा आचरण ऊंचा हो ।

= = अपील = =

जब मैं भारत सेवक समाज के कार्यकर्ताओं के आचरण के सम्बन्ध में कोई शिकायत सुनता हूं तो मुझे दुख होता है । हम सब समाज सेवा के काम में लगे हुये हैं और उस संस्था में हैं, जिसकी ओर जनता अपने सामाजिक स्तर को ऊंचा करने के लिए आशा से देखती है । इसलिए हम से आशा की जाती है कि हम अपना आचरण ऐसा रखें, जो दूसरों के लिए नमूने का काम दे और अपने कार्य क्षेत्र में हम अच्छा और पवित्र वातावरण पैदा करें । मेरी इच्छा उपदेश देने की नहीं है । कोई भी मानव पूर्ण नहीं हो सकता और स्वयं में मैं इसका अपवाद होने का दावा नहीं करता, पर अगर हमारे प्रयत्न हमेशा ईमानदारी और सच्चाई का आदर्श पेश करने की दिशा में हों, तो यह संस्था अपने लक्ष्य को पूरा कर सकेगी । यह संस्था तभी सुरक्षित है जब इस में काम करने वाले हम लोगों का आचरण सदैव से परे रहे और बेईमानी को कोई जरा सी कल्पना भी न कर सकें । झूठी अफवाये फैलाना भी बेईमानी है ।

कायदे कानून के द्वारा सदाचार के नियमों का बल पूर्वक पालन करना सम्भव नहीं है । इस लिए मैं अपने आप से और समाज के सब साथियों से अपील करता हूं कि वे ऐसा कोई काम न करें, जिससे भारत सेवक समाज के शुभ और बड़े नाम पर बट्टा लगे । हमारी संस्था से जनता बहुत आशा रखती है, इस लिए ईमानदारी के मापदंड के प्रति किसी प्रकार से स्खलन को सहन नहीं किया जा सकता । साथियों व जनता के द्वारा इस ओर तनिक भी उपेक्षा, हम सब के लिए बहुत निन्दा और कलंक की बात होगी ।

विनीत

(बी० डी० नन्दा)
महा मंत्री

नोट :- जहां तक मेरा बस चलेगा मैं ईमानदारी और मेहनत की कदर करूंगा तथा अनुशासन को प्रोत्साहन देता रहूंगा । जो लोग जीवन दानी बन सकेंगे उनकी जीविका की चिन्ता संस्था को होगी और उनकी जिम्मेदारी शेष परिवार (भारत सेवक समाज) की होगी । यह मेरा विचार है । इसके सम्बन्ध में मैं केन्द्रीय प्रधान मण्डल का निर्णय मालूम करूंगा ।

Since Sixty-first Birthday

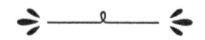

⇀——◦——↽

The tenth of December 1963, was my sixty-first birthday. I had recently returned from a tour of the South after having participated in the 8th All India Convention of the Bharat Sevak Samaj held at Bangalore about which I have already given my recollections in brief. I felt worn out physically but the session posed a number of problems which required mental exertion. Day in and day out I was working the new shape for the Bharat Sevak Samaj which no longer existed in secure obscurity but had come into prominence in a sceptical world.

Personally I had slipped through life comfortably without a great deal of effort, and considering that most people struggle hard for their very subsistence and only a small minority were really well off and fewer still were those who were fabulously rich, I reckoned myself among the lucky ones. Events like accidents, illness, losses in business etc. had never upset me and I could say with pride that people who make fuss about the normal happenings of life suffer from a kind of imbalance. But I was convinced that it was necessary for most of us to have mundane occupation to secure for self and dependents, the basic needs of life, and that material success required both energy and intelligence. Even those who held a spiritual view of life could not exist without procuring simple needs for existence whether they received them as gifts or alms. I was, therefore, very anxious that the workers of the Bharat Sevak Samaj must be provided with the optimum basic needs so that the organisation could draw the best out of them.

Like all complex tools, the body is subject to certain laws of maintenance, which I began to ignore. The nature of work to which I had now applied myself provided joy but I did not stop at that, I got addicted to it – brooding over the various problems facing the organisation during leisure thus destroying the latter. Early in February 1964, I had an attack of coronary thrombosis about which I have written elsewhere. The crisis was over within a couple of days, after which I was convalescing and remained in the Willingdon Hospital nursing home for over two months. I remained under the rigid discipline of the doctors in whose custody I was in the hospital. Complete rest, free of all kinds of anxieties about the social organisation to which I was devoted, was advised and by and large I acted on the advice, but this period of rest was a rare opportunity to look at the kind of work and the results produced by the organisation from a distance and a dispassionate mind.

I returned to my work in the Bharat Sevak Samaj. Besides my administrative work I made it a habit to write monthly letters/ circulars in addition to my contribution to our two journals *Bharat Sevak* (Hindi) and *Bharat Sevak* (English). I cannot recollect a single occasion when any of the workers of the Samaj sent me some kind of comments for or against my editorials, articles or circulars. I felt, and ultimately was convinced, reading as a habit was going to be a progressive rarity among the people. The kind of literature that I offered through those writings was intended to provide the kind of knowledge the social worker must acquire for its application in public cooperation programmes.

Having been shaped by events of the past sixty years I should have reached, I felt, a stage where I could have my views quite firm on most subjects related to society. I once possessed a desire to help the poor, the whole affair looked too gigantic to tackle. Another time I felt that I had far better make happy those in my own circle than sally forth giving battle to the hordes of outside misery, in which I could see my own defeat, and yet the fight in itself was a very noble act, and it did not matter if I was lost in it. I certainly lacked the determination of my father, who had sympathy with all sorts of curious people, whether he could or could not help them in their problems to the extent that they needed. I, on the other hand, could one moment be assailing the working classes and in another pouring out contempt for the rich.

My wife was as a child under the influence of Sikhism, and later after marriage she had the impact of Sanatan Dharma and Arya Samaj, with the result that she has a cosmopolitan outlook. My father's Vedantism combined with Sufism had its own effects on the whole family. The range and variety of thought was remarkable. Modern education in the family had brought western thought into our fold. Yet to look upon ourselves as conglomeration of thought un-connected with one another would not be the correct estimate. There is a blending, and compromise, which pervades to a great extent.

Maybe, because Sikhism follows Hindu pattern of life, I have not made any deep study about the distinctive features of that community. I came to know the Islamic customs – many of them in my boyhood. Unlike the Hindus, who observe different stages of individual life with ritual and prayers, the Muslims celebrate them. If I had my *mundan* ceremony described earlier, the Muslim lads also had '*aqiqa*', their heads shaved during the ceremony, and a goat slaughtered and the meat distributed without breaking the bones. This, I had been told, marks the commemoration of the sacrifice by Ibrahim of his son Ismail as a symbol of the love of God. The Mohammedan girls have the ceremony of piercing of the ears which I had at the time of my *mundan*. I have failed to trace the type of *mundan* ceremony among the Aryan community of old and believe that the custom of the sacred ceremony was modified by the Hindu community during the Muslim rule so as to bring some kind of similarity with the Muslim customs.

Being Metaphysical

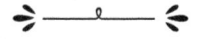

I see my reflection every day in the mirror. It is the reflector of my external form – my body which is made up of many mechanisms, some of which are visible to the naked eye. They can also be seen in the mirror. There are many invisible contrivances which with scientific discoveries have come to be known to us. The nervous system, the alimentary, relating to the digestive system, the circulatory and the respiratory systems, the skeleton and the muscular system. They are all independent in their functioning. Besides these physical systems there appears to be an interior master popularly known as the soul that acts automatically whose orders are obeyed whether they be good or evil. The master, although autocrat in functioning, is under the influence of an inborn heredity and of multitudinous outside environments. The autocrat has, therefore, a born-temperament which is not easily alterable, but the outside influences of the surroundings are alterable.

There is another mirror which consists of neighbour opinion, which reacts upon man not a great deal different from the optic mirror, as both of them assist the looker in gratifying his or her natural desire to appear agreeable to the neighbours around. There is a third mirror, the 'cosmic mirror' that is invisible and which reflects only the master's contentment and the autocrat (soul) in our body can only see. This mirror has an elasticity in its reflecting capacity which rivals the most sensitive device invented so far and it varies inversely in the ratio in which the looker is used to the other two types of mirrors.

Bodies of all human beings, that is, their physical equipment, are by and large quite identical notwithstanding physical environments which are responsible for shape and colour. There are also some manufacturer's defects, which account for certain ailments, quicker depreciation, or early end. The inborn heredity and the environment give us a variety of human beings, whose shape and intellect are largely influenced by the former while the latter chisel the internal master, whose growth in search for truth and goodness has produced saints among the human society. Those alone have an enduring place in the history of human culture.

Almost all the religions of the world submit to the concept that the creation of this whole universe and revolutionary changes in it are under the control and regulation of some superior power. All the religions adorn this Supreme Power with suitable superlatives, and a unique uniformity can be found in these descriptions. That power is omnipotent and omnipresent and all religions without exception instruct their followers to worship Him in their own particular and peculiar way. Further, from all the religious platforms, similar high ideals for human conduct such as truth, simplicity, honesty, restraint and cooperation are preached from day to day and unanimously deemed fit for human behaviour. And yet people with blind faith in their own religion become narrow minded and deficient in their appreciation of human brotherhood.

Religions are, in fact, losing hold upon the society to the extent that the State takes over relief from poverty, calamity, ignorance and disease. Besides, religions have, in their heyday, discouraged examination of even their dogmatic elements and have forbidden their followers to be critical about them and have, on the other hand, allowed their followers to be intolerant.

The obligations of morality and religion, which it is not always easy to distinguish from each other, largely influence conduct of the different communities. Circumstances are so changing that people have begun to feel happy or miserable through their own character and conduct and their growing tendency to limit the influence of religion and religious prayers to spiritual aspirations. This factor is bound to reduce fanaticism and promote greater understanding and coexistence among the communities.

Even during the mass frenzy of 1947, examples of high morality on the part of individuals in protecting the lives of those professing different religions may have exceeded those of bigotry which played such havoc. The mischief mongers always play upon their baser human feelings and arouse their co-religionists to hatred for the other communities. That is their make. From the cradle to the grave we as human beings are moulded very largely by our association with other men and women, by sermons, by books. The environments set the ideals and keep us on that road, and create our preferences, tastes, morals and religion.

Heart Attack

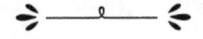

It was about four in the morning of the 8th February 1964, that I felt a severe pain in the region of the heart. Then I noticed that my left arm was numb, and felt pain running from my left shoulder to my elbow. Gradually I observed numbness in the other parts of my body and even began to lose vision. I could guess what was happening, therefore, I told my wife to telephone Dr. Singhi and tell him that I have a severe heart attack. I also told her to ring up my daughter and her husband, who were living on Pusa Road, Delhi at a distance of two to three miles of Connaught Place, where we were residing. The doctor arrived and slipped a small pill under my tongue and then he injected morphine into my left thigh. The morphine worked quickly and I was soon drowsy, only slightly conscious of the pain. My father, my aunt and my wife were living with me in the flat and before I had gone to sleep, my daughter and son-in-law arrived and assisted my wife in making the Willingdon Hospital cardiac expert aware of my illness and to arrange for the ambulance. I have no knowledge how and how soon I was removed to the Emergency Ward of the Willingdon Hospital. In the forty-eight hours following my attack the pain had died down. I was still alternating between sleep and wakefulness, and tests having shown that I was not in imminent danger of death, those attending on me felt relieved of the strain that they had been suffering from. The primary treatment consisted of prolonged rest in one of the rooms of the Nursing Home attached to the hospital. I was there for ten weeks before I was discharged. During the period of treatment I suffered a number of times with pain in the left arm (*anginal pectoris*), but gradually the pain became rare and had ultimately vanished during the last fortnight in the hospital. Emergency medicines were administered in large doses and pethidine was given to me almost every night for sleep. My sons, both of whom were in Bombay, remained in Delhi for attending to me during the illness for over a month. Whatever fears they may have had, none of my near ones showed any anxiety and I helped them in that direction by remaining calm and peaceful. It was coronary thrombosis and could have proved fatal but it never worried me. Occasionally after the event I have wondered why I had the attack when I have never been upset emotionally and have led an austere life. It could only be the result of rich food with little exercise. I could or could not have avoided it, would be crying over spilt milk. I was advised to watch my diet in the future, reduce my weight, avoid animal fats and several other small precautions of not great significance. The doctors explained to me that the attack was a result of the obstruction of the flow of blood in the coronary arteries, and that some cholesterol deposit had caused the obstruction. The heart, deprived of part of its nourishment, had begun to ache but as it began to obtain that part of the blood through other coronary arteries, the heart survived but one area had begun to die. In order to stop an increase in cholesterol formation I have been told to keep clear of anxiety, excitement, fear, and fatty foods (animal fats). This created no problem for me and I can hope to get through the passage of life without those emotions and in course of time I may forget the taste of animal fats.

Ever since the heart attack I began to think that I may not have plenty of time left to play my part in this world, and that I should act like the person who desires to complete his job. I realise the importance of my life which is not to be measured by its remaining duration. I must not waste my remaining strength. The question of my bequest is not really that important as a friend of mine keeps on harping. But how to beautify my remaining life, so that the end should be beautiful, should be my plan.

Being a Hindu I have imbibed a faith in the trans-migratoin of my soul, which gives promise of another life. I have never seriously applied my mind to the subject, and neither do I look forward to rebirth in another body in this world. I may, however, be reborn within the present span of life, if I can change from my present mundane to a life of complete ecstasy.

[Editor's Note: The following paragraphs were written when his hand is shaky. Perhaps this page are his notes during the period of his convalescence from his heart attack. They reflect his thoughts about a crisis that has emerged at Bharat Sevak Samaj – his health limitations frustrating him and preventing him from jumping in to fix the problem.]

Reports appeared about B.S.S. which brought the organisation from obscurity. It made me leave my compulsory rest at Chandigarh. I could not accept imbecility when there was demand for action. True, I was not strong in health but felt strong enough to put in normal days work free of mental fatigue and mental unrest, which I will avoid. But with an army of workers all over the country, I drew inspiration from them and take pride.

It is an ill wind that blows, does nobody any good. B.S.S. sprang as a non-political organisation out of the concept of public cooperation in the country's planned progress enunciated in the First Five Year Plan.

I am glad to say that it has not become a political organisation or machine. Its approach to national problems is promotion of construction effort by the people towards national problems. It has, therefore, to function as the heart of a movement for rebuilding life from the very function by stirring masses to act for themselves.

My colleagues in the organisation are making an exhaustive study of the Performance and Accountability Report regarding accounts, activities, expeditiously and I am convinced that the B.S.S. has to function as long as the State remains incapable of implementing a comprehensive scheme of social security for the entire population against all risks. A shock treatment would produce good results.

My Life's Inspirations

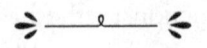

My Socialism

★

Land and All Property
is his, who will work for it

●

REAL Socialism has been handed down to us by our ancestors, who taught: "All land belongs to *Gopal* where then is boundary line? *Gopal* literary means cowherd; it also means God or *Janata Janardan* i.e., people. Land and all property is his, who will work for Janata Janardan.

My idea of Society is that while we are born equal, meaning thereby that we have a right to equal opportunity, all have not the same capacity. It is in the nature of things, impossible. Some will have ability to earn more and others less. People with talents will have more. If they utilise their talents not for the purpose of earning more but for philanthropic purposes, they will be performing the work of the State. Bulk of the earnings of such a man must be used for the good of the State, just as the income of all earning sons of the father goes to the common family fund.

I want to bring about an equalisation of status. The working classes have been relegated to a lower status, they have been termed *Shoodras*, which is iterpreted to mean persons of inferior Status. I do not want to allow, any difference between the son of a weaver, an agriculturist and a school master. I call it non-violent Swaraj.

This non-Violent Swaraj will not drop from heaven all of a sudden without working, but it has to be built up brick by brick by corporate self-effort. We have travelled a fair way in that direction, but a much longer and weary distance has to be covered before we can behold *Sarvodaya* in its glorious Majesty.

—M. K. Gandhi

●

An Appeal
To
All men & women of India

1. Inspite of political differences, everyone should unite for the defence and well-being of the country and co-operate with others to implement programmes for the common good.
2. The unity and good of the nation should be given first importance and people should, therefore, rise above differences of caste, creed, language and Province, and think more of the country as a whole.
3. Violence of any kind must be shunned and avoided. Violence creates hatred and is disruptive.
4. Religion is meant to raise an individual and to make him tolerant to others. Narrow prejudices and intolerance do not create respect for one's own religion in the eyes of others. We should honour not only our own religion but the religion of others also.
5. We should aim at equality of treatment and avoid feelings of high and low and touchable and untouchable.
6. We should aim at becoming good citizens, subordinating self-interest and aiming at the common good.
7. Women should be treated with respect and as comrades. They should not be kept in purdah or seclusion, but given opportunities to participate in national activities.
8. Children should be treated with affection and gentleness and not beaten or scolded
9. Liquor and all other intoxicants should be avoided.
10. Village and Cottage industries should be encouraged and as far as possible khadi should be used.
11. Adulteration of foodstuffs and other articles must be prevented.
12. The giving or accepting of bribes is bad, both for the giver and the taker, and must be vigorously dealt with.
13. The house, street and village or town should be kept neat and clean.
14. We should try to understand the great developmental work that is going on in the country, such as the Five Year Plan, the community development schemes etc., and co-operate in furthering and implementing it.
15. Manual labour should be respected and everyone should endeavour to engage himself in some form of manual labour for constructive work.

Jawaharlal Nehru

Problems unsolved!!

★

The progress that Science has been making has created problems which it has not been able to solve. Man has gained the power and strength not only of giants but of gods and unless man knows how to use that power and if instead of using it for the good of mankind he uses it for destructive purposes, this tremendous progress will prove a curse rather than a blessing.

Mahatma Gandhi struck at the root of the problem when he said that non-violence and not violence should determine the relationship between one individual and another and between one nation and another. There can be no peace and therefore no true progress so long as man continues to rely upon violence for fulfilment of his wishes, whether he is acting singly as an individual or as a member of a group collectively with others.

—*Rajendra Prasad*

S.K. Dey

Gulzari Lal Nanda

Work is Worship

"Power and things like that will come by themselves. Put yourself to work and you will find such tremendous power coming to you that you feel it hard to bear it. Even the least work, done for others awakens the power within; even thinking of the least good of others gradually instills into the heart strength of a lion. I love you all over so much, but I would wish you all to die working for others. I should be rather glad to see you do that."

—*Vivekanand*

The good people sustain the world by their austere life

There were many observers who forecast at the time of the transfer of power, that the Indian State would not be able to survive the effects of partition, that the country would get disorganised, that the administration would break down, that there would be no rule of law and no security of life and property. Many people feared and quite a few hoped for a sudden collapse. But these friends and foes have been confounded by the results. The country is held together. Instead of disintegration there has been integration. There is no part of the country where the writ of the Government does not run. The administration is still intact. A foreigner can travel from one end of the country to the other, without the least insecurity of life and property. Even in international affairs our stand may not be generally accepted, but it is widely respected. We have earned a reputation for honesty and independence. Our achievements in the economic and social spheres have not been spectacular but, they are not unsound.

It is not, however, for running things in the old routine ways, that we struggled for and achieved independence. Our aim is to bring about as speedily as possible a social and economic revolution. We wish to build a society free from caste and class, from exploitation of every kind, social and economic, racial and religious. We must admit that our society still suffers from grave economic injustices, social oppressions, caste prejudices, communal jealousies, provincial antagonisms and linguistic animosities. These are a challenge to our competence, our courage, our wisdom. If we are to survive as a civilised society, we have to get rid of these abuses as soon as possible and by civilised methods.

In the progress of societies three stages are marked, the first where the law of the jungle prevails, where we have the operation of selfishness and violence ; the second, where we have the rule of law and impartial justice with courts, police and prisons ; the third, where we have non-violence and unselfishness, where love and law are one. The rule of the jungle, the rule of law, the rule of love—these mark the three stages of social progress. The last is the goal of civilised humanity, and it can be brought nearer by the increase in the numbers of men and women who have renounced selfish ambition, surrendered personal interest, who die daily that others may live in peace and comfort. *The good people sustain the world by their austere life*, (*Santo bhumin tapasa dharayanti*). In Acharya Vinoba Bhave we have one such a *tapaswin*, who is striving to introduce the law of love in our social and economic life.

—*Radha Krishnan*

WE should create *Swatantra Jan-Shakti* (the self-reliant power of the people). It should be distinguished from the other two forms of power—the *Power of violence* (**Dand-Shakti**) and the *Power of the State* (**Hinsa-Shakti**). *Jan Shakti* (the power of the people) is the opposite of the power of violence. I, therefore, want to devote myself to the creation of *Jan Shakti*, the forging of the sanctions of enlightened public opinion.

Our work should proceed on the basis of *Vichar Shasan* or peaceful conversion of people to our views, by making them think about it; and *Kartritva Vibhajan* or distribution of work among individuals without creating an administrative Bureaucracy.

We should strive to create a State which would not need to exercise its coercive authority. Then only will we be said to have a non-violent State. With this end in view, we make the demand for investing the villages, with the power to manage their own affairs, so as to establish *Gram-raj*.

—*Vinoba*

Creation of a new spirit
★

Masses are awakening, showing a Healthy Discontent with their Living Standards

As a result of planned effort, the spell of stagnation has been broken and the economy has gathered momentum. India's National income has registered a climb, food grains production has gone up, the output of Cotton and major oil-seeds has also shown an appreciable increase. Millions of acres have been brought under the benefit of major irrigation. Industrial production has risen steadily. What is still more vital is the creation of a new spirit among the people a sense of enthusiasm and confidence engendered in the process of planned advance in all sectors. The progress of Community Development projects bears evidence of a resurgent community engaged in the tasks of constructive endeavour and National regeneration.

In this sphere, the quantum of voluntary contribution of the people in cash, manual labour and materials has been nearly half the Government's expenditure during the plan-period.

The masses are awakening, showing a healthy discontent with their living standards and conditions which are a legacy of past neglect and social inequalities. By touching the springs of popular enthusiasm and evoking public co-operation, both the plans have given a new dimension to our thinking and policy that enables the country to plan on a much bigger and bolder Scale for the next Quinquennium.

—Shriman Narayan

Pandit Nehru's Passing Away

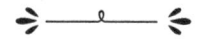

Wednesday, May 27, 1964, marked the passing away of Pandit Jawahralal Nehru, the first prime minister of Free India. In him the country lost a great leader and this day sounded the end of an epoch. The news of his death created a stir in the length and breadth of the country. With least regard to the scorching sun, large crowds assembled outside the Prime Minister's Residence in Delhi to pay their homage to the departed leader. Every man, every woman and every child broke down when informed about his death. Tears rolled down my cheeks. My people were puzzled because they feared that anxiety and grief may produce some adverse effects in view of my, not too distant, cardiac health.

The newspapers, without regard to their political views, paid homage to this National leader They were not content with eulogies but vied with one another in the prominence they gave to his portrait and biography. In a swift revolution of sympathy, the political parties, socio-religious organisations, schools and colleges, legislatures and innumerable other societies organised prayers and condolence meetings. Those bodies, to which Nehru ji was closely connected, used the occasion for expressing their grief in a way by which they monopolised the dead hero of the Nation and called attention to his services in a befitting manner.

The Bharat Sevak Samaj, of which I was the General Secretary, closed its offices and passed resolutions, besides condolence, his services to the Nation, expressing grief at the passing away of its founder President, who from the very inception of the Samaj in 1952 had nourished the organisation till the end.

A generation of politicians, who have deliberately cut themselves off from the people and whose attitude to political power is that of impoverished individuals to wealth made accidentally accessible, had begun to occupy seats of authority while Pandit Nehru was at the helm of affairs but this group, after his death abdicated the moral authority over public opinion and began to have and devote themselves to personal and petty ambitions at the cost of the Nation. We have lately witnessed secret efforts within the ruling party, I mean here the Indian National Congress, by one gang of political operators made against a particular leader or group of leaders. Even a public agitation was initiated with the limited objective of embarrassing a particular rival leader and that got out of hand and established its own momentum.

The public opinion, particularly since the passing away of Pandit Nehru and during the present regime of his daughter Shrimati Indira Gandhi, the Prime Minister of India, is in such a state of political discontent that any issue is enough to provoke the people to resort to violence. The ideal of non-violence used as a resistance and an expression of public grievance seems to have disappeared almost entirely from the Indian scene. The widespread agitational approach adopted by students and even the Delhi policemen's protest, produced law and order problems. The continuing disorder in our legislatures may appear unrelated to other forms of agitations but it shows that there is a collapse of national confidence.

The leader is dead.

My Aunt Lakshmi Devi

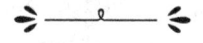

In the middle of the year 1967, my aunt Lakshmi Devi's health began to fail. She was in her hundredth year – a good old age, which I liked because it was wonderful, but it was very burdensome for her and, therefore, we were all sad about it. Her eyes were dim, cataract having already closed one eye completely and the other was also growing weaker day by day. She developed high blood pressure, which made her very uneasy. Her memory was almost as good as it ever was, although she now mixed up the different periods of her life – a very unusual thing for her to do. She continued with her habit of repeating the same events of her own life and those of many others over and over, again and by the process she seemed to have memorised the narrative so well that if one were to write down and compare with the repeated version after a couple of years, not a word would be missing and the story would be told by her in the same sequence as before. On the 16th of February 1968, she died.

Ten years ago she could not quit the kitchen for a minute without being afraid of something going wrong or down the drain. Later she acquired a position outside the kitchen in a verandah from where she could observe everything happening in the house and remained alert most of the time. She had, for the last several years, stopped going out of the house, but it was no longer safe for her even to go about in the house or the garden. She loved my grandson too well, that in spite of no strength left in her, she still had enough intelligence left in her to take good care of him. In fact, her devotion towards my family was of very high order, and she was observant about everything and every event visible or invisible, although she tended to overdo in her observations and was responsible for causing a certain amount of annoyance. At times she was unable to bear with patience even very minor lapses which make up a very large part of people's lives. I have seen her getting furious over trivial matters but it must be said to her credit that except on very rare occasions, no permanent tone of anger was harboured in her mind. She could exhibit that she was unhappy and even worry about the tiniest loss – the breaking of a cup, spilling of milk and the like, but she would ultimately reconcile herself with the loss.

My aunt created more misery for herself by finding faults in others or by blaming others. This defensive measure was so ingrained in her nature that even when it could be proved that her judgement was faulty, she would not easily bend. But what was true about her, was in some measure applicable to most of us. Lack of compassion in judging others arises from not knowing what lies behind a condemned one's actions. I have related elsewhere an anecdote in my own character where I was a victim of passing wrong judgement. Women can, by and large see, it is hard to say how, by some method of divination of which both the desire to please and desire to injure make them mistress of their homes. It is difficult to say whether that peculiarity is on the wane or not, but in the case of my aunt she had developed a habit of evil thinking to a remarkable intuition and possessed a marvellous power of analysis. In many cases her libel rested on no positive evidence, and yet there was all the appearance of truth. Whatever was sketched by her, had regard for probability. I resented at times and explained to her why her way of thinking was not beneficial for anyone and neither could she gain anything tangible by exercise of her inventive faculty.

We owe her gratitude.

Vishav Bhavan - A Family Album

Vishav Bhavan

Lalaji - Mathra Das. Bebeji - Lakshmi Devi

Mud Houses and Brick Walls

At Vishav Bhavan, four generations lived under one roof.

My children get married. Top: Shashi arrived as a new bride to Vishav Bhavan in 1956. Vinod and Shashi with Balbir, Sarla and Kailash. Bottom: Kailash and Shukla.

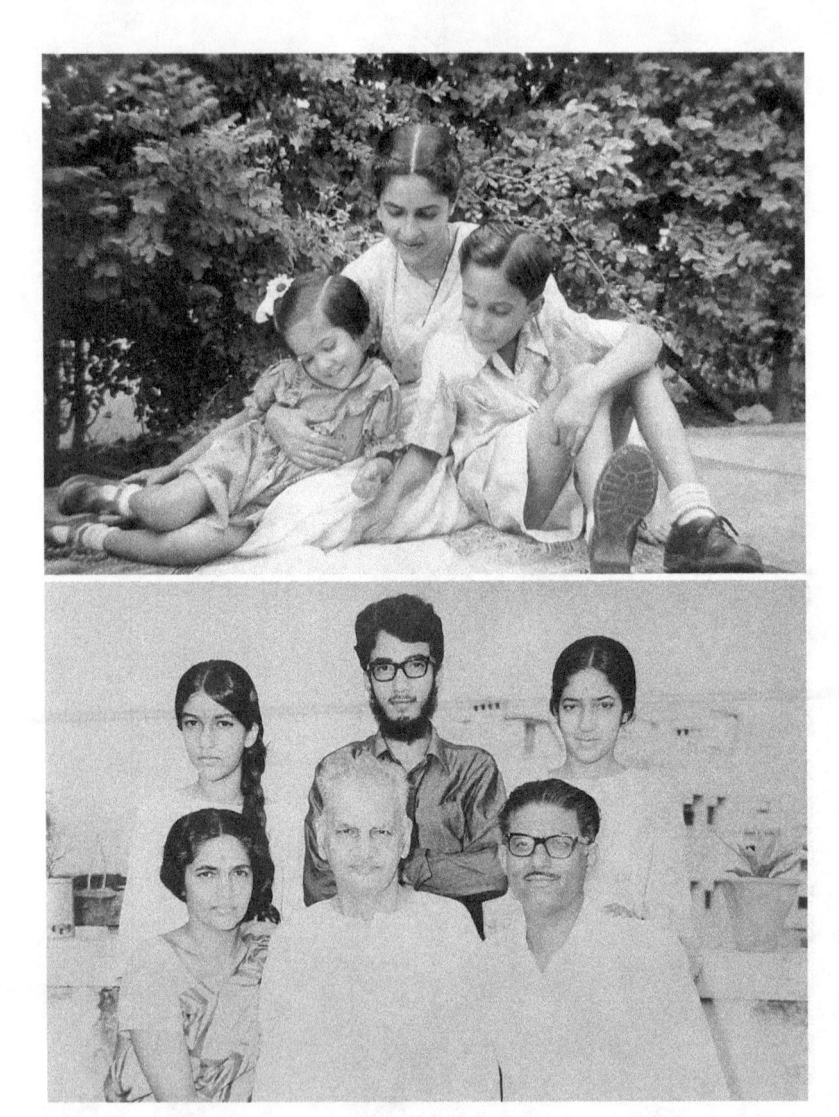

The Vadheras.
Bottom photo, back row: My grandchildren, Geeta, Sumant, Sarita.
Front row: I am flanked by Sarla and Balbir.

Vishav Bhavan - A Family Album

Photo day at Vishwa Bhavan in the mid-seventies.

Thirty Five Years of Independence

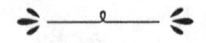

[Editor's Note: Meaning 1982, the year Pitaji passed away. However, it looks like these pages were first drafted in 1967 and titled, 'Twenty Years of Independence', the word 'Twenty' crossed out and replaced with 'Thirty Five', in the final version that we received. An indictment of the failure of a corrupted, socialist State, it's a commentary on the intervening years, 1967-82 that the text was left unchanged].

~~Twenty~~ Thirty Five eventful years have passed since the day of our National Liberation. We evolved for ourselves a pattern of political and social life under which the State is to "direct its policy in such a manner as to secure the rights of all men and women to an adequate means of livelihood, equal pay for equal work, and within limits of its economic policy and development, to make effective provisions for securing the right to work, education and public assistance in the event of unemployment, old age, sickness, disablement or other cases of underserved wants ..." The State has thus appropriated to itself the entire responsibility of developing the Nation to higher standards in all directions and with its power and splendour it has already eclipsed both religion and traditional family life of the people.

It has weakened the initiative and self reliance of individuals and social welfare organisations. The State being the biggest employer has taken away diligence and integrity from many of its employees with consequent results that great training in hard work, efficiency, and even character building seems almost lost. An official aristocracy indifferent towards the people with excessive power over them has gradually established itself in the country. Men of genius, whose opinions entitled them to the highest respect, had made forecasts about the establishment of *Ramraj*[27] after Independence. It is not even in sight and it can be said that socially and economically the community has tended to a state of things which is not quite desirable.

It would not be correct to say that we have not made any progress in material achievements, scientific learning and industry, but we have had a setback in our social and moral standards. Those who instinctively believe in a selfish outlook on life have been on the increase as they live by intellect only, they attach hardly any importance to community life. Those with utilitarian values as their motive power are apt to discard even the supernatural from their religious life and have no hesitation in making an unhealthy impact on the rest of society. Prior to Independence our leadership, which had occupied itself to drive the British out, practised their self imposed poverty or simplicity of life, higher code of conduct and devotion to ideals, and developed social enlightenment towards slavery. A stage has reached again when there is need for discouraging prestige attached to wealth and office, and to make sacrifices to fight all antisocial activities on the basis of emergency, shall we? Probably no other nation in the world spends so much time on

---

27 *Ramraj* - a virtuous government as in the reign of *Rama*.

discussions about the problems facing us. A constant stream of conferences, reports from working groups, symposia, speeches, articles, parliamentary debates and meetings of the National Development Council emerge almost to boredom. The press and controlled broadcasting media, produce imbalance in intellectual development of all those who receive these communications. We have a free press constitutionally but, in fact, it is directed by one section of the community who have over the years established vested interests. The result is that people, by and large, fall prey to the vociferous propaganda in making them believe what they desire, than to accept. We have thus grown unrealistic in our thinking and cold in our action.

I have often felt the need for complete detachment and yet I have failed to do it. Every morning I go through a daily newspaper and one of the weeklies every alternate day. During the war with Pakistan, I remember that the Press made us believe that those nations who did not support us in the justice of our case against Pakistan, were our enemies. I tried in vain to tell my friends that there was room to examine other people's point of view and that we may not be quite correct in our assessment of the reasons which count for their stand particularly in respect of problems relating to our country, and the anger which our press exhibited, was either the result of a directed national policy, or of exclusive attachment to our own problems. Who would listen to a detached view? What is true in our land applies equally if not more to many other nations. In spite of the United Nations Organisation, the world seems still intoxicated with Nationalism and within the Nation with narrower 'isms'.

The Princes and landlords representing loyalty to the British Government were liquidated, but those among them, who had eyes open to the writing on the wall, of the history in the making, readapted themselves long before the axe began to be sharpened.

They hold positions in the State, Commerce and Industry commensurate with their intelligence, acumen and financial assets. The others can be seen as vagrants of the lost empire. The Services – the Indian employees of the English *Raj* were not only adopted but given promotions with the exit of their masters. Some of them became aware of the mighty change that took place and have helped in shortening the transition, while many are blind to the writing on the wall. They seem to care for their selfish ends. The capitalists have become richer than before in spite of the high taxation policy of the Government. The poor in spite of higher wages or salaries have not been able to improve their lot on account of the sharp rise in the price of commodities.

The 'Question' arises how long shall this state of affairs last. Shall we go through an internecine bloodbath like the Russians did for changing the old order or shall we be able to evolve our Indian pattern on the non violent change over? Our dependence for military potential, food and economic assistance, on external powers, has led us to degeneration and consequent antipathy towards self reliance. The introduction of universal suffrage at the initial stage without proper preparedness for democracy has resulted in a mockery of that set up. The situation as it stands today is that the illiterate mass of people, unconscious of the valuable asset given to them under the Constitution, is wasted by them. The right to vote which means participation in the formation of the Government of the country is not fully understood by them. There ought to have been some limitations initially towards the suffrage and then gradually made universal. It appears to me that it is difficult to put the hands of the clock back in this case.

Those among the leaders who are wedded to the Gandhian ideals feel disgusted at the turn of events – Congressman wielding immense power and misusing the same either for personal or for party ends. Vinobaji and Jai Prakash Narain are making their own lonely furrow of the Sarvodaya movement, while those of the socialist 'ginger' group of the Congress like Acharya Kripalani, Acharya Narendra Dev, found themselves misfit for the National Congress after the demise of Mahatmaji.

Parochialism has taken hold of the people. The Maharashtra's Shiv Sena, Ramaswami Naicker's Tamil Sena are evils which destroy unity. Members of the Lok Sabha are influenced by these territorial organisations and in order to maintain their hold encourage provincialism and localism. Further, most of our elected legislators and Members of Parliament do not have adequate finances to invest in their elections and it is within my knowledge that they receive external financial support and even maintenance allowances, and even those who can afford the requisite expense for a mere seat in the Parliament are usually controlling industry and trade and own factories and vast business and enter the Parliament for building up political influence which is an asset for promoting their own interests.

For us to progress, and even to survive, we must have the right type of people in public life with adequate moral fibre. Whether they are officials or non-officials they come from the same stock and share basically the same virtues and vices. Whether they draw any remuneration in money for their work or they do honorary work is only a circumstantial distinction. The latter class of people do not necessarily have a qualitative edge over the former. We are a country divided by many loyalties and the centripetal force for unity is yet quite feeble as every now and then centrifugal forces come into play and we readily respond to them.

What we won on August 15, 1947, was Independence but Freedom has yet to be struggled for, and there is no shortcut to it. Freedom from hunger, disease and ignorance is a colossal task and to reach that height we shall pace along a winding and difficult road. Shall we reach that summit?

Gandhiji was right when he told his colleagues in the Congress that policial Indepence was only the first step towards the attainment of *'Ramraj'* of his dreams, and held that political power could and would corrupt rapidly those that wielded it if they did not place greater emphasis on moral and spiritual values of life. His advice has gone unheeded and there is a universal feeling of depression and frustration almost everywhere. It is in some measure due to the high cost of living and for not getting a sympathetic hearing or justice from the administration but a good deal of depression is due to widespread and ever increasing evils of corruption and nepotism, black market and adulteration.

When I was holding the office of the Vice President of the Sanyukt Sadachar Samiti many causes of corruption and adulteration were dealt with by me and referred to the Vigilance Section of the Home Ministry of the Government of India. In all these cases, the Devil was in operation – the illusory belief that the gains of utilitarianism was the base. While I addressed a gathering on the subject of giving standing to integrity in a growing utilitarian society, someone among the audience said that *"Sadachar* is too dearly bought if we give it a higher standing than material possessions." One could only remedy this state of mind through a long term programme of renaissance, by an overhaul of our educational system.

Anti-cow slaughter movement, which was led by religious organisations and backed by political organisations, gathered large public support and backward sections in North India were enraged. The enlightened people, who have no faith in maintaining crores of unproductive cattle at the cost of humanity, either did not raise their voice or it was so feeble that it was not audible. The Government also could not afford to ignore the passions that had been aroused in the country. One feels disgusted with the political leadership who would not fearlessly express their inner feelings based on reason. Surprisingly enough, each party, even the Jan Sangh, denied having any hand in organising the agitation. Some *Sadhus* and *Shankaracharyas* were heading the movement. They called on President Radhakrishnan and met Shri Gulzari Lal Nanda, the Union Home Minister and both of them expressed full sympathy with their cause. Both these leaders, if I remember alright, even suggested to these deputationists that they should create strong public opinion, which would be difficult for the Government to ignore. I do not suppose that the Home Minister was looking forward for the kind of public opinion which turned on him and his exit from his high office, after the agitation took a serious violent turn. I have personal knowledge that Nandaji's close associate in the *Sadachar* movement, namely Swami Ganeshananda, helped to work up the movement.

Recently two ministers from Uttar Pradesh went to Delhi for an anti-English demonstration. Fancy, ministers breaking the law of the land, I said to myself. This kind of resistance to the Centre's authority by a State government would surely rebound by *Panchayats*, Block *Samitis* and *Zila Parishads* revolting against the authority of the State's Chief Minister.

Fight Corruption Through Moral Regeneration

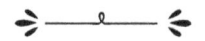

⇒——❦——⇐

[Editor's Note: This essay was published as an opinion piece in the Nagpur Times on 15th November 1965 under the column People and Their Problems, authored by B. D. Nanda, Vice President, All India Sanyukta Sadachar Samiti. The writer pleads for a vigorous campaign to restore moral values so that the nation-wide crusade against corruption can be waged to a successful conclusion].

'Sadachar' in society is valuable not because it adds to the good of the community but because it is eternally good. Corruption, as opposed to *Sadachar*, spells great harm to the community. In fact, it is a form of theft which, on this account, should not be tolerated anywhere. It is contrary to the laws of organised societies.

To wage a relentless all-out war against corruption in all its various aspects, the people must mobilise their reserves of honesty and integrity, and their emotional resources as well. Corruption must die so that honesty can flourish.

There is a considerable body of opinion which accepts the existence of bribery and corruption without question holding that it does not matter. It is even argued that these evils have existed throughout history and that they are rampant throughout the world today even among the most advanced nations of the earth. We must, however, proceed on the assumption that corruption and bribery do matter, and that it is necessary to eradicate them.

Both moral uplift and social reform remained for a long time, the preserve of our religious leaders. But with the gradual decay of religious faith, people have begun to scoff at life in the hereafter and to clutch greedily at power and wealth. Yet, religious institutions can play a very useful part in spreading the cult of self-purification and austere living. They can urge people to abjure mal-practices, and invoke the community's disapproval against the corrupt. Saintly persons, who exercise a great influence over people must act, and act together.

Motive Power

The motive power is however, shifting more and more to politics and administration; religion and family life are gradually losing their power as factors in shaping the affairs of society. As the Nation has begun to develop its physical and financial resources, attachment to idealistic values is tending to decline. There is little indication that people are trying to combat the grip of the philosophy of utilitarianism. Integrity may seem to people with a utilitarian outlook a logical monstrosity.

More virtues are more needed among those engaged in administrative work, who constitute the vital element in society for the promotion of good living. Social and moral standards ought to be observed in full both in administration and politics. If the administration is clean, the other components in society will become equally healthy. An administration imbued with a sense of purity and austerity will have a wholesome effect on the entire nation.

Apart from the Government in a welfare State, it is the function of social welfare and religious institutions as well to face the problem of corruption boldly. Examples alone can generate ardour for social reform, and social workers must display faith in physical purity and in austere living.

In the century before independence persons like Raja Ram Mohan Roy, Sir Syed Ahmad, Swami Dayanand, Gokhale, Annie Besant, Tilak, Tagore, Mahatma Gandhi and Badshah Khan worked untiringly and dedicatedly in almost all spheres of constructive work. They not only strove to free the country from the foreign yoke but they also laid the greatest emphasis on improvement of the people's moral and social standards.

Our food resources would be adequate to meet the country's needs if corrupt officials and corrupt traders could be persuaded to become honest. (The penalties of law rarely carry enough stigma to deter the wrong-doer from doing wrong again.) Similarly, the country could double its financial resources if there were no tax evasion. The Nation would be healthier if food were not adulterated. National integration would be a reality if nepotism became a myth.

Vigilant Electorate Wanted

People will, however, fail to get any redress of their grievances from the administration unless they assert themselves courageously. They must be prepared to fight the opponents of *Sadachar* regardless of personal inconvenience. Only an enlightened and vigilant electorate can make a real democracy function. People have to be fearless and alert if corruption is to be rooted out. A movement for moral regeneration must not be compartmentalised; it must not restrict itself to problems relating to one particular section of society. Those engaged in politics or administration are as much a part of the Nation as are the rest of the people. Corruption, being highly infectious, affects all sections of the community.

The whole Nation cannot be made moral by force of law; the problem of corruption is much bigger than can be handled by the law alone. We must launch a programme for re-establishment of fundamental values. We should take moral values from all religions, synthesise them and teach them to our youth, who are citizens of tomorrow. This means remoulding character. The task may appear difficult, but it is better to make even a humble beginning than to sit back and moan. It also means that the personal life of every worker in this crusade must be linked to group life of the community, and that all must pull together on the common pilgrimage towards purifying the community.

The Santhanam Committee had made several suggestions such as a specific code of conduct for Ministers, a ban on donations to political parties, prompt disciplinary action against corrupt officials, regulations to restrict the grant of permits, licences etc. The State has already implemented some of its recommendations. Bsides, the consensus opinion of several Seminars held during the past two years is that the Government and the ruling party must refrain from using political patronage. Suggestions have also been made for the setting up of a permanent commission to go into allegations against Ministers and Secretaries of the Government, and Government is considering the adoption of the system of Ombudsman to deal with complaints against civil servants.

Assurance

The relationship between Legislatures and the Administration is exceedingly unsatisfactory. Assurances given by Ministers of

Parliament and State Legislatures about improving efficiency in the Administration or even important policy statements concerning the community are not transmitted quickly to functionaries for execution. There are more than four thousand 'leaders' in the State Assemblies and Councils. Some are encouraged to work to gain their own selfish ends; some are busy in factional strife. They are all 'leaders'. Though we have such a great number of leaders it is difficult to persuade even a few among them to divert their attention to moral reconstruction.

When people do not get two square meals a day, what can you expect from them? In the struggle for existence they accept slavery as their lot. Consequently, they lack faith in themselves and resort to lies, flattery and begging to secure favours. They dare not protest as they have been used to accepting authority just or unjust. They are helpless. Raising their living standards however will make an impact on their character. It is here that a great effort is called for.

An organisation, namely, the Sanyukta Sadachar Samiti has been set up in the country. Its programme is promotion of *Sadachar* and eradication of corruption. Its plan is beyond the present resources of the organisation, and calls for cooperation from the entire Nation. It therefore looks to all who are engaged in service to the community to strive for the eradication of corruption. This work will be an exacting master and will demand great sacrifice which must be cheerfully made.

PEOPLE AND THEIR PROBLEMS

Fight Corruption Through Moral Regeneration

By B. D. Nanda
(Vice-President, A.-I. Sanyukta Sadachar Samiti)

'Sadachar' in society is valuable not because it adds to the good of the community but because it is eternally good. Corruption, as opposed to Sadachar spells great harm to the community. In fact, it is a form of theft which on that account should not be tolerated anywhere. It is contrary to the laws of all organised societies.

To wage a relentless all-out war against corruption in all its various aspects, the people must mobilise their reserves of honesty and integrity, and their emotional resources as well. Corruption must die so that honesty can flourish.

There is a considerable body of opinion which accepts the existence of bribery and corruption without question holding that it does not matter. It is even argued that these evils have existed throughout history and that they are rampant throughout the world today, even among the most advanced nations of the earth. We must however, proceed on the assumption that corruption and bribery do matter, and that it is necessary to eradicate them.

Both moral uplift and social reform remained the only time the preserve of our religious leaders. But with the gradual decay of religious faith, people have begun to scoff at life in the hereafter and to clutch greedily at power and wealth. Yet, religious institutions can play a very useful part in spreading the cult of self-purification and austere living. They can urge people to abjure malpractices, and invoke the community's disapproval against the corrupt. Saintly persons,

(The writer pleads for a vigorous campaign to restore moral values so that the nation-wide crusade against corruption can be waged to a successful conclusion.)

who exercise a great influence over people must act, and act together.

MOTIVE POWER

The motive power is, however, shifting more and more to politics and administration; religion and family life are gradually losing their power as factors in shaping the affairs of society. As the nation has begun to develop its physical and financial resources attachment to idealistic values is tending to decline. There is little indication that people are trying to combat the grip of the philosophy of utilitarianism. Integrity may seem to speak with a utilitarian outlook a logical anomaly.

More virtues are more needed among those engaged in administrative work, who constitute the vital element in society for the promotion of good living. Social and moral standards ought to be deserved in full both in administration and politics. If the administration is clean, the other components of society will become equally healthy. An administration imbued with a sense of purity and austerity will have a wholesome effect on the entire nation.

Apart from the Government in a welfare State, it is the function of social welfare and religious institutions as well to face the problem of corruption boldly. Example alone can generate ardour for

social reform, and social workers must display faith in chastest purity and in austere living.

In the century before independence persons like Raja Ram Mohan Roy, Sir Syed Ahmad, Swami Daya Nand Gokhale, Annie Besant, Tilak, Tagore, Mahatma Gandhi and Badshah Khan worked untiringly and dedicatedly in almost all spheres of constructive work. They not only strove to free the country from the foreign yoke but they also laid the greatest emphasis on improvement of the people's moral and social standards.

Our food resources would be adequate to meet the country's needs if corrupt officials and corrupt traders could be persuaded to become honest. The penalties of law rarely carry enough of a stigma to deter the wrongdoer from doing wrong again.) Similarly,

(Contd. on Page 3 Col. 2)

[between] the Administration [is] sadly unsatisfactory given by [govern]ment and about [it]. In the [gi]ven importance concerns are not by func[t]ion. There [are] thousand to Assem[bly]. Some are gain their some are of life. They though we [n]umber of [i]t to ter[minate] them [...] attention to moral reconstruction.

When people do not get two square meals a day, what can you expect from them? In the struggle for existence, they accept slavery as their lot. Consequently they lack faith in themselves and resort to lies, flattery and begging to secure favours. They dare not protest as they have been used to accepting authority just or unjust. They are helpless [...]

[...] made moral by force of law, the problem of corruption is much bigger than can be handled by the law alone. We must launch a programme for re-establishment of fundamental values. We should take moral values from all religions, synthesise them and teach them to our youth, who are the citizens of tomorrow. This means remoulding character. The task may appear difficult, but it is better to [...]

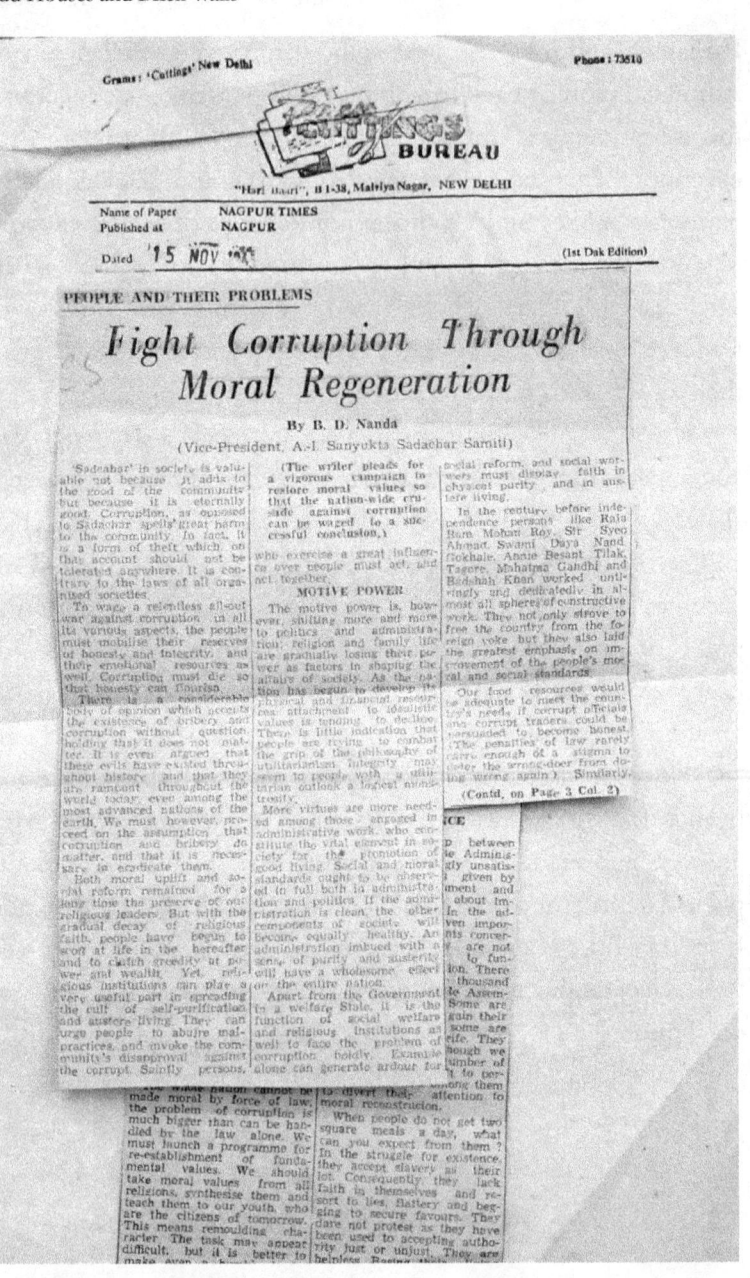

Op Ed in The Nagpur Times written as All India Vice President of the Sanyukta Sadachar Samiti, formed with the goal of bringing moral regeneration back in public life.

Our Country

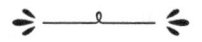

➤ ——o—— ⟵

Post Independence, India still lives in its villages, more than eighty percent of its people being denizens of villages. But that is not because there is no wish to urbanise but because of poverty. It is merely a question of time because our planning is in that direction. Whether you talk to a villager or a townsman, a rustic or an intellectual, a Jan Sanghi[28] or a Communist, they all desire to have good roads, bus services, schools, hospitals, railways, cinemas, for rural areas. Aping the western nations in transforming our countryside seems to have general acceptance and people are mentally alert in adopting modernism. But the grim economic fact is that potential economic energy of more than two hundred million employable people has not been put to use and probably it is difficult, if not impossible, to do so within the existing framework of the economic system which we are attempting to adopt. Here, it would not be right to say that it is the general low technical efficiency which stands in the way, but the lack of employment or full time occupation for them that is responsible for their miserable condition. Our planning

---

28 Jan Sangh was a Nationalist political party that existed until 1977 when it merged into the Janata Party.

in this direction, that is to harness the economic energies of the employable population for conservation of the resources of the country, has lacked consciousness. More land should be brought under cultivation, subsidiary agrarian occupations such as horticulture, epiculture, pisciculture, sericulture, afforestation should have been stepped up.

The concept of community development is quite in keeping with our tradition. I have not been able to understand why it is being lately decried. Maybe that its administrative set up is not indigenous. It is certainly in line with the rural development programme in Sriniketan set up under the guidance of late Guru Rabindra Nath Tagore. Mahatma Gandhi who advocated rural rejuvenation by providing Cottage Industries and the cult of *Swadeshi* had an identical approach but desired to succeed in his mission through a people's movement. F.L. Brayne in Gurgaon district of Haryana had, during the Alien *Raj*, also realised the importance of developing rural areas but he had a pathetic faith in the government machinery. I have also described elsewhere the experiments that have been carried out in this direction in Etawah (U.P.) and Nilokheri (Haryana) in the post-Independence period. The programme of rural development is a must, it should be aided self-help projects and unless the responsibility for its execution rests on the people or on the people's organisation, namely the *Panchayat*, it will not become a movement.

What form of society is in the making in our country? Is it socialism, which is repeated *ad nauseam*, by our leaders – Congress or Socialists. Is Communism having a foothold? Must we imitate others who have made a success of their 'isms'? Why should we! Are we not worthy progeny of our own culture which achieved a synthesis of all the divergent components of society from the child to the old man, from the untouchable to the Brahmin? Left to ourselves we are bound to rediscover our anchorage again in keeping with our own philosophy of life. We should aim at compatibility, at a total synthesis of all the elements of life that function within its orbit, the head, the arms, the thighs and the feet each developing to the highest stature in its 'natural' station in society and all pulling together like the human body for the benefit of the entire community. This is Indian-ism. There should be no slaves in society purchased with the coins but instead the relationship should be that of brothers and sisters of a common fraternity to share the victuals from out of the common family pool according to the station held for the genuine needs. There will then be no heartburning for the trivial discrepancies in the society. One may need grape juice, and the other buttermilk, according to his or her station in work. Equality, in everyone wanting grape juice or for that matter buttermilk, would create problems both for the Communist and the Socialist, but not for those that believe in a joint family. All the members – Indian men and women are entitled to a livelihood in the country they belong to. Communism breeds and flourishes with starvation, misery and degradation – the real inequalities of society. If we spend more in looking after the criminals in prison, than those who have no work and are ignored, they would prefer to resort to lawlessness so they can enter the prison gates both for work and livelihood, as long as they are unable to topple the existing system of government.

Living among the elite I observe that there are plenty of fancy ladies who pay fees to doctors to put them on slimming diets. From my own experience, after my recovery from thrombosis, for reducing my bodily weight I had recourse to a voluntary cut in my food or partial starvation. I could bring it down from 180 pounds to 140 pounds without the use of any pills. Those who starve under force of circumstances and suffer malnutrition are constantly slimming towards bare skeletons. Those fancy ladies could be put on this well-tried and known course free of any charge.

The basic needs of all human beings are alike. This is unquestionable, and this we are apt to forget and it looks so easy to forget. Those who are prosperous, can well afford to do so. They support the religious institutions and vice versa to have spiritual tenets in their favour. They can and do buy God, and they seem to believe that, when luck continues to favour them it becomes easy to ignore the fact that at bottom they are no different from the poor. We keep on struggling for maintenance of hypocrisy – provincialism, linguism, casteism, cow protection and the like, and seem to forget that nothing else is so serious a malady as the lack of basic needs for the members of this joint family. How can we keep them together?

Now and Then in Retrospect

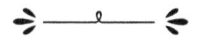

This chapter brings me more or less to the completion of this story, which was visualised to be a sequence of the evolution that has taken place in this country during the present century.

I can well recall to memory the days when wheat in Punjab was sold at Rs. 150 per maund (Rs. 400/= per quintal) and ghee at Rs. 30 per maund (Rs. 80 per quintal). Even during World War II, wheat prices did not rise beyond Rs. 20 per maund (about Rs. 52 per quintal). But prices, in many parts of the country, of wheat have touched a new high. Among the pulses, *moong* dal which is being sold at Rs. 2.25 per kilo and mustard oil at Rs. 4.50 per kilo. The sugar scarcity is causing great anxiety throughout the country. A good pair of shoes is a luxury these days. The cost of education has gone up. The fees, text books, note books, paper, pencils etc. have become so costly that our hearts begin to sink while purchasing them.

While there will be no coming back of the good old days, will ever the level of our incomes rise so high as to match the rise in prices? It appears that none of the two alternatives can be expected in the foreseeable future. I am also sure that the villages are in no different a plight, for if there was prosperity in rural areas, the movement of the population from urban to rural would have taken place.

High prices are not the only problem. An even worse problem is adulteration. Inferior stuff is marketed without fear. Bottles of medicines have been found not containing what the label shows. Cases have come to notice where things like sugar, salt, wheat flour are adulterated with powdered glass and chalk and sold openly in the market. I have seen papaya seeds being mixed with peppercorns. A seed closely resembling mustard seed, milled as 'mustard oil' has led to thousands of unsuspecting people to develop beriberi. The dishonest grocer may weigh out the genuine article but his balances may be deliberately wrong or the balance may be accurate and the article adulterated. Dishonesty can come in small packages, but it is still dishonesty, and gradually the mind becomes benumbed.

'Sadachar' in society is valuable not because it adds to the good of the community but because it is eternally good. Corruption as opposed to *Sadachar* spells great harm to the society and in fact, it is a form of theft which on that account should not be tolerated. Unfortunately there is a considerable body of opinion which accepts corruption without question holding that it does not matter. It is even argued that these evils have existed throughout history and that they are rampant throughout the world, even among the so-called civilised societies.

Both moral uplift and social reform remained for a long time the preserve of our religious leaders but with the gradual decay of religious faith, people have begun to scoff at life in the hereafter and to clutch greedily at power and wealth. As the Nation has begun to develop its physical and financial resources, attachment to idealistic values is tending to decline. There is little indication that people are trying to combat the grip of the philosophy of utilitarianism. In the century before Independence, persons like Raja Ram Mohan Roy, Sir Syed Ahmed, Swami Dyanand, Gokhale, Annie Besant, Tilak, Tagore, Mahatma Gandhi and Badhsha Khan worked untiringly and dedicatedly in almost all spheres of constructive work. They belonged to the people. Unless the people fight the opponents of *Sadachar* regardless of personal embarrassments and start a movement for moral regeneration of the whole nation, the society will not establish *Sadachar*.

Many years ago matrimony was arranged between boys and girls by the parents. Their families were generally well acquainted with each other and the union of the opposite sexes further strengthened the family ties. Now, marriages between strangers are quite common. I recollect that a newly married young couple stayed with us as guests at Quetta for about a fortnight or so. The wife belonged to the aristocratic stock and she never forgot this fact. Neither did her husband, who lived in a state of timid admiration of the woman who, despite his lowly origin, on account of his good education and post, had married him and who gave him to understand on every possible occasion the extent of her sacrifice. This had endowed him with deep respect for the nobility, of whom the type to him was his wife's stately and commanding features and an authoritative voice. This reminds me of another lady, the wife of a class fellow of mine, who very alike the woman already described told me that her match with my friend was unbecoming as she not only belonged to the noble and aristocratic family of Bedis but was also a graduate of Punjab University among the very few that there were in the teens of the twentieth century.

These ladies, described above, had refused to accept their restricted role and felt strongly that the Hindu system of matrimonial relationship and of joint family was hard towards their individuality and stifled women's personality. While I admit that it had led to injustice and even ill treatment, the credit side of the systems must also be given their due place. In the absence of any system which would provide the individual an insurance against old age, handicap, widowhood, loss of parent, etc., the joint family, however imperfectly, gave shelter and security. After Independence we have placed a Hindu Code Bill to remove certain inequalities between the rights of the two sexes, but the Bill was mooted by those advanced in modern learning and is put to practice primarily in that group. The Bill has its debit side too. The Hindu traditional system is not static and like the symbol of the Ashok Chakra – the wheel of life has no beginning or end.

I have lost contact with the rural life of my country and now in my advanced age with well-educated daughters-in-law brought into our family fold from urban areas and my own children having lived and been brought up in urban society, I have to shed my own rural conservatism to prevent the younger elements from rebelling. Luckily I did not have to observe blind obedience towards my own parents. My father had always been very liberal and this helped me to perpetuate his nature in meeting the emotional needs of my own children. But for this balance, companionship would not have grown between us.

My two daughters-in-law took up their own careers for some time, in which they had the full support of their parents. Shashi, the elder of the two partakes in the maintenance of our home, home life, being a good hostess and in tending to the development of her sons – Sanjiv and Vipul, my grandsons. The younger, Shukla lives with her husband in Delhi, and maintains her home and a companionship for Kailash.

My daughter Sarla is an artist and her son Sumant has qualified from Arts College in Delhi. On my 65th birthday he sent me greetings on a card with a picture in modern art painted or scribbled by himself. Sarita is married and has two daughters. Geeta is an artist in Delhi.

Sanjiv, after having spent some time in the kindergarten and then a year in the preparatory school entered St. John's – a missionary convent school in Chandigarh. He carried a satchel with seven to eight books besides exercise books – neat and clean. He always wears a coat and pants, a tie, and has to be well groomed. In my days these provisions for school going children were just unknown. Later, he joined I.I.T. at Kanpur.

On 18th March 1968 at 12:15, Shashi gave birth to another son, to whom we gave the name Vipul in the presence of a ceremonial gathering. He is fourteen years old now.

My grandsons and granddaughters are all an intelligent lot and I am blessed with two great-granddaughters Sumati and Sukriti, daughters of my daughter's son Sumant, whose wife Sandhya belongs to the Kapoor family of Solan (Himachal Pradesh). Besides my granddaughter Sarita has two daughters, my great-granddaughters, Priyanka and Priyamvada. They belong to the Puri family.

A few years before Independence conditions in Kakrali were none too good for Hindus, who did not feel quite secure. Most of my relations who had a financial setback, and being too fastidious to live as working people and not clever enough to earn sufficient for living as gentlemen, looked completely lost. Having had a glorious inheritance they felt uncomfortable among the lower classes, who sensed their grace; and equally uncomfortable among the upper classes in the towns, who had a poise and composure they felt difficult to assume. They felt quite tormented whenever I met them. The Partition, in spite of the accompanying hardships, brought about a solution to their difficult problem. They were thrown away from their village among the people who were completely indifferent towards them. Most of them set down to work and earn a livelihood by sweat and are no longer tossed here and there about their status. They have become hard working people. One of my father's cousins is working even as a carpenter without the least discomfort.

I tried to believe that I would not become a creature of circumstances. That I never considered myself master of my fate or the captain of my soul. I alternated between intelligent arguments of my brain such as it was and the continuous upsurging of my emotions.

A Final Word

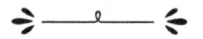

We lighted the sacred fire together in 1925, and have kept it lit by our joint devotion. According to the customs of our society I had a duty towards my parents and a duty towards the needs of my own *Atma* (spirit), and my wife's role was to help me in that dual task. Her role was no less important and was in no way considered less important to my own. We were united by 'bandaged' love but by tradition for parenthood. Every one of our children was a rarity for us. We made every effort to create for our children an environment that was fresh, gay and frank.

While the breath of life is in me, I shall thank God for giving me wonderful parents, such a wife, such a daughter, such a son-in-law, such sons, and such daughters-in-law. We have been happy. We have not come across misfortune. My sons are successful in their careers and like their grandfather and I go about carefree. Even after the most weary days at work they remain quite happy.

One greatest single factor providing so far a tranquillity in our home life is the sprint of devotion and renunciation of my father, my aunt (both now dead), my wife, who always looked upon the family above self. I have also looked upon the home as family security in storms of life that face every one of us. I am, also, glad to say that the children, too, seem to accept this view to some extent, but with the passage of time and without any coercion from my side are bound to treat the inevitability of their own role of the spirit of sacrifice in their own interest and that of their progeny.

May God bless them.

Epilogue: Seventy Years of Vishav Bhavan

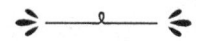

Forty years have gone by since Pitaji passed away. The brick walls of Vishav Bhavan, built in 1953 in Sector 16, Chandigarh are now seventy years old. The civil engineer laid a firm foundation for the lives that were built here.

A house needs more than just bricks and mortar, lives and relationships need sustenance and nurturing.

Shashi, our mother, arrived as a new bride to Vishav Bhavan in 1956. After Pitaji suffered his heart attack in 1964, our parents, Vinod and Shashi moved back to Chandigarh from Bombay. Sanjiv was 3.

The daughter of the highly respected physician and philanthropist Dr. Sadhu Chand Vinayek of Ferozepur Punjab, Shashi became homemaker to the family, nurse to the ailing, innkeeper to the guests at Vishav Bhavan, and a respected professor to thousands of students at M.C.M. D.A.V. College for Women.

As she often says – while she was not herself a doctor, she was the daughter of, and mother, mother-in-law, and now grandmother to doctors. She has been a nurturer and nurse throughout her life. To her, we lovingly dedicate this book. We are truly blessed.

— *Vipul Nanda and Sanjiv Nanda*

Shashi Nanda, front lawn at Vishav Bhavan

Glossary

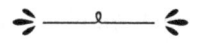

ahimsa	non-violence
Arya Samaj	Arya Samaj was founded by Dayanand Saraswati in the 1870s as a monotheistic Indian Hindu reform movement that promotes values and practices based on the belief in the infallible authority of the Vedas.
Azadi Bachao Andolan	Azadi Bachao Andolan (Save Freedom Movement) was launched in the early 1990s as a campaign to protect Indian industries, at a time when multi-national corporations were increasing their presence in India as a part of a trend towards globalisation.
bhaiya	an elder brother
Bharat Sevak Samaj	Bharat Sevak Samaj was established in 1952 by India's Planning Commission as an agency tasked to ensure public co-operation for implementing government plans. https://www.bharatsevaksamaj.org/
charan amrit	Literally, the nectar from the feet of the gods. A teaspoon of the elixir is placed in the palms of the devotee by the priest in the temple.

charkha	The hand-driven cotton spinning wheel used by Gandhi. The *charkha* was also printed on the white panel on the flag of the Indian National Congress, and was replaced by the Ashok *chakra* (wheel) on the Indian national flag.
didi	an elder sister
madrassah	an Islamic school or college
mamaji	uncle, mother's brother
mantras	sacred verses from Hindu scriptures.
massi	aunt, mother's sister
mataji	a term of respect for mother, but in this case referring to Sanjiv's grandmother.
panchayat	Literally an assembly of five, the panchayat is the oldest system of local village self-government in India.
pandit	a Hindu priest
phupha, phuphaji	uncle, *phuphi's* husband
phuphi	aunt, father's sister
pitaji	A term of respect for father. In this context, B.D. Nanda's grandchildren referred to their parents as papa and mummy, and their grandparents as pitaji and mataji.
prasad, parshad	Sweet foods or fruits consecrated through *puja* or offering in a temple. The blessed sweets and fruits are shared with others.
puja	A family prayer cermony usually in front of a Hindu idol.
sadachar	good conduct, good behaviour
sadhu	a holy man, sage
samaj	society

Sanyukta Sadachar Samiti	An organisation established by Union Home Minister Gulzari Lal Nanda in response to deep anxiety about the damage that corruption in administration and business was doing to the social, economic and political fabric of the nation.
sarai	inn
Sarvodaya	Literally *sarva* (all) + *udaya* (ascent or uplift), *sarvodaya* was a word coined by Mahatma Gandhi for a policy of economic and social development of the community as a whole. Vinoba Bhave, Jayaprakash Narain and other followers created a movement to implement Gandhi's principles for community development.
satyagraha	Literally, *satya* (truth) + *agraha* (insistence), *satyagraha* was a word coined by Mahatma Gandhi for his policy of passive political resistance as a tool to demand *swaraj* (self rule) or Independence from British occupation.
seva	Service, particularly to society
sevak	A servant
shayari	Urdu poetry, from *sher*, a poem in two lines where the first line sets up a thought, and the second completes it.
shraddhanjali	homage or tribute
Shri	short for *Shriman*, it means respected, and is used in lieu of Mister or Mr. It is also abbreviated to Sh.
Shrimati	Meaning respected, it is used in lieu of Mrs. It is also abbreviated to Smt.

Shuddhi movement	Literally, purification, a reform movement in Hinduism to abolish the practice of untouchability, but also designed to bring back lower caste Hindus back from Islam and Christianity to which they had converted.
swaraj	Literally, self-rule, but Gandhi meant the word freedom to include freedom from want - self-sufficiency of each human being to live a life with dignity of labour and a concomitant birthright to nutrition, shelter, clothing, health and education
swastika	A Hindu symbol for the sun signifying prosperity and good fortune, often rendered in white or coloured powders at the entrance to a home or business.

Bishambar Das Nanda was a civil engineer who built earthquake resistant housing in Quetta following the devastating earthquake in 1935, and built new townships in Nilokheri, near Kurukshetra, and Fulia in West Bengal, to rehabilitate refugees following Partition. When he built his home Vishav Bhavan in Sector 16, Chandigarh, in 1953, it was the first private home in the newly planned city, a new capital for the Indian state of Punjab. He was a member of India's Planning Commission and General Secretary of the Bharat Sevak Samaj.

Artist: Sumant Vadhera, grandson of the author.

Sanjiv Nanda loves to hike and explore the Borrego Badlands. He is a popular hike leader and likes to rate his hikes on a Wow! scale. To share this love, he writes appreciations of awe-inspiring desert landscapes and the resilience of the flora and fauna that make these harsh environments home, which are published in *The Sand Paper* published five times a year by the Anza-Borrego Desert Natural History Association. When he is out walking in the desert or in the mountains, he cannot stop smiling.

He is inspired by the dedication of his grandfather Bishambar Das, and his father Vinod Chander, to the pursuit of Gandhian social justice.

Connect with him at: https://www.linkedin.com/in/sanjiv-nanda/ or via email: borregosand@gmail.com

Printed in the USA
CPSIA information can be obtained
at www.ICGtesting.com
LVHW091407271223
767436LV00058B/1000

9 789358 966329